JOHN CALVIN AS SIXTEENTH-CENTURY
PROPHET

John Calvin as Sixteenth-Century Prophet

JON BALSERAK

OXFORD
UNIVERSITY PRESS

OXFORD

UNIVERSITY PRESS

Great Clarendon Street, Oxford, OX2 6DP,
United Kingdom

Oxford University Press is a department of the University of Oxford.
It furthers the University's objective of excellence in research, scholarship,
and education by publishing worldwide. Oxford is a registered trade mark of
Oxford University press in the UK and in certain other countries

Published in the United States of America by Oxford University Press
198 Madison Avenue, New York, NY 10016, United States of America

British Library Cataloguing in Publication Data
Data available

Library of Congress Control Number: 2013945564

ISBN 978-0-19-870325-9

As printed and bound by
CPI Group (UK) Ltd, Croydon, CR0 4YY

To the memory of David F. Wright

Acknowledgments

The first thing I ever read from Calvin was the preface which he wrote to his commentary on the Psalms. I had no idea at the time that what I was perusing held such a unique place within his body of writings. I recall reading quite personal details about this man and his calling to serve within the Christian church and being, if I may say, charmed by his openness. Twenty-seven years later, it is interesting for me to ponder the influence which that first encounter with Calvin may have had on me and on the writing of this book. I interpret it as an influence for good. My wife usually has other ideas, particularly when she sees that I have purchased yet another tome about this strange individual. While writing the present study, I have benefitted enormously from that same wife, Bilgay (despite her misgivings about Calvin); from her unselfish encouragement and her probing questions.

I have also profited from the wealth of erudition and acumen that Calvin scholars, medievalists, and Early Modern historians have lavished on the subjects of prophecy, French history, religious identity, war, and church reform. I am particularly grateful to Erik de Boer for allowing me to read the manuscript of his new monograph on Calvin's *congrégation* before its publication. Thanks are also due to Bruce Gordon for directing my attention to discussions of prophecy written by Theodor Bibliander of which I was unaware and for allowing me to read his excellent treatment of Bibliander on prophecy prior to its publication. Max Engammare, Sujin Pak, and Barbara Pitkin participated, with me, in a session at the 2011 Sixteenth Century Studies Conference (SCSC) in Fort Worth at which some of the ideas found in this book were presented and discussed. I am grateful to them for their constructive comments and also to those who attended our session. Presentations at three other conferences— the International Colloquium on Calvin Research (in Bloemfontein, South Africa, 2010), the Renaissance Society of America Conference (in Washington, DC, 2012), and the Society for French Historical Studies Conference (in Boston, USA, 2013)—also yielded very helpful results. In relation to these, and other, gatherings throughout the last four years, I should express my appreciation to a number of people including Olivier Millet, Peter Wilcox, Emidio Campi, Peter Opitz,

Acknowledgments

Robert Kingdon, Randall Zachman, John Thompson, Shannon Miller, Amy Nelson Burnett, Ann Blair, and Sara Beam. Herman Selderhuis' invitation, in late 2008, to speak at the "Saint or Sinner" conference, in Puten celebrating John Calvin's birth is what spawned my interest in this topic, so sincere thanks are due to him as well.

Research for this monograph was made possible, in part, by a generous University Research Fellowship which I won from The Institute for Advanced Studies, University of Bristol, and which allowed me to take research leave for the academic year 2011 to 2012. My leave, which I took in Philadelphia at the University of Pennsylvania, was made easier by the help of their librarians. Specifically, John Pollack and Lynne Farrington have been tremendously helpful, as has Lapis David Cohen, who assisted me in gaining access to the 1551 printing of Calvin's Isaiah commentary, *Ioannis Calvini Commentarii in Isaiam prophetam*...(Geneva: ex officina Ioannis Crispini, 1551). Ann Matter and Tom Safley helped make my time at Penn both fruitful and enjoyable. I thank them for their friendship and for sharing their insights into so many areas of scholarship. My colleagues at the University of Bristol are due my thanks as well for their constant encouragement.

Lizzie Robottom, of Oxford University Press, has been a pleasure to work with. My thanks are also due to three anonymous readers of my manuscript for their invaluable suggestions and comments.

I have dedicated this work to my doktorvater and friend, David F. Wright, who passed away on 19 February 2008. I recall, at the start of my Ph.D. studies at the University of Edinburgh, being so terrified of my first Latin reading session with David that I contemplated skipping it. I'm glad I didn't. I count it an enormous privilege to have studied under him. He is still, in my eyes, an absolute giant both as a scholar and an individual.

J.B.
30 May 2013, the feast day of St Joan of Arc
Philadelphia, USA

Why are prophets and teachers sent?
That they may reduce the world to order.

Calvin, from his lecture on Jeremiah
1: 9–10; CO 37: 480

Contents

Abbreviations

Aquinas Opera	*Sancti Thomae Aquinatis doctoris angelici Opera Omnia* ... (Parma: Typis Petri Fiaccadori, 1852–73).
Bonaventure Opera	*Doctoris seraphici S. Bonaventurae Opera Omnia* ... (Ad claras Aquas (Quaracchi): Ex typographia Collegii S. Bonaventurae, 1882–1902).
CO	*Corpus Reformatorum: Ioannis Calvini Opera quae supersunt omnia*, ed. W. Baum *et al.* (Brunswick: C. A. Schwetschke & Filium, 1863–1900).
Gwalther (1 Cor.)	Rudolph Gwalther, *In Epistolam D. Pauli Apostoli ad Corinthios Priorem* (Zurich: Froschouerus, 1590).
Isaiah 1551	*Ioannis Calvini Commentarii in Isaiam prophetam* ... (Geneva: ex officina Ioannis Crispini, 1551).
Lyra Biblia Latina	*Biblia Latina cum postillis Nicolai de Lyra* ... *et additionibus Pauli Burgensis replicisque Matthiae Doering* (Nuremberg: Anton Koberger, 1483).
Musculus (1 Cor.)	Wolfgang Musculus, *In ambas apostoli Pauli ad Corinthios epistolas, commentarii* (Basel: Joannem Hervagium, 1559).
OS	*Joannis Calvini opera selecta*, ed. P. Barth *et al.* (Monachii: C. Kaiser, 1926–59).
PG	*Patrologia Graeca*, ed. J. P. Migne (Paris: Garnier, 1857–99).
PL	*Patrologia Latina*, ed. J. P. Migne (Paris: Garnier, 1844–79).
PMV (1 Cor.)	*In Selectissimam D. Pauli Apostoli Primum ad Corinthios Epistolam Commentarii* (Zurich: Froschouerus, 1579).
PMV (Gen.)	*In Primum librum Mosis, qui vulgo Genesis dicitur, commentarii doctissimi D. Petri Martyris, Vermilii Florentini,* ... *nunc denuo in lucem editi* (Zurich: Froschouerus, 1579).
PMV (Rom.)	*In Epistolam S. Pauli Apostoli ad Rom. D. Petri Martyris, Vermilii Florentini,* ... *commentarii doctissimi, cum tractatione perutili rerum & locorum, qui ad eam epistolam pertinent* (Basel: Apud Petrum Pernam, 1560).
PMV (1–2 Sam.)	*In duos libros Samuelis prophetæ qui uulgo priores libros Regum appellantur D. Petri Martyris*

1

The "I" of Calvin

For I am persuaded that the "I" of Calvin is inseparably tied to
his doctrine.[1]

(Alexandre Ganoczy)

Historians writing on prophets and prophetic movements have
approached their subjects in different ways, depending on what
their subjects have left behind.[2] Did their subjects leave written
records, either authored by them or penned about them by their
contemporaries? Oral traditions of some kind? A community who
adheres to their teachings? Physical artifacts such as icons, statues, a
temple, or a coat or other garment? Expanding our thinking somewhat: did their subjects leave behind reports of miracles performed by
them? Did they leave mysterious proverbs in need of deciphering?
Did they leave a new kind of mystical lifestyle, filled with visions and
ecstatic experiences, or an example of austerity, fasting, and self-
flagellation? Did they die as a martyr? Did they pass down a new
rule for the Christian life, or a unique understanding of evangelical
doctrine? Did they vigorously condemn the church and society of

[1] Alexandre Ganoczy, *Le Jeune Calvin: genèse et évolution de sa vocation réformatrice* (Wiesbaden: Franz Steiner Verlag, 1966); ET: *The Young Calvin*, tr. David
Foxgrover and Wade Provo (Philadelphia: Westminster Press, 1987), 242. Throughout this study, all translations, unless otherwise specified, are my own.
[2] E.g. compare Robert E. Lerner's *The Powers of Prophecy; The Cedar of Lebanon
Vision from the Mongol Onslaught to the Dawn of the Enlightenment* (Berkeley, Calif.:
University of California Press, 1983) and Richard Kagan's *Lucrecia's Dreams; Politics
and Prophecy in Sixteenth-Century Spain* (Berkeley, Calif.: University of California
Press, 1995). The work by Lerner is focused on seven known copies of a prophecy
produced in different languages and spanning several centuries. Kagan's work de-
pends, as he tells us, "almost entirely from evidence compiled during the course of
[Lucrecia's] trial by the Spanish Inquisition, a process that began in 1590 and lasted
for five years." (Kagan, *Lucrecia's Dreams*, p. ix).

their own age, and insist that God was speaking afresh through them and was using them to call the church to radical repentance and renewal? Did they prophesy an imminent end of the world and pinpoint the date of the final Armageddon? The answers to all of these questions invariably have a profound influence on the resulting scholarly monograph.

Naturally, such requirements and constraints attend the present study. The character of Calvin's life, work, and legacy close off some approaches one might take to him. One such closure which I might identify has to do with the mining of Calvin's resources; that is, the movements, *scholae*, individuals, and writings that influenced him. Calvin left behind an enormous cache of writings, but he simply said nothing about influences in those writings, nor did he leave many hints. He moved around from one university to another as a student; he wandered through France, Basel, portions of Italy, and Strasbourg, drinking in ideas but leaving us with no way of discerning their sources with any confidence. The scholarly aspiration to identify influences, therefore, is an extraordinarily difficult one to pursue, if not impossible. Not surprisingly, then, whereas scholars during the last century[3] often pursued this line of approach in their research on Calvin, it has now largely been adjudged to be a dead end.[4] Accordingly, while I have enormous respect for those in the past who took up such work (what Oberman called a "pedigree pursuit"),[5] I will not follow it here. This study will explore prophecy as discussed in the Western Christian tradition, but will content itself with identifying broad streams of thought and placing Calvin within them in order to help elucidate his thinking and his self-awareness.

There are other approaches which might, equally, be set aside as impossible or impractical. But here surely one might be inclined to think that an attempt to scrutinize Calvin's sense of prophetic calling

---

[3]   One thinks of Karl Reuter, *Das Grundverständnis der Theologie Calvins* (Neukirchen-Vluyn: Neukirchener Verlag, 1963) or Alister McGrath, "John Calvin and Late Mediaeval Thought: A Study in Late Mediaeval Influences upon Calvin's Theological Development," *Archiv für Reformationsgeschichte*, 77 (1986), 58–78, or T. F. Torrance, *The Hermeneutics of John Calvin* (Edinburgh: Scottish Academic Press, 1988).

[4]   The standard work on the topic is Anthony N. S. Lane, *John Calvin: Student of the Church Fathers* (Edinburgh: T&T Clark, 1999), 1–66 *et passim*.

[5]   Heiko Oberman, *John Calvin and the Reformation of the Refugees* (Geneva: Droz, 2009), 93–102, esp. 93.

is one of them. Such a psychologically oriented subject might be legitimate in researching Luther, since he spoke quite frequently about himself.[6] But Calvin is on record as virtually opposed to self-disclosure.[7] Even his correspondence, which will be an important resource for all that follows, is remarkably void of explicit and unequivocal information about his sense of self. Therefore, such psychologizing in relation to him might seem inappropriate. And yet, Calvin scholars have produced their fair share of such work— whether one thinks of earlier efforts like Oskar Pfister's *Das Christentum und die Angst: Eine religionspsychologische, historische und religionshygienische Untersuchung*, Richard Stauffer's "Les Discours à la première personne dans les sermones de Calvin," or Ganoczy's *Le Jeune Calvin,* or more recent titles such as Suzanne Selinger's *Calvin Against Himself,* William Bouwsma's *John Calvin: A Sixteenth Century Portrait,* or Denis Crouzet's *Jean Calvin: Vies parallèles.*[8]

It will come as little surprise to learn that these attempts at unearthing Calvin's psychology have frequently been censured for *inter alia* being wildly speculative.[9] Indeed, one can understand why. For it might be argued that material for such a pursuit simply is not present in Calvin's corpus. Being absent, it has had to be manufactured (or so the argument goes).

While I grasp the criticism, I am not dissuaded by it from investigating Calvin's prophetic awareness. Here I concur with Ganoczy (cited at the head of this chapter). Even though Calvin refrains from explicit self-disclosure, he seems nevertheless to divulge much about

---

[6] One thinks of Erik H. Erikson, *Young Man Luther: A Study in Psychoanalysis and History* (Norton, NY: Norton, 1958).

[7] "De me non libenter loquor" (*Responsio ad Sadoleti Epistolam*, OS 1: 460.42).

[8] Oskar Pfister, *Das Christentum und die Angst: Eine religionspsychologische, historische und religionshygienische Untersuchung* (Zurich: Artemis, 1944); ET: *Christianity and Fear: A Study in History and in the Psychology and Hygiene of Religion* (London: Allen & Unwin, 1948); Richard Stauffer, "Les Discours à la première personne dans les sermones de Calvin," in *Regards contemporains sur Jean Calvin: Actes du Colloque Calvin* (Paris: Presses Universitaires de France, 1965), 206–38; Ganoczy, *Le Jeune Calvin*; Suzanne Selinger, *Calvin Against Himself: An Inquiry in Intellectual History* (Hamden, Conn.: Shoe String Press, 1984); William Bouwsma, *John Calvin; A Sixteenth Century Portrait* (Oxford: OUP, 1988); Denis Crouzet, *Jean Calvin: Vies parallèles* (Paris: Fayard, 2000).

[9] NB the widely different reviews of Crouzet's *Jean Calvin: Vies parallèles*: Max Engammare, "Review of Jean Calvin. Vies parallèles," *Bibliothèque d'Humanisme et Renaissance,* 62/3 (2000), 732–9; Michael Monheit, "Review of Jean Calvin: Vies parallèles," *Sixteenth Century Journal,* 33/3 (2002), 854–6.

himself, and his sense of self, in his corpus and his behavior. Thus, unlike the question of his influences, issues related to his psychology are things about which he provides us hints. The self is, it should be said, difficult to hide, especially for someone who left behind such an enormous body of oral and written communication (fifty-nine volumes in the CO of letters, sermons, treatises, and other writings, plus additional material found in the *Supplementa Calviniana* and elsewhere[10]). Therefore, while I am wary of the legitimate concerns that have been raised in relation to labors such as this one, I am convinced that these worries cannot possibly be taken to indicate that all such scholarly exploration of Calvin is illegitimate. This monograph will, then, aim to explore Calvin's psychology and, specifically, his sense of prophetic vocation and authority.

A glance at the publications produced in the last one hundred years suggests that other scholars might not agree. For they have not flocked to the topic of prophecy in their work on Calvin—quite the opposite, in fact. When one ponders extant examinations of his life, times, and thought, one finds immediately that the vast majority of such studies do not treat, or even raise, the idea of his prophetic standing. One does not find it mentioned in Émile Doumergue's *Jean Calvin, les hommes et les choses de son temps.*[11] The same must be said of Fritz Büsser's more modestly sized *Calvins Urteil übersich Selbst* as well as François Wendel's *Calvin: Sources et évolution de sa pensée religieuse.*[12] Moreover, even following the exploration of Calvin's prophetic consciousness by Ganoczy, Stauffer, and Peter in the mid-1960s, others within the world of Calvin scholarship exhibited little enthusiasm for the idea. It makes no appearance in T. H. L. Parker's *John Calvin: A Biography* or in Randall Zachman's *John*

---

[10] When I began this study, since I did not have access to any of the volumes of the *Opera omnia denuo recognita*—and also since so many of the works on which this study would focus have yet to appear in this new edn—I decided, when I arrived at Penn, not to switch over from the CO to these newer volumes.

[11] Émile Doumergue, *Jean Calvin, les hommes et les choses de son temps*, 7 vols. (Lausanne: G. Bridel & Cie., 1899–1927).

[12] Fritz Büsser, *Calvins Urteil über sich Selbst* (Zurich: Zwingli-Verlag, 1950); François Wendel, *Calvin: Sources et évolution de sa pensée religieuse* (Paris: Presses Universitaires de France, 1950); ET: Wendel, *Calvin: The Origins and Developments of his Religious Thought*, tr. Philip Mairet (Durham, NC: Labyrinth Press, 1987).

Calvin as Teacher, Pastor, and Theologian.[13] It does not appear in Heiko Oberman's scholarly labors on Calvin, nor can it be found in more recent short works by authors such as Christian Link.[14] Obviously, it would be tedious and unnecessary for me to continue listing titles ad infinitum; the point has been made.

One could conclude, therefore, either that Calvin's prophetic awareness is of little to no significance or that the very idea of Calvin believing himself to be a prophet is simply wrong-headed. While that might seem to be the natural conclusion to draw, anyone hastening towards such a verdict too rapidly needs to be aware of the fact that there were individuals who lived in the sixteenth century (some who knew Calvin quite well) who believed that he was. Antoine Fumée, a contemporary and friend of Calvin, refers to him as a prophet in an undated letter to the reformer. Jean Morely calls Calvin a prophet in his *Traicté de la discipline & police chrestienne.*[15] Moreover, Theodore Beza writes the following about Calvin in August 1564 after his passing.

The following night, and the day after as well, there was much weeping in the city. For the body of the city mourned the prophet of the Lord, the poor flock of the Church wept the departure of its faithful shepherd, the school lamented the loss of its true doctor and master, and all in general wept for their true father and consoler, after God.[16]

The city "mourned the prophet of the Lord," Calvin's compatriot and protégé declares. Could this be hyperbole; an overzealous expression

[13] T. H. L. Parker, *John Calvin: A Biography* (London: J. M. Dent & Sons, 1975); Randall Zachman, *John Calvin as Teacher, Pastor, and Theologian* (Grand Rapids, Mich.: Baker Academic, 2006). This comment is not intended to be a criticism but merely an observation on the contents of these studies.

[14] Christian Link, *Johannes Calvin—Humanist, Reformator, Lehrer der Kirche* (Zurich: TVZ, 2009). See also, Peter Opitz, *Leben und Werk Johannes Calvins* (Göttingen: Vandenhoeck & Ruprecht, 2009).

[15] Millet cites an undated letter from Fumée to Calvin in which he calls Calvin a prophet, "plus grand prophète de notre époque." See Olivier Millet "Eloquence des prophètes bibliques et prédication inspirée: La 'Prophétie' réformée au XVIᵉ siècle," in *Prophètes et prophétie au XVIᵉ siècle* (Paris: Presses de l'École Normale Supérieure (Cahiers V.-L. Saulnier, 15), 1998), 65–82; esp. 65. Also: Jean Morely, *Traicté de la discipline & police chrestienne* (Lyon: Jean de Tournes, 1562), book 3, ch. 4, 257.

[16] CO 21: 45–6 cited in Max Engammare, "Calvin: A Prophet without a Prophecy," in John Leith and Robert Johnson (eds), *Calvin Studies IX: Papers Presented at the Ninth Colloquium on Calvin Studies, Davidson College, January 30–31, 1998* (Davidson, NC: Davidson College, 1998), 88–107; esp. 88.

of the high regard which individuals, like Beza, possessed for Calvin? Listening to the majority of scholars from the last hundred years would nudge one decidedly towards this conclusion. A handful of contemporary authors, however, *do* contend that Calvin believed himself to be a prophet. Although the celebration in 1959 of the 450th anniversary of Calvin's birth produced the publication of *John Calvin Contemporary Prophet: A Symposium*,[17] it was Alexandre Ganoczy's 1966, *Le Jeune Calvin*, that brought Calvin's prophetic awareness into the consciousness of Reformation and Early Modern scholars. Around the same time, Richard Stauffer and Rodolphe Peter wrote on the topic, pointing to allusions from Calvin's sermons to this self-belief.[18] A short section in Peter Opitz's work on Calvin's hermeneutics is devoted to the reformer's thinking on the prophetic role of interpretation. Olivier Millet in three engaging publications—*Calvin et la dynamique de la parole*, "Eloquence des prophètes bibliques et prédication inspirée: La 'Prophétie' réformée au XVIe siècle," and most recently "Calvin's Self-Awareness as Author"—treats the topic.[19] Max Engammare has produced an exceptional piece, which is perhaps the best known piece on the subject outside of Ganoczy's, in his "Calvin: A Prophet without a Prophecy." Calvin's prophetic consciousness makes appearances in Denis Crouzet's *Jean Calvin: Vies parallèles* and Bernard Cottret's *Calvin: Biographie* and is an important element in Bruce Gordon's *Calvin*

[17] *John Calvin Contemporary Prophet: A Symposium* (Grand Rapids, Mich.: Baker, 1959), which contains pieces by G. C. Berkouwer, Jean-Daniel Benoît, Philip Edgcumbe Hughes, and Pierre Marcel among others.

[18] Ganoczy, *Young Calvin*, 287–312; Ganoczy wrote a second piece as well, "Calvin avait-il conscience de réformer l'Eglise?" *Revue de Théologie et de Philosophie Lausanne*, 118/2 (1986), 161–77. See also, *Sermons sur les livres de Jérémie et des Lamentations*, ed. Rodolphe Peter, SC 6: XIV–XVI; Richard Stauffer, "Les Discours à la première personne dans les sermones de Calvin," 206–38; Philippe Denis, "Calvin et les églises d'étrangers au XVIe siecle: Comment un ministre intervient dans une église autre que la sienne," in *Calvinus Ecclesiae Genevensis Custos: Die Referate des Congrès International des Recherches Calviniennes . . . Vom 6. bis 9. September 1982 in Genf* (Frankfurt am Main: Peter Lang Verlag, 1984), 69–92, esp. 87–8.

[19] For Opitz, see Peter Opitz, *Calvin: Theologische Hermeneutik* (Neukirchen-Vluyn: Neukirchener Verlag, 1994), 273–81. For Millet, see Olivier Millet, *Calvin et la dynamique de la parole: Étude de rhétorique réformée* (Geneva: Editions Slatkine, 1992), 324–9, 447–9, *et passim*; Millet, "Eloquence des prophètes bibliques," 65–82; Millet, "Calvin's Self-Awareness as Author," in Irena Backus and Philip Benedict (eds), *Calvin and his Influence, 1509–2009* (Oxford: OUP, 2011), 84–101.

and Jean-Luc Mouton's *Calvin*, both published in 2009.[20] The present author has also written on the topic.[21] Most recently the subject has been treated in Marco Hofheinz's "*De munere prophetico*—Variationen reformierter Auslegung des prophetischen Amtes. Zur theologiegeschichtlichen Entwicklung eines dogmatischen Topos vor der Aufklärung (von Zwingli bis Lampe)."[22] Thus, a handful of studies exist which address this subject. In my judgment, a number of these are outstanding contributions to research on Calvin and the Early Modern era produced by some of the best Reformation scholars in the business today. Moreover, all of them confirm both the scholarly interest in, and the importance of, the subject.

CALVIN'S PROPHETIC AWARENESS REVISITED

Despite the excellence of many of these studies on Calvin's prophetic awareness, they manifest a debilitating shortcoming. None of these pieces of research address the problem that Calvin's corpus contains

---

[20] Engammare, "Calvin: A Prophet," 88–107; Crouzet, *Jean Calvin: Vies parallèles*, 115–19, 139–40; Bernard Cottret, *Calvin: Biographie* (Paris: Éditions Jean-Claude Lattès, 1995), 268; Bruce Gordon, *Calvin* (New Haven: Yale University Press, 2009), 2, 3, 94, 114, 145, *et passim*; Jean-Luc Mouton, *Calvin* (Paris: Gallimard, 2009), 21–2, 71–83, *et passim*.

[21] Jon Balserak, "'There will always be prophets:' Deuteronomy 18: 14–22 and Calvin's Prophetic Awareness," in Herman Selderhuis (ed.), *Saint or Sinner? Papers from the International Conference on the Anniversary of John Calvin's 500th Birthday in Putten, the Netherlands* (Tübingen: Mohr Siebeck, 2010), 85–112; Balserak, *Establishing the Remnant Church in France: Calvin's Lectures on the Minor Prophets, 1556–1559* (Leiden: Brill, 2011), 65–107. In the present study I set out conclusions which supersede those found in both of these earlier pieces.

[22] Marco Hofheinz, "*De munere prophetico*: Variationen reformierter Auslegung des prophetischen Amtes. Zur theologiegeschichtlichen Entwicklung eines dogmatischen Topos vor der Aufklärung (von Zwingli bis Lampe)," in M. Hofheinz, W. Lienemann, and M. Sallmann (eds), *Calvins Erbe. Beiträge zur Wirkungsgeschichte Johannes* (Göttingen: Vandenhoeck & Ruprecht, 2011), 115–68. Hofheinz's lengthy (53 pages) essay does not strictly aim to address the question of Calvin's prophetic consciousness. It, rather, analyses Calvin's views on the prophetic office. Hofheinz does this in a theologically oriented fashion, locating a prophetic ministry in Calvin's thinking on the Christian church and, thus, in Calvin as well. He takes as his starting point Calvin's understanding of the *munus triplex* of Christ, and works from there to see the ways in which a prophetic ministry flows from that understanding. His study focuses almost exclusively on the *Institutio*, taking only a brief glance at other texts (such as the 1545 Genevan Catechism). It also frames its discussion of Calvin within modern troubles currently percolating within the European church—a frame which feels somewhat restricting in terms of producing a penetrating historical analysis of Calvin's thought.

within it views on prophecy that are disparate, if not contradictory. Several of these studies, I hasten to add, *do* discuss the related issue of Calvin's apparently ambiguous feelings towards his own prophetic awareness, whereby he sometimes "considered his vocation as being based on an extraordinary prophetic ministry, sometimes simply as a pastoral and teaching ministry."[23] But the concern which I am highlighting here has not been addressed.[24] Its existence has the effect of moving one prima facie to hold in suspicion any of the currently existing discussions of Calvin's prophetic consciousness. For, how—the complaint could be registered— could he have considered himself a prophet, when he does not seem to be clear on what a prophet actually *is* and, in fact, seems in some of his writings clearly to deny the existence of prophets in the post-apostolic period.

Thus, although I hold the conclusions of a number of these studies to be correct and the studies themselves to be excellent in many ways, it is my judgment that the weight of the burden of Calvin's prophetic awareness cannot be supported by any of them. It might be noted additionally that, even if it could, the subject really needs to be expanded upon and contextualized if it is to begin to hold the place of importance within a scholarly understanding of Calvin that it should. It should also be advanced that no one has treated the aggressive character of Calvin's reforming efforts in relation to his prophetic authority, as I will do in Chapters 4 and 5.

The present study will, then, strive to build upon, supplement, and develop the findings of the existing collection of studies, also correcting them in a few areas where their findings are imprecise or in need of qualification. Despite Calvin's conflicting statements on the locus, it will argue that he did believe himself a prophet. While not disparaging other approaches, this study will adopt an approach which aims to examine Calvin's sense of vocation with his context foremost in mind; extracting his sense of prophetic self-identity from his religiously and culturally contextualized observations and conduct.

---

[23] Engammare, "Calvin: A Prophet," 91, summarizing Millet, *Calvin*, 449.
[24] I address the problem briefly but insufficiently; see my *Establishing the Remnant Church in France*, 84–94.

Calvin on Prophecy: Revealing his Apparent Inconsistency

Unlike thinkers like Cassiodorus, Thomas Aquinas, François Lambert of Avignon, Heinrich Bullinger, and Peter Martyr Vermigli,[25] Calvin did not write a specific treatise, or locus, dedicated to prophecy. The sources for Calvin's views on the subject come from his oral and written communications. As one begins to examine these sources, one finds a curious mixture of ideas. There are places in the Frenchman's corpus where he seems to articulate unequivocally the position that prophecy has ended. For instance, we read in Calvin's comments on Daniel 9: 24 that the phrase "to seal up the vision and the prophecy" should be taken to mean that, with Christ, all prophecies have ceased. He, then, in order to further expound his position, notes that Rabbi Barbinel[26] has an argument which the rabbi believes defeats Christians on this point, namely, that it would be absurd to assume that God would deprive himself of something like prophecy which is such a remarkable blessing. Thus, here Barbinel is arguing for the continuation of prophecy—the very position which I contend Calvin holds—and yet one discovers Calvin arguing against this position.[27] Calvin registers the same opposition to the continuance of prophecy in his remarks on Acts 7: 37. In expounding the passage, he comments on Moses' promise of prophets in Deuteronomy 18: 15 in the following manner:

> now it is certain that the ministry of the prophets was temporal, as was also that of the law; until Christ should bring the full perfection of wisdom into the world. . . . The prophets, surely, were interpreters of the law and all their doctrine was, as it were, an addition or appendage of those things taught by Moses. But this was also certain, that Christ should bring a more perfect kind of doctrine in order that he should

---

[25] The works of these and other writers will be examined in Ch. 2.

[26] On Isaac Barbinel (1437–1508), whose surname is spelled variously but most often as Barbinel or Abravanel, see Benzion Netanyahu, *Don Isaac Abravanel: Statesman and Philosopher* (New York: Cornell University Press, 1998). On Early Modern engagement (including Calvin and others) with Jewish exegesis, see Max Engammare, "Humanism, Hebraism and Scriptural Hermeneutics," in Torrance Kirby, Emidio Campi, and Frank A. James III (eds), *A Companion to Peter Martyr Vermigli* (Leiden: Brill, 2009), 161–74; Bernard Roussel, "Des auteurs," in Guy Bedouelle and Bernard Roussel (eds), *Bible de Tous les Temps: Le Temps des Réformes et la Bible*, 8 vols. (Paris: Beauchesne, 1989), v. 199–282, esp. 215–33; specifically the section entitled "Une école Rhénane D'exégèse (ca 1525–ca 1540)."

[27] CO 41: 171–2.

make an end of all the prophecies (*ut qui finem impositurus esset prophetiis omnibus*) ... lest gospel faith should be doubtful.[28]

The same sentiment is replicated by Calvin in comments on Acts 3: 22 and in *Institutio* 2.15.1.[29]

This, then, is one strand of material which one finds in Calvin's œuvre. While it may seem fairly conclusive, it is not. Calvin can also speak of prophecy as still existing within the Christian church of his day. He does this in comments on Romans 12: 6. He first asserts that "Christ and his gospel have put an end to all the former prophecies and to all the oracles of God," but follows this by arguing for a continuation of the spiritual gift. In "the Christian Church today prophecy is (*prophetia hodie ... est*) almost nothing except a correct understanding of the scriptures and a singular ability in explaining them well."[30] Plainly by referring to prophecy "today," he intimates that prophecy and, hence, prophets still exist. Further support for this second strand of material can be garnered from the Frenchman's sermons. In a sermon on Deuteronomy 18: 14–22, Calvin teaches that God promises prophets to the New Testament church. He summarizes the basic point of God's promise to the church with the declaration that: "there will always be prophets."[31] To make his point more explicit, he declares: "God promised a prophet not only to the Jews but also to us ... "[32] "I have proved already," he says in a later sermon on the same chapter, that Deuteronomy 18: 15 "is not meant of Moses alone, and of those who lived under the Old Testament but that it extends even to us also and comprehends in it the whole reign of our Lord Jesus Christ."[33] The same basic point is expressed in his exposition of 1 Corinthians 14: 29–31.[34] These examples provide hints of a second strand, or trajectory, of material which one can find in the Frenchman's œuvre; a trajectory which not only allows for the existence of prophets in the Early Modern church but seems to

---

[28] CO 48: 149; also SC 8: 316 (Sermon on Acts 7: 35–7).
[29] CO 48: 74–5; CO 2: 362.
[30] *Iohannis Calvini Commentarius in epistolam Pauli ad Romanos*, ed. T. H. L. Parker (Leiden: Brill, 1981), 270.
[31] CO 27: 499 (Sermon on Deuteronomy 18: 9–15).
[32] CO 27: 519 (Sermon on Deuteronomy 18: 16–20).
[33] CO 27: 527 (Sermon on Deuteronomy 18: 16–20).
[34] CO 49: 499–500 (Commentary on 1 Corinthians 12: 10) and CO 49: 529–30 (on 1 Corinthians 14: 29–31).

take for granted that they do exist and have been promised by God to "us."

But Calvin can also speak on the question of the existence of prophets in a third manner, namely, with ambivalence. He declares, for example, in a sermon on Ephesians 4: 11–12 that prophets are rare.

> Now in regards to the office of prophets, we do not have the office today as excellently as they did then, as one can see . . . [God has taken this gift away because of the ingratitude of the world] . . . The prophets served as expounders of the will of God, and they had a much better understanding of the Scriptures than the common teachers, whose office was to instruct.[35]

Thus, the Early Modern era is blessed with some prophets, but only to a minimal degree. While the view expressed here does not contradict outright the position asserted in support of the second trajectory of thought, it raises significant questions about it. The weight of these questions becomes considerably heavier when we look at the year 1543. For in that year, in the 1543 edition of his *Institutio*, Calvin makes his uncertainty explicit by producing lines which remain in all subsequent editions of his magnum opus: "By prophets, he means not all interpreters of the divine will, but those who excelled by special revelation; none such now exist or they are less manifest (*quales nunc vel nulli exstant, vel minus sunt conspicui*)."[36] Thus, here Calvin would seem to confess confusion, or perhaps at the very least, uncertainty on the topic. He seems simply not to know whether prophets exist in his own day or not.

It would appear, then, that for Calvin all of the following positions may be accurately ascribed to him. (1) Prophets do *not* exist any longer in the Christian church. (2) Prophets *do* exist in the Christian church today (with the qualification also asserted: Prophets exist but *are rare* in the Christian church today). (3) Prophets *may or may not* exist in the Christian church today. Naturally, one can interpret this material in different ways, but the point is that it requires careful interpretation.

---

[35] CO 51: 556.
[36] CO 2: 779. This is cited from *Institutio* 4.3.4, but the quotation is from material which was added in Calvin's 1543 editing of his magnum opus.

Analysis of Calvin on prophecy may be continued for a moment longer by noting the different senses which Calvin seems to have ascribed to it. We have seen that, for Calvin, prophecy is *interpreting*. I have shown this in relation to Romans 12: 6, for instance. He makes the same point in comments on 1 Thessalonians 5: 20, observing that, by the term prophesying, the writer of Thessalonians does not mean the "gift of foretelling the future" but, as in 1 Corinthians 14: 3, the science of the interpretation of scripture, so that a prophet is the interpreter of the divine will.[37] Yet, when expounding Daniel 7: 10 ("And I, Daniel, alone saw the vision"), Calvin clearly holds that prophecy is *prognostication*. He states that Daniel "alone was the recipient of these prophecies, as he alone was endued with the power of predicting future events."[38] Calvin can also express a broader conception of prophecy. In his homily on Deuteronomy 18: 21–2, he can ascribe to prophecy a *range of activities*.

> The office of prophet was not only to tell of things to come, but also to give people good instruction, to exhort them to amend their lives, and to edify them in the faith. As, for example, we see that the prophets did not only say such a thing will befall you but also confirmed the covenant by which God had adopted the people of Israel and told them of the coming of the redeemer on whom the hope of all God's children was grounded. Moreover, they comforted the sorrowful by preaching the promises of God's favor to them; further they threatened the people when they became disordered; they discovered their faults and transgressions; they cited sinners to God's judgment to make them humble themselves.[39]

Here prophecy would appear to include a range of activities including urging hearers towards personal reform, predicting the coming messiah, comforting, threatening, preaching, and other actions. Hence, we might ascribe to Calvin various positions. (1) Prophecy is the special gift of interpreting the divine will. (2) Prophecy is predicting the future. (3) Prophecy is a range of activities which includes not only predicting the future but also comforting, warning, and other functions which are often associated with preaching and the preaching office. Again, one can interpret this material in different ways. But so long as it remains unexamined, it is impossible for one to conclude

---

[37] CO 49: 517–18.   [38] CO 41: 55–7.
[39] CO 27: 529–30 (Sermon on Deuteronomy 18: 21–2).

with any degree of certainty that Calvin believed *himself* to be a prophet. For, what kind of prophet might he have held himself to be? Indeed, how could he have believed himself to be one, if he may well have held that prophets did not exist in his own day?

STRUCTURE AND AIMS

The remaining chapters may be outlined in the following way. Chapter 2 will explore the Christian church's handling of the locus of prophecy, outlining the two major trajectories I have found within thought on prophecy during the patristic and medieval eras and identifying the changes which occur in thinking on the locus among a number of Early Modern thinkers. The historical, social, and intellectual milieu within which these views on prophecy were developed will be attended to so that the chapter's findings are appropriately contextualized. These findings are vital because they will assist me in Chapters 3, 4, and 5, in which I explain Calvin's thought on prophecy and his belief that he had been raised up by God to be a prophet.

With this accomplished, Chapter 3 turns to Calvin himself. This chapter will demonstrate that, like a number of his contemporaries, Calvin saw himself as a prophet raised up by God to reform the church through authoritative scriptural interpretation and application. His was specifically a calling like that given to Old Testament prophets. He was raised up, he believed, to fight Roman Catholic "idolatry," just as Isaiah, Jeremiah, and the other prophets had been called to fight the idolatry prevalent in their own church. The chapter will contend that Calvin, again like contemporaries, was drawn to the Old Testament office and steered clear of the Pauline office of prophet in part due to the Anabaptists' appropriation of the latter. It will also demonstrate, in concert with Chapters 4 and 5, that Calvin's fundamental conviction in relation to his vocation was that he had been set "over nations and kingdoms to tear down and destroy, to build and to plant" or, as he indicated in his lecture on Jeremiah 1: 10, "to reduce the world to order."[40] Here my aim is not to resurrect Rodolphe Peter's idea that Calvin identified strongly with Jeremiah,[41] though

[40] CO 37: 480.
[41] Peter, *Sermons sur les livres de Jérémie et des Lamentations*, SC 6: XIV.

I contend that this passage from Jeremiah's prophecy is a particularly important one for conceptualizing Calvin's understanding of his own prophetic commission.

Delving deeper into Calvin's sense of his prophetic authority, Chapters 4 and 5 take up his work on behalf of France. They demonstrate how, commencing likely in the 1550s, Calvin developed a plan to win France for the gospel; a plan which included the possibility of war. Part of his pursuit of this plan involved his training of a group of "prophets" whom he, and the Venerable Company of Pastors, sent into France. This training commenced in late 1555, or early 1556, and was still being carried out when he died in 1564. These minister-prophets were sent into France with the mandate to support the Huguenot churches and also to displace the Catholic priests as the authoritative voice of God within the country. They were to be God's heralds, being sent into the country to labor intensely to undermine the king's authority, on the grounds that he was an indefatigable supporter of idolatry, convince the French Reformed congregations that they were already in a war with the monarch and his government, and prepare them for a possible military uprising. An additional part of this plan saw Calvin search for a high-ranking French noble who was willing to support the evangelical religion, even if it meant initiating a coup. From as early as 1536, Calvin had indicated that it was the "duty" of such a noble— referred to more generally by Calvin as a lesser, or popular, magistrate (*popularis magistratus*)—to protect the people from the king when that king had become tyrannical.[42] Accordingly, Calvin was not, here, supporting rebellion initiated by private individuals, though his adherence to the command to submit to the "governing powers" (Romans 13: 1) could still very plausibly be questioned, since he was knowingly working to foment a kind of legal insurrection. The end result of these two chapters will be to elaborate upon the discoveries of Chapter 3 on Calvin's prophetic consciousness, particularly along the lines of analyzing the character of Calvin's prophetic authority. This study's findings will be summarized in Chapter 6.

The study seeks to break new ground on two levels. First, it seeks to contribute to the "quest for the historical Calvin" (to borrow Bouwsma's

[42] CO 1: 248 (from 1536 *Institutio*) which appears in *Institutio* 4.20.31 of the 1559 edn.

phrase[43]) through a thorough examination and critical analysis of his prophetic awareness. This monograph will unearth something of the character of this man who seemed so obsessed with imposing his version of the *regimen Dei* upon European Christendom. He was, it seems to me, an individual who thought of himself as possessing a role of profound, almost unparalleled, significance to his own and subsequent eras. But scholarship has, until recently, largely avoided considering the nature of that role. This monograph aims to contribute to our understanding of it, and (therefore) of him. The portrait produced is of a Calvin who fits within a non-mystical, non-apocalyptic prophetic tradition which aligned itself with the Old Testament prophets, whom he saw as authoritative biblical interpreters. This portrait requires one to reflect on the sense of authority Calvin believed himself to possess, which I will contend was akin to that of Elijah, Isaiah, or Paul.

Second, reflecting on Calvin's work on behalf of France and his efforts to secure fundamental change within that country, this monograph offers a meditation on his understanding of reformation or, to put it another way, of his vocation as a reformer. It argues that in his work for France he pursued an expansionist, insurrectionist reforming agenda which blended the religious, political, and social towards the end of making France Protestant at all levels of society. Here, I might note that considerable scholarly work has been done on Calvin's views on civil government and on the question of whether or not he supported active resistance against the civil magistrate.[44] While the present study owes much to these engaging investigations, it contends that too much emphasis has, at times, been placed on this specific issue, over emphasizing its significance and, in so doing, obscuring the connections which exist between political, religious, and social *topoi* in Calvin's reforming labors.[45] These connections can

---

[43] Bouwsma, *John Calvin*, 1.

[44] Recent works include Max Engammare, "Calvin monarchomaque? Du soupçon à l'argument," *Archiv für Reformationsgeschichte*, 89 (1998), 207–26; Philip Benedict, "The Dynamics of Protestant Militancy: France, 1555–1563," in Philip Benedict *et al.* (eds), *Reformation, Revolt and Civil War in France and the Netherlands 1555–1585* (Amsterdam: Royal Netherlands Academy of Arts and Sciences, 1999), 35–50; John R. Witte, *The Reformation of Rights* (Cambridge: CUP, 2007), 39–80; Paul-Alexis Mellet, *Les Traités monarchomaques: Confusion des temps, résistance armée et monarchie parfaite (1560–1600)* (Geneva: Droz, 2007).

[45] Sheldon Wolin speaks of "Calvin's thought . . . revealing . . . the interpenetration of political and religious modes of thought" in "Calvin and the Reformation: The

be seen, I contend, when one takes a broader view, considering him and his work on behalf of the Evangel; and I think a particularly intriguing and insightful angle from which to approach things is to consider his work on behalf of the Evangel *in France*. While I concede that Calvin was generally opposed to individuals rising up of their own accord against the king,[46] I will set forth evidence in this monograph which shows that this opposition is only a small piece of a larger puzzle, and must be understood as such. Indeed, Calvin seems to push distinctions between individual resistance and resistance led by a popular magistrate to their limits through his own tireless campaign to prepare the Huguenots for war against the Catholic king led by a high-ranking noble (referred to as a Prince of the Blood), who ended up being Louis of Condé. And when one considers, moreover, that his reforming work included at least one attempt to raise money and troops to place at the disposal of a noble around the time of the ill-fated Conspiracy of Amboise,[47] one begins to obtain a clearer sense of the character of this work. This study, then, will contend that Calvin's fight against French Catholicism possessed a (cryptic) seditious and imperialistic quality and that this was an outworking of his beliefs concerning his mission. "The city of Geneva is" for Calvin, as Oberman observed, "a bridgehead for the expansion of the kingdom of Christ."[48]

Political Education of Protestantism," *American Political Science Review*, 51/2 (1957), 428–53; esp. 429.

[46] Though his position shifts in later life; see Willem Nijenhuis, "The Limits of Civil Disobedience in Calvin's Last-Known Sermons: Development of his Ideas on the Right of Civil Resistance," in *Ecclesia Reformata*, ii. *Studies on the Reformation* (Leiden: Brill, 1994), 73–94. One of the citations from Calvin's sermons used by Nijenhuis to establish his position did not seem to me to be sufficiently clear, but, that being said, the remainder of his citations and references were impressive and convincing.

[47] See Alain Dufour, "L'Affaire de Maligny (Lyon, 4–5 septembre 1560) vue à travers la correspondance de Calvin et de Bèze," *Cahiers d'Histoire*, 8 (1963), 269–80. This will be discussed further below.

[48] Heiko Oberman, "One Epoch: Three Reformations," in *The Reformation: Roots and Ramifications*, tr. Andrew Colin Gow (Edinburgh: T&T Clark, 1994), 217. This study's findings will, in part, concur with Oberman on the fact that it is false or, at the very least, extraordinarily careless to label Calvin a "magisterial" reformer according to the typology of George Williams, *The Radical Reformation* (Philadelphia: Westminster Press, 1975), pp. xxiii–xxxi, esp. xxiv.

2

Prophets and Prophecy up to Calvin

In order for someone to believe he, or she, is a prophet, they must have some conception of what a prophet is. Such a conception will invariably be linked with contemporary historical events, biblical interpretation, various other contextual factors, and of course the beliefs held by one's contemporaries. The present chapter will examine these issues as they relate to Calvin. Taking center stage in these considerations will be the thought on prophecy of several of Calvin's contemporaries. Ulrich Zwingli, Johannes Oecolampadius, Heinrich Bullinger, Theodor Bibliander, Conrad Pellican, Martin Bucer, Rudolph Gwalther, Peter Martyr Vermigli, and Wolfgang Musculus will all receive attention; some brief consideration will also be given to Martin Luther, Philip Melanchthon, and some other Lutherans. Discerning the character of their thought on the locus will help us to excavate Calvin's prophetic awareness and the character of his prophetic ministry. But before approaching these individuals, attention must be paid to other church authorities who wrote on the *topos* before Calvin or any of his fellow reformers were born.

PROPHECY IN EARLY AND MEDIEVAL WESTERN CHRISTENDOM[1]

Prophecy has ever been a part of the church's life. In the judgment of many within Christendom, prophets continued to exist in the

---

[1] There is need for a new outline of prophecy in the Middle Ages. See *inter alia*, Paul Alphandéry, "Prophètes et ministère prophétique dans le Moyen Age latin," *Revue d'Histoire et de Philosophie Religieuses*, 12 (1932), 334–59; Marjorie Reeves, *The*

post-apostolic era and would exist until the end of time. "The charism of prophecy," Apollinarius observed, "must exist in all the Church until the second coming: this is the view of St Paul."[2] The church has thought carefully about what it means to be a prophet. The positions which one finds within writings on the topic from the ancient to the Early Modern eras are diverse but generally fall into two traditions or trajectories. Coverage of these, which will be referred to as Tradition 1 and Tradition 2 for the sake of convenience, is not intended to be exhaustive, but sufficiently thorough to provide an understanding of the intellectual and institutional context from within which Calvin did his thinking on prophecy. It should be noted at the outset that these two traditions are by no means mutually exclusive. In fact, it is quite common to find thinkers who could appropriately be placed in both. What ultimately determines my treatment of an individual under one category or the other is the emphasis which characterizes his, or her, thought.

Early and Medieval Thinking on Prophecy: Tradition 1

The understanding of prophecy which one finds in early and medieval Christian writings in the West exhibits a profound interest in knowledge, specifically knowledge of a supernatural character. This understanding spawns a significant amount of reflection upon the character of this knowledge, as anyone who examines the writings of major figures throughout the period can see. Augustine produces important reflections on this theme in his *Super Genesim ad Litteram*,[3] which would be repeated by thinkers throughout the medieval and Early Modern eras. Likewise, Cassiodorus' influential short

---

Influence of Prophecy in the Later Middle Ages: A Study in Joachimism (Oxford: OUP, 1969); Reeves, "History and Prophecy in Medieval Thought," *Medievalia et Humanistica*, NS 5 (1974), 51–75; Reeves, "The Medieval Heritage," in Reeves (ed.), *Prophetic Rome in the High Renaissance Period* (Oxford: Clarendon Press, 1992), 3–26; Bernard McGinn, "Awaiting an End: Research in Medieval Apocalypticism 1974–1981," *Medievalia et Humanistica*, NS 11 (1982), 263–89; McGinn, *The Calabrian Abbot: Joachim of Fiore in the History of Western Thought* (New York: Macmillan Publishing Co., 1985).

[2] The opinion of Apollinarius as cited by Eusebius in *Ecclesiastical History* 5.17, which is cited in *St Thomas Aquinas Summa Theologiae*, vol. 45 *(2a2ae. 171–178) Prophecy and Other Charisms*, tr. Roland Potter OP (Cambridge: CUP, 2006), 159.

[3] In his *Super Gen. ad litt.*, book 12, chs 6–9, esp. 9 (PL 34: 458–61).

chapter on prophecy in the preface to his *Expositio Psalmorum* contains material upon which the church would ponder for centuries, including the assertion: "Prophecy is divine revelation."[4] The same focus can be seen in Gregory the Great's reflections on prophecy in his homilies on Ezekiel.[5] By the beginning of the thirteenth century, one finds these notes emphasized by Albertus Magnus[6] and Bonaventure.[7] Thomas Aquinas' first question in his treatment of prophecy is: "Is prophecy a matter of knowledge?," which he answers affirmatively, making clear it is *scientia* which surpasses all human knowledge and which is revealed by God.[8] Many medieval thinkers connect the knowledge possessed by the prophet with that possessed by the angels. Thus William of Auxerre introduces his discussion of prophecy (his sixth treatise in book 2 of his *Summa Aurea*) by stating that "because prophets see what they see in the mirror or eternity, like angels do, after we have treated the knowledge of angels," which William had done in treatise 5, "we ought to go on to treat prophecy."[9] By the fourteenth century, one finds this emphasis on knowledge in statements such as this one from Nicholas of Lyra, who discusses prophecy in terms of God "elevating the mind to supernatural knowledge (*elevens ad supernaturalem cognitionem*)."[10] This understanding is in line with analyses of the basic meaning of the word prophet, *prophētēs*, which one finds in authors from Eusebius to Basil, Chrysostom, Isidore, and Gregory.[11] Though deriving the word's meaning from slightly different Greek origins, all of these thinkers maintain that the basic sense is predictor of the future (i.e. by divine revealing of knowledge about that future). The work of Isidore seems to have been particularly influential here.[12]

[4] Cassiodorus, *De Prophetia* in his Psalms *praefatio*, PL 70: 12.
[5] *Homélies sur Ézéchiel*, ed. Charles Morel SJ (Paris: Éditions du Cerf, 1986), 50–64.
[6] Albertus Magnus, *S.D.E. Alberti Magni . . . Opera Omnia*, 19 vols. (Mon. Westfalorum in aedibus aschendorff, 1952), 19: 2, 85, 637.
[7] *Bonaventure Opera*, 9: 564. [8] *Aquinas Opera* ST II-II q171 a1.
[9] William of Auxerre, *Summa aurea*, 2: fo. 53ʳ.
[10] Nicholas of Lyra in "Prohemium" to his postillae on the Psalms in *Lyra Biblia Latina*. See, as well, the *Additiones* and *Replicae* of Paul of Burgos and Matthew Doering, respectively.
[11] See Eusebius, *Demonstratio Evangel. v Prol.* (PG 22: 345); Basil, *Comm in Is* 102 (PG 30: 284); Chrysostom, "*Vidi Dominum*" *Hom* 2.3 (PG 56: 111); Isidore of Seville, *Etymologiarum* 7.8.32 (PL 82: 283); Gregory, *In Ezekiel* i, *Hom* 1, 1 (PG 76: 786).
[12] His derivation is followed, or interacted with, by a number of thinkers throughout the history of the church such as Thomas and Suarez. See Anthony John Maas, *Christ in Type and Prophecy* (New York: Benziger Brothers, 1893), 1: 82.

This prophetic knowledge is, however, not normally restricted to knowledge of the future. In more thorough treatments of the locus, prophetic knowledge is said, more precisely, to be knowledge of what is hidden. It can be knowledge of the past or the present as well as knowledge of the future. One can find this spelled out very clearly in Junillus Africanus' *Instituta regularia divinae legis*[13] and in Gregory the Great's first homily on Ezekiel. "Prophecy has three tenses; the past, of course; the present and the future."[14] Continuing, Gregory explores these three tenses, and elaborates on how prophecy can be understood according to each of these tenses. He points to interesting scriptural examples in order to argue his case that revelation of the present or the past can still be labeled as prophecy. Similar thoughts are found in Theodoret,[15] and in Aquinas' handling of the *topos*, specifically his raising of the question: Whether prophecy only relates to future contingencies.[16] Aquinas also addresses it in his comments on 1 Corinthians 14: 1–2.[17] Moreover some writers, like William of Auxerre, argue that the knowledge of prophets is a knowledge of the divine essence (referred to as the mirror of eternity[18]), and thus it is clearly a knowledge which amounts to more than a knowledge of the future alone.

The identification of prophecy as supernatural knowledge divinely conferred upon the prophet does not stop these thinkers from subjecting it to exhaustive analysis. Prophecy is often divided by them into kinds. Jerome, for instance, divides prophecy into predestination, foreknowledge, and denunciation.[19] Similar divisions appear in a myriad of other writers, such as Peter Lombard, William of Auxerre, Hugh of St Cher, and Thomas Aquinas.[20] Prophecy is also defined

---

[13] See Junillus Africanus, *Exegesis and Empire in the Early Byzantine Mediterranean*; *Junillus Africanus and the Instituta Regularia Divinae Legis*, ed. Michael Maas *et al.* (Tübingen: Mohr Siebeck, 2003), 128–31.

[14] Gregory, *Homélies sur Ézéchiel*, 56.

[15] Theodoret, *In Psalm. Praef.* (PG 80: 861).

[16] *Aquinas Opera* ST II-II q171 a3.

[17] Aquinas, *Expositio in Epistolam I ad Corinthios* 14, in *Aquinas Opera* 13: 281; Lanfranc of Bec, *In epistolam I ad Corinthios* 14 (PL 150: 202); Herveus Burgidolensis, *In epistolam 1 ad Corinthios expositio* 14 (PL 181: 958–9); Peter Lombard, *In 1 epistolam ad Corinthios* 14 (PL 191: 1659).

[18] William, *Summa aurea*, 2: fo. 53^r.

[19] *Commentaire sur Saint Matthieu*, ed. Émile Bonnard (Paris: Éditions du Cerf, 1977), 80.

[20] Lombard, *Prologo super Psalmos* (PL 191: 59); William of Auxerre, *Summa aurea*, 1: fo. 53^v; Hugh of St Cher "De prophetia," in Jean-Pierre Torrell OP (ed.),

according to the mode of prophesying (*secundum modum prophe-tandi*) as one finds in Isidore of Seville's *Etymologiae*, where he distinguishes prophecy as (1) ecstasy; (2) vision; (3) dreams; (4) through a cloud; (5) a voice from heaven; (6) the receiving of an oracle; and (7) being filled with the Holy Spirit.[21] Such divisions appear throughout the Middle Ages; thus one finds theologians discussing the grades or degrees (*gradus*) of prophecy.[22] William of Auxerre, for instance, sets out four different modes (*modis*) of proph-ecy and later five different kinds (*genera*) of prophecy.[23]

In this thorough analysis, patristic and medieval thinkers exhibit concern for several issues. Among these is the state of the recipient of such supernatural knowledge. As early as Origen, one finds thought-ful reflection on the prophet as one who must be pure, wholehearted in devotion to God, earnest in his or her spiritual exercises, in abstinence, particularly sexual abstinence, and in holiness.[24] Likewise, there is copious discussion of the state into which the prophet is brought upon receiving this charism. That state was sometimes referred to as ecstasy, though serious debate occurs over precisely what this means, with the question of Montanism and the opinions of Plato and Middle Platonism clearly providing some of the back-ground for these debates. Thinkers like Tertullian, in his *De anima*, enter into consideration of the question, linking it with the common issues surrounding understanding of sleep, dreams, ecstasy, and the soul.[25] Such issues were still the topic of serious discussion and debate in the thirteenth century.[26] These debates raised a number of

Théorie de la prophétie et philosophie de la connaissance aux environs de 1230: La Contribution d'Hugues de Saint-Cher (Ms. Douai 434, Question 481) (Leuven: Spici-legium Sacrum Lovanense, 1977), 32; see also, *Aquinas Opera* ST II-II q174 a1.

[21] *Etymologiarum* 7.8.32 (PL 82: 283–7; esp 285–7).

[22] *Aquinas Opera* ST II-II q174 a3; also Denis, *D. Dionysii Carthusiani insigne opus commentariorum in Psalmos omnes Davidicos* (Cologne: apud Haeredes J. Quentelii & G. Calenium, 1558), 3.

[23] He adds a fifth to his list, hesitantly; see William, *Summa aurea*, 2: fo. 53ʳ.

[24] See the discussion in Gunnar af Hällström, *Charismatic Succession: A Study on Origen's Concept of Prophecy* (Helsinki: Finnish Exegetical Society, 1985), 10–21.

[25] Plato, it will be recalled, discusses mania in *Phaedrus* and contrasts it with sober mindedness. See Laura Nasrallah, *An Ecstasy of Folly: Prophecy and Authority in Early Christianity* (Cambridge, Mass.: Harvard University Press, 2003), 29–60. Also, J. L. Ash, "The Decline of Ecstatic Prophecy in the Early Church," *Theological Studies*, 37 (1976), 227–52.

[26] Aquinas devotes a whole question to the topic of ecstasy (de *raptu*) in, *Aquinas Opera* ST II-II q175.

questions, including ones having to do with whether the prophet, given that he, or she, is experiencing a kind of special communion with God, descends into a kind of madness, loses self-control, or receives a revelation which supposes in some way separation from their senses (*abstractio a sensibus*).[27] While variation in responses to these questions can be found, paramount among the concerns detected in these responses is an interest in differentiating God's revelation to a prophet from the experience of demonic possession. This concern issued in a number of questions being asked about whether demons could ever prophesy, whether they could prophesy anything that was true, whether a true prophet of God knows what he, or she, is prophesying, and so forth. Here again, as so often was the case, Augustine's thoughts on these matters would prove enormously important.[28]

Intimately intertwined with interest in the state of the prophet was interest in the character and manner of the prophet's knowledge. Augustine's reflections played a pivotal role here as well, as did those of Jerome. In *Super Genesim ad Litteram*, Augustine discusses prophetic knowledge in terms of signs being manifested in the human spirit through likenesses of corporeal objects and light being given to the mind of the prophet so that the images can be understood. Continuing his reflections, Augustine produces a sophisticated analysis of corporeal, spiritual, and intellectual vision, treating along the way, *inter alia*, the prophet Daniel's interpreting of the king's dream and Moses' vision of God.[29] One can also find discussion of such matters in the commentaries of Jerome.[30] In taking up such themes, these fathers set the agenda for the treatment of prophecy in the medieval West, an agenda which exhibits a profound interest in the figurative character of prophetic knowledge. Examining the later works of any number of theologians, one finds nuanced elaboration upon the themes canvassed by Augustine. Characteristic of reflections on these matters is Aquinas' comment:

> It ought to be said that prophetic revelation happens in four ways: by the inflowing of intellectual light, by the emission of intellectual species,

[27] Augustine, *Super Gen. ad litt.* 12.9 (PL 34: 461).
[28] Augustine, *Super Gen. ad litt.* 12.9 (PL 34: 461).
[29] Augustine, *Super Gen. ad litt.* 12.9 and 12.10–27 (PL 34: 461–4).
[30] Jerome, *Comm. Amos* 1.2 (PL 25: 1041).

by the impression or ordination of forms in the imagination, and by the expression of sensible images.[31]

In his handling of the next question (on the divisions of prophecy), Aquinas queries, "whether prophecy which has intellective and imaginative vision is more excellent than that which is only intellective?"[32] In both, Aquinas dialogues with Augustine and Jerome as well as with his medieval dialogue partner, Peter Lombard. Augustine had asserted that the prophet who enjoyed both intellective and imaginative vision was superior to the one who enjoyed only the intellective. He said Daniel was a good example of one who experienced both.[33] Likewise, Jerome had distinguished between prophets and hagiographer (*hagiographos*), with only the former having both intellective and imaginative vision.[34] Yet the *Glossa* and Lombard,[35] in their prefaces to the Psalms, speak in a manner which seems to indicate that any imaginative vision detracts from the purity of the Spirit's revelation of an intellective vision to the prophet. In adjudicating the various issues at stake in this debate, Aquinas argues against—or at least, does not concur simply and in a straightforward manner with— Augustine and Jerome. He qualifies his handling of Augustine, explaining what the eminent North African father had really intended to say in his comments on intellective and imaginative vision. Aquinas' intention in doing so is clearly to imply that his position and that of Augustine's are not at odds with one another. But the question of whether Aquinas' position represents a discernible shift away from that of Augustine, or not, is not important enough for us to spend much time on it. Suffice it to say, then, that Aquinas *does* seem to favor the idea of the superiority of a bare (*nude*) contemplation of the truth which does not require mediating corporeal imagines. This, he seems to indicate, approaches what the blessed enjoy in the vision which they have of God in heaven.[36]

Deeper analysis of the character of the prophetic vision also appears in the writings of several theologians. In Aquinas' engagement with the character of prophetic knowledge, for example, he takes up, in article 3 of question 174, a query related specifically to the imaginative vision and whether distinctions can be made with

---

[31] *Aquinas Opera* ST II-II q173 a3.   [32] *Aquinas Opera* ST II-II q174 a2.
[33] Augustine, *Super Gen. ad litt.* 12.9 (PL 34: 461).
[34] Jerome, *Prolog.I & II Para.* (PL 28: 598) as cited in *Aquinas Opera* ST II-II q174 a2.
[35] PL 191: 58.   [36] *Aquinas Opera* ST II-II q174 a2.

regards to it.[37] The same is true not only of Dominicans but also Franciscans. Bonaventure weighs in on the subject as well, adding his own appraisal of the character of the prophetic vision, which he argues is threefold, *secundum sensum exteriorem, imaginationem et intellectum*.[38] The point is that for many medieval thinkers supernatural knowledge was integral to the idea of prophecy and was, for that reason, scrutinized with intricacy, intensity, and precision.

This fact might be lingered over for a moment longer, because in so doing it will allow us to craft a brief but helpful picture of what these thinkers held a prophet to be, in the most elemental sense. This can be discerned if we take note of the fact that many of the thinkers who have been examined here are quite willing to comment on who the greatest prophet might be. Augustine was willing to mention the name of Daniel as a pre-eminent example of one in whom was embodied the highest qualities of a prophet, though he does not specifically designate Daniel as *the* greatest. Others in the Middle Ages identified David as the greatest of all prophets. This number includes the *Glossa Ordinaria* and Peter Lombard.[39] Others called Moses the greatest, as can be seen through the analysis of the question provided by Aquinas.[40] The answers of these thinkers differ, but their reasoning is invariably similar. For all of them, the decision as to who the greatest prophet was is reached by taking their conceptions of what the highest form of prophetic knowledge is and then endeavoring to find the prophet who embodied that form most perfectly. Thus, the prophet can be conceptualized *simpliciter* through the lens of knowledge.

Early and Medieval Thinking on Prophecy: Tradition 2

A second tradition of thought on prophecy exists. This tradition also focuses on knowledge, though in a manner quite different from Tradition 1. The two traditions are not mutually exclusive. In fact, as mentioned earlier, a sizeable portion of those examined in this

---

[37] *Aquinas Opera* ST II-II q174 a3.   [38] *Bonaventure Opera* 1.281, arg 4.

[39] David, it was asserted, prophesied "on a more exalted and distinguished level (*digniori atque excellentiori modo*)," Lombard, *Prologo super Psalmos* (PL 191: 55). On the figurative character of much prophetic knowledge see Aquinas, *Expositio in Epistolam I ad Corinthios* 13, in *Aquinas Opera* 13: 263.

[40] *Aquinas Opera* ST II-II q174 a4.

chapter possess views which place them within both traditions. More will be said on the relationship between the two traditions in a moment, but first the basic character of this second trajectory will be expounded.

The prophet, according to this tradition, is conceived as one who interprets the scripture. This view, like Tradition 1, garners support from a number of important early and medieval sources. Among the former, the names of John Chrysostom and Ambrosiaster should be mentioned. Ambrosiaster, for example, declares: "Prophets however, are those who explain the scriptures. In the beginning there were, though, prophets such as Agabus and the four virgins who prophesied, as is found in the Acts of the Apostles [21: 9]. This was for the purpose of commending the beginnings of the faith [Acts 7: 2ff.]. Now, however, those who interpret scripture are called prophets."[41] The views of Ambrosiaster and Chrysostom are repeated throughout the Middle Ages.

This tradition does not exhibit a sophisticated concern for the character of prophetic knowledge, as we saw among proponents of the first tradition. One finds no discussion of the differences between intellectual and imaginative knowledge being produced in relation to this tradition. Rather, adherents to this second tradition betray a different range of interests. One of the foremost is a concern for precisely what the prophet is called to do. While the views set forth by these thinkers on this question reflect a considerable amount of overlap, some differences do appear. We find that some thinkers give prominence to the work of revealing the mysteries found in scripture while others emphasize proclamation and practical application. The latter category, for example, includes Sedulius Scotus, Bruno, Rhabanus, Lanfranc, Strabo, Haymo, Pseudo-Jerome, and (to some extent) Aquinas.[42] Concerning the content of the prophet's proclamation, some hold that it is primarily doctrinal in nature, while others see it as

---

[41] Ambrosiaster, *Divi Ambrosii episcope Mediolanensis omnia . . .* (Basel: A. Petri, 1516), 2, fo. 208ᵛ as cited by Elsie McKee, *Elders and the Plural Ministry: The Role of Exegetical History in Illuminating John Calvin's Theology* (Geneva: Droz, 1988), 65.

[42] Some citations: Bruno (PL 153: 192); Rhabanus (PL 112: 116), Lanfranc (PL 150: 199); Strabo (PL 114: 542) and Haymo (PL 117: 580); Pseudo-Jerome (PL 30: 788); Aquinas, *Expositio in Epistolam Romanos* 12.6 (vol 13, 123); William of St Thierry (PL 180: 673). In contrast, some, like Herveus Burgidolensis, argue for prediction of the future alone (PL 181: 767–8). For additional references to medieval exegetes see McKee, *Elders*, 44, 65.

moral instruction, and still others do not comment explicitly on the question.[43] In all the writers known to the present author, Tradition 2 is associated with the New Testament, specifically Paul. Many writers, in fact, make an explicit distinction between the Old Testament prophet and the New Testament prophet, with the former being identified as a recipient of supernatural knowledge and the latter as an interpreter.[44] This is a virtual commonplace.

But the fact that the character of this knowledge was not inspected more thoroughly leaves its mark upon the tradition in ways which are, arguably, not entirely helpful. For while this second tradition avoids what may, in the eyes of some, be considered an unhelpful speculative quality which characterizes Tradition 1, it leaves itself open to the accusation of being vague. What, precisely, *is* prophetic about this work of interpreting or exhorting or preaching which is done by the Christian prophet? How is the prophet's interpreting distinguished from that offered by a pastor? These sorts of questions were, occasionally, taken up, but not as often as one might expect. Some argued for a kind of special enlightenment which is given to the prophet so that he, or she, can plumb the depths of the mysteries of scripture; a divine illumination by which they were aided in their understanding of scripture. It was sometimes explained that this was what distinguished the New Testament "prophet" from "doctor," the latter having to study in order to come to an understanding of the scriptures. As early as Chrysostom, one discovers this distinction,[45] and it is also found in later thinkers, like Nicholas of Lyra.[46] This would be argued when treating texts like 1 Corinthians 12: 28 ("first apostles, second prophets, third teachers (*doctores*)"). But while those who represent this second tradition hold that the doctor must study and labor for his understanding of the scriptures, they do not spell out in careful detail what precisely it means for the prophet to gain understanding without such study and labor. How are the truths of

---

[43] Additionally, some writers argue that the prophet engages in private proclamation while other writers see the office as entailing public proclamation, i.e. preaching of the gospel. John Thompson, *John Calvin and the Daughters of Sarah: Women in Regular and Exceptional Roles in the Exegesis of Calvin, his Predecessors, and his Contemporaries* (Geneva: Droz, 1992), 190–7.

[44] See the brief discussion in McKee, *Elders*, 64–5.   [45] PG 61: 265.

[46] Lyra's treatment of 1 Cor. 12: 10 in *Lyra Biblia Latina*, where he remarks simply: "second prophets. These are those receiving revelations immediately from God (*accipientes a deo immediate revelationes*)."

the Bible revealed to him or her by the Spirit? Do they, at least, have to read the scriptures, and (if so) must they read them in the original languages or does the Latin Vulgate suffice? Of course, by the Early Modern era a host of humanist-trained exegetes would argue that the ability to read the languages (Hebrew and Greek) was essential to understanding the scripture. Martin Luther, in fact, argues that that is what distinguishes the prophet from the ordinary teacher.[47] But such specific questions are simply not taken up in explanations of this second tradition. This tradition also does not query who the greatest prophet is.

The Two Traditions in the Middle Ages

Many patristic and medieval theologians believe that both kinds of prophets exist within Christendom; that both represent legitimate forms of prophecy. Common is the custom found in an author like Rhabanus Maurus, who comments on the existence of both traditions (*duo prophetarum genera*, is the phrase) and leaves one with the feeling that they exist in happy agreement with one another. "We understand prophecy in a two-fold manner, not only as predicting the future but also as revealing the Scriptures."[48] The same can be found in writings by Bruno Carthusianorum, Herveus Burgidolensis, Lanfranc, and Peter Lombard. These are, one presumes, citations of Ambrosiaster, who made this assertion in his comments on 1 Corinthians 12: 28.[49] Yet, the remarks by Herveus Burgidolensis on the relationship between the two traditions strike an interesting note worth lingering over for a moment. In expounding 1 Corinthians 14: 1–6, he writes that "as a prophet predicts the future which is unknown, so also a doctor when he reveals the sense of the Scriptures,

[47] *An die Radherrn aller Stedte deutsches lands: dass sie Christliche schulen auf-frichten und halten sollen* in WA 15: 40.
[48] Rhabanus Maurus, *Enarrationum in Epp. Pauli lib XI—Epist. 1 ad Corinthios* 12 (PL 112: 116).
[49] See Lanfranc of Bec (PL 150: 197); Herveus Burgidolensis (PL 181: 944); Bruno (PL 153: 192); indeed, Bruno differs from one place to another; in comments on 1 Cor. 14: 1–6 (see PL 153: 197) he argues that prophecy is interpretation, while in comments on Romans 12: 6 (see PL 153: 102) it is prediction of the future. Lombard, when writing on 1 Cor. 12: 18–30, points out that both those who reveal future and who interpret scriptures are prophets (PL 191: 1657); see also his comments on 1 Cor. 14: 6–14 (PL 191: 1665). The exposition of Ambrosiaster is in Ambrosiaster, 2, fo. 208ᵛ.

which contains much that is hidden (*occultus*), is said to prophecy." Herveus makes it clear in the next sentence that the doctor's labors here are not the result of unaided human effort. He "prophesies things which are useful for many people, not from the human spirit but the things he teaches are from the Holy Spirit."[50] The distinction which Herveus' language would seem to suggest between a prophet and a doctor who prophesies is fascinating. He clearly states that a doctor, not a prophet, can be said to prophesy when he expounds scripture. Here, then, Herveus throws confusion into the distinction set down between prophets and doctors by Chrysostom and those who follow him. In so doing, he reminds us of the ambiguity which is occasionally apparent in Christian thought on this locus.

More elaborate, and yet striking a similar note to what was just found in Hervaeus, is Aquinas' discussion of prophecy from his handling of 1 Corinthians 14.[51] There he discussed the idea of prophecy as scriptural interpretation within his larger treatment of prophecy as the reception of supernatural knowledge. He explains that in order to understand the Pauline passage one must understand several things, one of which is what prophecy consists of. Elaborating, he first sets down that prophecy is "the sight of things far off, whether they be future contingents or beyond human reason."[52] This sight requires four things, Aquinas argues. The first two relate to Aquinas' epistemology. It is required that in the prophet's imagination is formed the bodily likeness of things which are shown (*quae ostenduntur*). Second is the requirement that intellectual light be given in order to enlighten the prophet's intellect to know these things. Third is courage to announce the things revealed. And the fourth is the working of miracles which lends credence to the prophecy.[53] With this understanding in place, Aquinas goes on to argue that individuals can be called prophets in various ways. Some are called prophets because they possess all four of these qualities. But sometimes, he explains,

---

[50] PL 181: 959 (on 1 Cor. 14: 3). Herveus' assertion is: "sicut enim propheta praedicit futura quae nesciuntur, ita et doctor dum Scripturarum sensum, qui multis occultus est, manifestat, dicitur prophetare. Et iste ad multorum utilitatem *sic* prophetat, nec ab homine, sed a Spiritu sancto est sensus dictorum eius."

[51] Cf. section 924 in *S. Thomae Aquinatis . . . super Evangelium S. Matthaei Lectura*, ed. P. Raphaelis Cai OP (Taurini: Marietti, 1951), 145, with *Aquinas Opera* ST II-II q. 174, a.6, ad3.

[52] See Aquinas, *Expositio in Epistolam I ad Corinthios* 14, in *Aquinas Opera* 13: 281.

[53] See Aquinas, *Expositio in Epistolam I ad Corinthios* 14, in *Aquinas Opera* 13: 281.

someone is called a prophet even though he does not possess all four. Within his discussion of such instances, Aquinas remarks that one may be called a prophet if he possesses the intellectual light to explain imaginary visions made to someone else. He then adds: "or for explaining the sayings of the prophets or the scriptures of the apostles."[54] He adds to this the fact that one could be called a prophet if one merely announced the statements of the prophets or explained them or, even, sang them in church.[55] Aquinas, it can thus be seen, sets out a fairly elaborate conception of prophecy which aligns him with both Tradition 1 and Tradition 2.

Views differing from those held by theologians like Rhabanus Maurus, Lanfranc, Peter Lombard, and Thomas Aquinas can also be discovered. William of Auxerre, for example, openly disagrees with the position that scriptural interpretation could ever rightly be called prophecy. In fact, he argues explicitly against it, though without naming anyone in particular as his opponent. Both Maurus and Aquinas asserted that the interpreting of the scriptures occurs prophetically by means of the same Spirit who brought forth the scriptures. But William argues in his *Summa Aurea* that such an argument is a paralogism.[56] He does not elaborate on this, unfortunately, but makes it clear that he does not think interpreting the scriptures is prophecy in *any* sense. William, therefore, contends that a Tradition 1 understanding of prophecy is the only legitimate position one can hold.

The Existence of Prophets in the Middle Ages

Many during the Middle Ages believed that prophets still existed and defended their beliefs from the scriptures. Jerome, for instance, comments on Matthew 11: 13 ("The prophets and the law prophesied until John"), declaring: "This does not mean that there were no more prophets after John."[57] This sentiment was repeated throughout the Middle Ages,[58] and seen to support the post-apostolic continuation of

[54] See Aquinas, *Expositio in Epistolam I ad Corinthios* 14, in *Aquinas Opera* 13: 281.
[55] See Aquinas, *Expositio in Epistolam I ad Corinthios* 14, in *Aquinas Opera* 13: 281.
[56] Auxerre, *Summa aurea*, 2: 55^r column 2.
[57] Jerome, *Commentaire sur Saint Matthieu*, 222.
[58] In the *Glossa Ordinaria*, Hugh of St Cher, Thomas, Denis, etc. See, for instance, the *Glossa* on Matt. 11: 13 or *Aquinas Opera* ST II-II q. 174, a.6, ad3.

prophecy. "The charism of prophecy must exist in all the Church until the second coming: this is the view of St. Paul," Apollinarius asserts.[59] And Aquinas notes in his *Summa Theologica* that "at no time have persons possessing the spirit of prophecy been lacking, not indeed for the declaration of any new doctrine of faith (*non . . . ad novam doctrinam fidei depromendam*) but for the directing of human acts."[60]

For some theologians this belief was aided through the drawing of a distinction between different kinds of prophets or prophetic functions. This can be seen in the distinction just noted from Aquinas. He helpfully elaborates on that distinction in his *expositio* on the Gospel of Matthew, where he asserts:

> It ought to be said that the prophets were sent for two reasons: to establish faith and to correct behavior: Prov. 29: 18: "When prophecy fails, the people are scattered (*dissipabitur*)." To establish the faith, as is said in 1 Peter 1: 10: "Concerning that salvation, the prophets. . . ." Thus, prophecy had served two purposes, but now the faith is established (*iam fides fundata est*), since the promises have been fulfilled in Christ. Prophecy that aims to correct behavior (*mores*), however, has not ceased, nor will it ever cease.[61]

Here Aquinas contends that prophets are directed to be correctors of behavior or, in other words, reformers. The necessity of this office continues to the end of time. Much the same is seen in comments by Denis the Carthusian: "Prophecy also contains those things which have to do with the instruction of human behavior, such as 'break your bread with the hungry . . .' and Micah says 'he has shown you, man, what is good and what the Lord requires of you.'"[62]

This reforming "spirit of prophecy" was common in the Middle Ages, and especially the later Middle Ages.[63] One thinks of the rise of the papacy to a position of ultimate authority, the moral decline of the

[59] Apollinarius cited by Eusebius in *Ecclesiastical History* 5.17, cited by Aquinas, *St Thomas Aquinas Summa Theologiae*, vol 45 (II-II, 171–8), 159.

[60] *Aquinas Opera* ST II-II q. 174, a.6, ad3.

[61] Section 924 in *S. Thomae Aquinatis . . . super Evangelium S. Matthaei Lectura* 145.

[62] Denis, *Commentariorum in Psalmos omnes Davidicos*, 2.

[63] On reform, see Gerhart Ladner, *The Idea of Reform: Its Impact on Christian Thought and Action in the Age of the Fathers* (New York: Holt, Rinehart & Winston, 1967); also Thomas M. Izbicki and Christopher M. Bellitto (eds), *Reform and Renewal in the Middle Ages and the Renaissance Studies in Honor of Louis Pascoe, SJ* (Leiden: Brill, 2000).

monasteries, the Avignon papacy, Western schism, and the appearance of groups like the Albigensians, Cathari, and others, in response
to which prophets like Hildegard of Bingen,[64] Joachim of Fiore,[65]
Francis of Assisi,[66] Birgitta of Vadstena,[67] Jan Hus,[68] Savanarola,[69]
and others[70] arose. As Kathryn Kerby-Fulton has stated "often thinking and working within an eschatological or apocalyptic framework,"
the motivating factor for prophets during these eras "will nearly
always be an overwhelming concern with Church reform and the
question of renewal."[71] Kerby-Fulton's point reminds us that in the
Middle Ages the prophet-reformer model was one which belonged,
by and large, to those who were apocalyptic prognosticators; to those
whose authority was largely based on the fact that they were able to
predict the future through the light given them by the Spirit of God
(experiencing visions, dreams, etc.). The existence of these prophets
led to concerns about the presence of false prophets, with Myrddin
(more commonly known as Merlin) being possibly the foremost
example of one who raised such concerns.[72] But the possibility of

[64] Pope Eugene III acknowledged Hildegard of Bingen as a prophet, as did Bernard
of Clairvaux; see Beverly Mayne Kienzle, "Defending the Lord's Vineyard: Hildegard
of Bingen's Preaching against the Cathars," in Carolyn Muessig (ed.), *Medieval
Monastic Preaching* (Leiden: Brill, 1998), 178. See also Kathryn Kerby-Fulton,
"Prophet and Reformer; 'Smoke in the Vineyard'," in Barbara Newman (ed.), *Voice
of the Living Light: Hildegard of Bingen and her World* (Berkeley, Calif.: University of
California Berkeley Press, 1998), 70–90.

[65] McGinn, *The Calabrian Abbot: Joachim of Fiore in the History of Western
Thought* (New York: Macmillan Publishing Co., 1985).

[66] Bonaventure asserts St Francis's prophetic gifts in ch. 11 of his "Life of
St Francis," in *Bonaventure Opera* 8: 535–8.

[67] Ingvar Fogelqvist, *Apostacy and Reform in the Revelations of St Birgitta* (Stockholm: Almqvist & Wiksell International, 1993).

[68] Heiko Oberman, "Hus and Luther: Prophets of a Radical Reformation," in
C. Pater and R. Peterson (eds), *The Contentious Triangle: Church, State, and University* (Kirksville, Mo.: Truman State University Press, 1999), 135–67.

[69] See Girolamo Savonarola, *Compendio di Rivelazioni: Trattato sul Governo della
città di Firenze* (Casale Monferrato: Piemme, 1996), 37 et passim.

[70] One could also point to things like the *Apocalypsis Nova*, on which see Anna
Morisi-Guerra, "The *Apocalypsis Nova*: A Plan for Reform," in *Prophetic Rome in the
High Renaissance Period*, 27–50.

[71] Kathryn Kerby-Fulton, *Reformist Apocalypticism and "Piers Plowman"* (Cambridge:
CUP, 1990), 4. See also Bernard McGinn, "Early Apocalypticism: The Ongoing Debate,"
in C.A. Patrides and J. Wittreich (eds), *The Apocalypse in English Renaissance Thought and
Literature* (Ithaca, NY: Cornell University Press, 1984), 2–39.

[72] Jan Ziolkowski, "The Nature of Prophecy in Geoffrey of Monmouth's Vita
Merlini," in James Kugel (ed.), *Poetry and Prophecy: The Beginnings of a Literary
Tradition* (London: Cornell University Press, 1990), 151–62.

false prophets did not squelch the conviction among the medieval church that true prophet-reformers had been, and would be, raised up by God.

Theological reflection on the existence of prophets whose labors focus on interpretation of scripture (Tradition 2) is noticeably different from this. While it is always difficult to speak in generalities, we may nonetheless say that the movement of these thinkers is towards the ordinary. In other words, prophets still exist, many believed, but they exist merely in the form of the ordinary pastor, bishop, or even the ordinary parishioner. So, for instance, Haymo declares that whereas there used to be evangelists, prophets, and pastors, now the fact is that whoever tells someone the good news is an evangelist and whoever speaks to his hearers about the joys of the elect and the punishments of the reprobate "is a prophet (*propheta est*)."[73] Rhabanus Maurus follows a line of argument set out by Ambrosiaster in drawing one to one correspondences between the New Testament offices and their modern equivalents, and in this schema the prophet becomes a presbyter, namely, one who interprets the scriptures.[74] Herveus Burgidolensis, Aquinas, and Lyra also draw a correspondence between the New Testament office of prophet and the modern interpreter of scripture.[75]

THE EARLY MODERN PERIOD

The remainder of this chapter represents, in one sense, my answer to the question: what happens to the prophet as we move from medieval into Early Modern Europe? My answer, in brief, is that at least among a particular group of theologians (the collection including Zwingli, Bibliander, and Pellican mentioned at the beginning of this chapter), the prophet continues to exist as a kind of creative blending of what was set forth by early and medieval theologians. To put it another way, he continues to exist as a scripture-interpreting prophet-reformer; he exists as a merging of the two traditions. My longer

---

[73] PL 117: 720.   [74] PL 112: 430.

[75] For instance, see Herveus Burgidolensis' treatment of Ephesians 4: 11 (PL 181: 1246). For details on Aquinas and Nicholas of Lyra, see McKee, *Elders*, 143–5, to which I am indebted for the material in this paragraph.

answer will endeavor to map out the idiosyncratic qualities which set this Early Modern prophet apart from his medieval counterpart. Calvin, I will eventually demonstrate, is one of these Early Modern prophets.

Attention will be predominately paid in this chapter to the Swiss, though interest will be shown to theologians from Strasbourg and Germany. Those treated here, irrespective of their confessional allegiance, have been selected because they hold views on prophecy which are comparable and in some cases very similar, to those held by Calvin. My interest in similarity here is (to reiterate once again) *not* on the level of searching for sources from whom Calvin adopted his own position but rather it is a simple interest in finding the proper intellectual context from within which Calvin can be examined in greater detail and with greatest benefit. That is to say, if these theologians hold views on prophecy similar to those espoused by Calvin, this realization provides us with a suitable platform upon which to conduct our analysis of Calvin. It, in some ways, legitimizes my analysis of him because it demonstrates that what I am saying about Calvin can also be said about a number of his contemporaries. Calvin does not appear entirely at odds with the rest of his generation. In this way, my analysis of him is strengthened by virtue of the fact that I can begin to see nuances of how his thinking is expanded upon, supported, echoed, and explained by others who hold views similar to his.

Because mention of the Swiss invariably raises the spectre of Ulrich Zwingli, whose influence within the Swiss Confederation was so pronounced, a brief comment on his relationship to Calvin is in order. I do not intend to posit a strong relationship between Calvin and Zwingli.[76] Calvin is known to have had some disagreements with

---

[76] For comparison between the two, see Gottfried Locher, *Zwingli's Thought: New Perspectives* (Leiden: Brill, 1981), 190–5. By contrast, little is said on Calvin (Geneva was, of course, not a part of the Swiss Confederation during Calvin's life) in Gottfried Locher, *Die Zwinglische Reformation im Rahmen der europäischen Kirchengeschichte* (Göttingen: Vandenhoeck & Ruprecht, 1979) and Rudolph Pfister, *Kirchengeschichte der Schweiz*, ii. *Von der Reformation bis zum zweiten Villmerger Krieg* (Zurich: Zwingli Verlag, 1979). On Calvin's relationship with the Swiss, see Paul Wernle, *Calvin und Basel bis zum Tod des Myconius 1535–1552* (Basel: Reinhardt, 1909); Wilhelm Kolfhaus, "Der Verkehr Calvins mit Bullinger," in Josef Bohatec (ed.), *Calvinstudien: Festschrift zum 400. Geburtstage Johann Calvins* (Leipzig: Haupt, 1909), 27–125. More recent work includes Bruce Gordon, "Calvin and the Swiss Reformed Churches," in Andrew Pettegree, Alastair Duke, and Gillian Lewis (eds), *Calvinism in Europe 1540–1620* (Cambridge: CUP, 1994), 64–81; Peter Opitz (ed.),

Zwingli, distancing himself from the Zurich reformer fairly early on.[77] That being said, it is well-known that Calvin's relationship with Zwingli's understudy, Heinrich Bullinger, was among the closest and most valued of all his relationships. It seems certain that Calvin met Bullinger, as well as figures like Leo Jud, in 1536 in Basel.[78] Jud, in the preface to his *Catechismus brevissima Christianae religionis formula* (1539), praises Calvin's *Institutio*[79] suggesting a shared esteem between the two men. While Jud died in 1542, the friendship which Calvin develops with Bullinger throughout their lives until Calvin's death was plainly suggestive of the mutual respect they bore for one another. The two undoubtedly had their differences, as the dispute over Jerome Bolsec attests. But they still enjoyed a strong friendship. Calvin also maintains a warm friendship with Conrad Pellican, exchanging letters and asking advice. In one such letter, he lends his support to another man who would eventually relocate to Zurich to

Calvin im Kontext der Schweizer Reformation: Historishe und theologische Beiträge zur Calvinforschung (Zurich: TVZ, 2003); Emidio Campi and Christian Moser, "Loved and Feared: Calvin and the Swiss Confederation," in M. E. Hirzel and M. Sallmann (eds), *Calvin's Impact on Church and Society, 1509-2009* (Grand Rapids, Mich.: Eerdmans, 2009), 14–34; Wilhelm Neuser, *Johann Calvin: Leben und Werk in seiner Frühzeit 1509-1541* (Göttingen: Vandenhoeck & Ruprecht, 2009), 144–51. Neuser focuses on Calvin's early writings. His reflections are not particularly historical in character, in contrast to Wernle, but he does discuss his early schooling and attachment to humanism. One does not find a significant discussion of Calvin's burgeoning friendship with Bullinger or with Oswald Myconius, but there is a brief one of Calvin's ultimately trying relationship with Louis du Tillet (Neuser, *Johann Calvin*, 302–5). Emidio Campi, "Calvin, the Swiss Reformed Churches, and the European Reformation," in *Calvin and his Influence, 1509-2009* (Oxford: OUP, 2011), 119–43. Fritz Büsser's impressive 2-vol. study of Bullinger makes relatively little mention of the relationship between Bullinger and Calvin: *Heinrich Bullinger (1504-1575): Leben, Werk und Wirkung* (Zurich: TVZ, 2004-5), but he does treat that relationship in his earlier work, Fritz Büsser and Alfred Schindler (eds), *Die Prophezei: Humanismus und Reformation in Zürich. Ausgewählte Aufsätze und Vorträge* (Bern: Lang, 1994), 183–99 (comparison of basic ideas of Zwingli found in Calvin's *Institutio*), 200–3 (comparing Calvin and Bullinger on a number of issues). Likewise, Alexandre Ganoczy compares Calvin and Zwingli, see *Young Calvin*, 151–8.

[77] Calvin does, we might notice, come close to defending Zwingli (along with Oecolampadius) on one occasion considerably later (CO 12: 11).

[78] Some uncertainty surrounds the question of whether Calvin made a return trip to Basel in 1536 on his way back to Ferrara; cf. CO 21: 125 with CO 21: 58 (this information comes from Wernle, *Calvin und Basel*, 95 n. 37).

[79] See A2^{r-v} of Jud's preface (to Johannes Frisio on this relationship between Jud's catechism and Calvin's Cat. Genev. Prior), see *Ioannis Calvini Epistolae*, i (1530–Sept. 1538), ed. Cornelis Augustijn and Frans Peter van Stam (Geneva: Droz, 2005).

be the pastor of the Italian congregation there, Bernardino Ochino.[80] He also knew Rudolph Gwalther, Conrad Pellican, Theodor Bibliander, and Gemma Phyrisius. Outside of Zurich, he expresses great regard for individuals such as Johannes Oecolampadius of Basel.[81] Calvin was also friendly with Oswald Myconius, having met him in Basel. They continued to write to one another until 1552, Myconius passing away in that year. He also had good relations with Wolfgang Musculus and Peter Martyr Vermigli (inviting the latter to teach Hebrew in Geneva) and with Strasbourg theologians such as Wolfgang Capito and, of course, Martin Bucer, with whom he was particularly close.[82] Calvin's views on prophecy, as I will show, are probably most closely aligned with those of Zwingli, Bullinger, Bibliander, and Pellican, but it is worth remembering that he had strong contacts with theologians throughout the Swiss Confederation, Strasbourg, and Germany, from Geneva north and east to Bern to Zurich, Basel, and Strasbourg.

General Context: The Early Modern Era and the Two Traditions on Prophecy

The later Middle Ages saw increased concern about numerous aspects of the church and church life, as has to some degree already been indicated. Continuing worries about corruption, not to mention other fears such as the appearance and spread of the Turks and rise of the Antichrist,[83] called forth prophets who believed themselves to be raised up to purify the church. They were often given terrible visions of divine wrath and of the end of the age (following a Tradition 1 sense of prophecy) on the grounds of which they warned their world

---

[80] See Calvin's letter to Pellican, on 18 Apr. 1543 (CO 11: 527–9).

[81] CO 12: 11. He also praised Oecolampadius' commentary on the Psalms.

[82] Calvin's friendship with Capito is not known to have been especially strong; he did write to Capito in relation to the idea of publishing his recently written *Psychopannychia* (see CO 10b: 45–6). Bucer, however, is commonly regarded as a good friend and mentor. Research on Calvin's stay in Strasbourg includes Doumergue, *Jean Calvin*, ii. 293–8, 376–524; Jacques Pannier, *Calvin à Strasbourg* (Strasbourg: Impr. alsacienne, 1925); Daniel Benoit et al., *Calvin à Strasbourg, 1538–1541* (Strasbourg: Oberlin, 1938); Wendel, *Calvin*, 57–68. I owe knowledge of these references to Wulfert de Greef, *The Writings of John Calvin: Expanded Edition*, tr. Lyle Bierma (Philadephia: Westminster/John Knox, 2008), 13.

[83] See Bernard McGinn, *Antichrist: Two Thousand Years of the Human Fascination with Evil* (New York: Columbia University Press, 2000).

and called it to repentance. Apocalyptic prophecy continued in the late medieval and into the Early Modern eras throughout Europe, as a glance at the work of Meister Theodorius[84] and Anabaptists like Melchior Hoffman[85] and Thomas Müntzer[86] confirms. Mention of Melchior Hoffman raises the specter of Anabaptist prophecy, which will occupy us in the remainder of this chapter. Here let me consider the Strasbourg theologian Hoffman, who produced an exposition of Daniel 12, *Das XII. Capitel des propheten Danielis ausgelegt, . . . christen nutzlich zu wissen*, and also produced his *Weissagung aus heiliger gotlicher geschrift* and *Prophetische Gesicht und Offenbarung*.[87] In these and other works, Hoffman sets out an interpretation of Europe as already in the end times (which he divides into two periods of three and a half years) and predicts the precise date of Christ's second coming. His intense apocalypticism and anxiety over the wickedness of contemporary society brought him in contact with many individuals and groups, one of whom—the Strasbourg prophets—would have an impact upon him and, likewise, spread his own influence within Germany. Within the Strasbourg prophets, predictions uttered by a number of the members, but particularly by two female visionaries, Ursula Jost and Barbara Rebstock, resulted in Strasbourg being held to be the New Jerusalem from which would proceed 144,000 apostolic messengers. Indeed, Hoffman's *Prophetische Gesicht und Offenbarung* was actually a collection of the recorded visions of Ursula Jost.[88] Eventually Jost, in her

---

[84] Robert E. Lerner, "Medieval Prophecy and Religious Dissent," *Past and Present*, 72 (1976), 3–24.

[85] Klaus Deppermann, *Melchior Hoffman: Soziale Unruhen und apokalyptische Visionen im Zeitalter der Reformation* (Göttingen: Vandenhoeck & Ruprecht, 1979); ET: Klaus Deppermann, *Melchior Hoffman: Social Unrest and Apocalyptic Visions in the Age of Reformation*, tr. Malcolm Wren (Edinburgh: T&T Clark, 1987).

[86] Hans-Jürgen Goertz, *Thomas Müntzer: Mystiker, Apokalyptiker, Revolutionär* (Munich: C. H. Beck, 1989); ET: Hans-Jürgen Goertz, *Thomas Müntzer: Apocalyptic Mystic and Revolutionary*, tr. Jocelyn Jacquiery (Edinburgh: T&T Clark, 1993). For a new treatment of Müntzer which engages briefly with his work as prophet, see Günter Vogler, "Thomas Müntzer: Irrweg oder Alternative? Plädoyer für eine andere Sicht," *Archiv für Reformationsgeschichte*, 103 (2012), 11–39.

[87] Melchior Hoffman, *Das XII. Capitel des propheten Danielis ausgelegt, . . . christen nutzlich zu wissen* (Stockholm: Königliche Druckerei, 1526).

[88] See Sigrun Haude, "Gender Roles and Perspectives among Anabaptist and Spiritualist Groups," in James M. Stayer and John D. Roth (eds), *A Companion to Anabaptism and Spiritualism, 1521–1700* (Leiden: Brill, 2007), 425–66, esp. 434–5.

prophecies, would identify Hoffman as one of the two coming witnesses, Elijah (the other is Enoch), who was predicted in Revelation 11: 3.[89]

The rise of an Anabaptist prophetess like Ursula Jost was indicative of a development which had commenced several centuries earlier. Women visionaries had begun to increase in number in the late Middle Ages and this continued into the Early Modern era. What Europe witnessed with the rise of Hildegard of Bingen, Mechthild von Magdeburg, and Birgitta of Vadstena, it continued to see with the Maid of Lorraine prophecies and the rise of Joan of Arc as well as Maria de Santo Domingo, Teresa of Avila, and others. Much of their reforming work was moral in its focus. Birgitta of Vadstena and Catherine of Siena are good examples of this.

Their work represented a worrying trend for authorities.[90] At times, the tensions seem to have been minimal, as was broadly the case with Catherine of Siena, whose preaching and visionary experiences were investigated and found not to offend orthodoxy.[91] But on other occasions, these prophets were deemed far too inflammatory and seditious to be allowed to continue. Here, one thinks of someone like Lucrecia de León, the political visionary. It is not surprising that our remaining source of knowledge about her is primarily inquisitorial records.[92] In England, "radical" figures such as Margery Kempe and Julian of Norwich would test the resolve of authorities both civil and ecclesiastical. Kempe especially caused problems for the authorities throughout her life. Later English women mystics, such as Eleanor Davies, would continue this trend. Davies was repeatedly imprisoned and placed in Bedlam (the London mental hospital) for warning her contemporaries of the coming Day of Judgment and criticizing King

---

[89] See Rodney Peterson, *Preaching in the Last Days: The Theme of the "Two Witnesses" in the Sixteenth and Seventeenth Centuries* (New York: OUP, 1993), 90–6.

[90] Despite this, their work was not infrequently supported by patrons, clergy, and wealthy donors; see, for instance, Jodi Bilinkoff, "A Spanish Prophetess and her Patrons: The Case of Maria de Santo Domingo," *Sixteenth Century Journal*, 23/1 (1992), 21–34.

[91] For an interpretation arguing that some women prophetesses learnt to conform to the expectations of the discerning of the spirits, see Rosalynn Voaden, *God's Word, Women's Voices: The Discernment of Spirits in the Writing of Late-Medieval Women Visionaries* (Rochester, NY: Boydell & Brewer, 1999). On Catherine of Siena in particular, see George Ferzoco, "The Processo Castellano and the Canonization of Catherine of Siena," in Carolyn Muessig, George Ferzoco and Beverly Mayne Kienzle (eds), *A Companion to Catherine of Siena* (Leiden: Brill, 2009), 185–201.

[92] See Kagan, *Lucrecia's Dreams*.

Charles I and Parliament. She also predicted the deaths of several leading clerics, including William Laud, Archbishop of Canterbury.[93] Accordingly, visionaries and preachers of a coming apocalypse, irrespective of their professed desire to bring something good (such as a reform of morals), tended to be classed as troublemakers by the governments of their day.

This rise in the number of female mystics corresponded with other shifts and occurrences. With the growth of cities during the period, discernible changes occurred in the religious expression of the populace. No longer were intense expressions of religious devotion confined to monasteries. Rather, they could be seen on city squares and street corners, a fact which led to greater disruption in the view of some of those within the ecclesiastical hierarchy.[94] In order to combat this, literature on the *discretio spirituum* proliferated, representing a continuation of the kind of concerns that I mentioned earlier in relation to individuals like Merlin. This is nicely illustrated in writings such as Jean Gerson's *De probatione spirituum* and *De distinctione verarum visionum a falsis*. Along with this, Europe witnessed a rise in magic and the occult, as seen in the work of figures like Heinrich Cornelius Agrippa of Nettesheim and Paracelsus. Likewise, one finds a continued concern for the apocalyptic within Europe, sometimes expressing itself in intense apocalyptic anxiety. This was the case, as Denis Crouzet has exhaustively shown, in France in the late medieval and Early Modern eras, with French Catholics coming to believe that the world would shortly come to an end, a worry which contributed eventually to the commencement of the French Wars of Religion. There existed among Catholics a sense that the church was engaged mystically and prophetically in a struggle against the powers of darkness—a sense which Crouzet's examination of hundreds of pamphlets, contemporary historical accounts, and sermons reveals. From this vantage point, the early Protestants and (eventually) Huguenot preachers were identified as portents of coming judgment.[95]

---

[93] I am grateful to Shannon Miller of Temple University for my knowledge of Eleanor Davies.

[94] See Voaden, *God's Word, Women's Voices*, and Nancy Caciola, *Discerning Spirits: Divine and Demonic Possession in the Middle Ages* (New York: Cornell University Press, 2003).

[95] Denis Crouzet, *Les Guerriers de Dieu: La Violence au temps des troubles de religion (vers 1525–vers 1610)*, 2 vols. (Seyssel: Champ Vallon, 1990), see esp. i. 103–236; ii. 330–60, 428–64, 464–539.

Likewise, in Zurich, Conrad Grebel, George Blaurock, and Felix Mantz, fueled by a similar kind of zeal, led a rebellion against Zwingli and his colleagues, as I will discuss in more detail later. Meanwhile a continuation of the prophet-interpreter (i.e. Tradition 2) within Europe during the Early Modern era appears particularly, it would seem, among those influenced by humanism. What influenced this is a matter of speculation, but one discovers in the first several decades of the 1500s thinkers from various theological camps articulating the position that prophecy is interpretation: Erasmus, Tomasso De Vio Cardinal Cajetan, Martin Luther, François Lambert of Avignon. Erasmus, for instance, articulates this position in a number of places, including his paraphrase of Romans 12: 6 and his annotations on 1 Corinthians 14: 1, the latter dating from 1516.[96] (Others take one or both of these biblical passages to be referring to prophets who interpret the scriptures, including Guilielmus Estius, Johann Bugenhagen, Matthias Illyricus, Johannes Brenz, and Caspar Olevianus.[97]) By 1524, however, Erasmus was urging in his debate with Luther that the charism of prophecy had actually ceased—a fact which may reveal more about Erasmus than it does about sixteenth-century views on prophecy.

Several qualities which distinguished this continuation of Tradition 2 can be identified. First, an emphasis upon proclamation can be found among some of these thinkers. François Lambert of Avignon is one of them. Writing in his preface to a commentary on the prophet Hosea, he interrupts his train of thought and turns to raise the question: But what is prophecy (*sed quid est prophetia*)? His answer follows a Tradition 2 (possibly Erasmian) line of thought, but

---

[96] Erasmus, *In Epistolam Pauli Apostoli ad Romanos Paraphrasis* (Basel: Johann, Froben, 1518), 110. For the 1 Cor. 14 reference: "prophetiam vocat, non praedictionem futurorum, sed interpretationem divinae scripturae" (Erasmus, *In Novum Instrumentum* (Basel: Johann Froben, 1516), 477 see Engammare, "Calvin: A Prophet," 94).

[97] For Guilielmus Estius, see: *Estius in Omnes Canonicas Apostolorum Epistolas* (Paris: Mogunriae, 1841), i. 369; for Johannes Bugenhagen, see: *Annotationes Ioan. Bugenhagii Pomerani in X. epistolas Pauli, scilicet, ad Ephesios, . . . Hebraeos* (Strasbourg: Iohannem Hervagium, 1524), 13[r]. The views of Matthias Illyricus are discussed in Olivier Millet, "Eloquence des prophètes bibliques," 65–82. For Brenz: Johannes Brenz, *In Epistolam, quam apostolus Paulus ad Romanos scripsit, commentariorum libri tres* (Tübingen: Georgius Gruppenbachius, 1588) 723. For Gaspar Olevianus: *In epistolam D. Pauli Apostoli ad Romanos notae, ex Gasparis Oleviani concionibus excerptae, & a Theodoro Beza editae . . .* (Geneva: Apud Eustathium Vignon, 1579), 614.

expands it to focus on *annunciatio* and *praedicatio*. Prophecy, he avers, is the announcing of the truth according to the command of God.[98] Lambert wrote this in 1525. The year following, he produced an entire treatise *Commentarii de Prophetia, Eruditione et Linguis etc.*[99] which focuses primarily on erudition, but sets out the same interpretation of prophecy found in his 1525 commentary. Second, an emphasis on the biblical languages appears in the thinking of some on prophecy, such as Martin Luther. He produces comments similar to those treated above which see prophecy as interpretation of scripture. But in addition, he avers that that which distinguishes the prophet from the simple preacher is that the former knows the biblical languages. Luther also links this position with the Apostle Paul's letters. Those whom God wishes to contend for the faith, the German insists, must have the languages. This being so, "there must always be such prophets in the Christian church who can dig into Scripture, expound it, and carry on disputations. A saintly life and right doctrine are not enough. Hence, languages are absolutely and altogether necessary in the Christian church, as are the prophets or interpreters."[100] A third trait found among these thinkers is an anti-speculative disposition, which seems even more pronounced among many of these sixteenth-century thinkers than it was among their medieval counterparts.

It is with these scripture-interpreting prophets that my focus will narrow, looking at Zwingli, Bullinger, Bibliander, Pellican, Bucer, Gwalther, Vermigli, Musculus, and others in what follows. Intriguing developments occur among the thinking of these theologians on prophecy, which will be crucial to my reading of Calvin. It was difficult to decide whether to begin a discussion of their thinking by situating it within Tradition 1 or Tradition 2, but the latter seems to serve as a slightly better point of departure than the former, since their focus is so profoundly oriented towards scripture.

[98] François Lambert of Avignon, *Praefatio in In Primum Duodecim Prophetarum, nempe, Oseam...* (Strasbourg: Johan Hervagium, 1525), 8ʳ.

[99] François Lambert of Avignon, *Commentarii de Prophetia, Eruditione et Linguis...* (Strasbourg: Johan Hervagium, 1526).

[100] Luther, "To the Councilmen of All Cities in Germany That They Establish and Maintain Christian Schools," in *Selected Writings of Martin Luther*, ed. Theodore Tappert, 4 vols (Philadephia: Fortress Press, 1967), iii. 55, tr. from: *An die Radherrn aller Stedte deutsches lands: dass sie Christliche schulen auffrichten und halten sollen* (WA 15: 40).

IDOLATRY, ANABAPTISTS, AND PROPHECY

Theologians like Zwingli, Oecolampadius, and Musculus studied and worshiped in, and reacted to, an environment which they found to be profoundly corrupt. Their views on prophecy seem to be shaped by this experience. These theologians developed thinking on prophecy and the character of the prophet's callings which focuses significantly, as I will demonstrate, on fighting idolatry. This, to some degree, aligns these men with medieval prophets like Hildegard of Bingen and Joachim of Fiore, who also fought certain abuses within the church of their own day (though this time without, by and large, the mystical visions). There is, additionally, a second experience which also influenced the theology of these individuals on the topic of prophecy— that is, the experience of having to deal with the Anabaptists. Both of these experiences will shape the contents of the remainder of this chapter. I shall begin with idolatry.

One of the elements of late medieval piety that was a profound part of the Christian experience and became a focal point for nearly every theologian living and writing during these years was the Eucharist. Always important to the Christian church, its place in European Christendom was significantly strengthened by the decisions set down by the Fourth Lateran Council. The fifteenth century, moreover, saw the full development of the feast of Corpus Christi. "Popular piety seized on the theological and liturgical idea of transubstantiation with unrestrained fervor, but often without a proper understanding of its meaning."[101] To have Christ present on earth and even marched through the center of one's town was expressive of a nearness which was eagerly embraced by worshipers. Miracles were attributed to the consecrated host. All of this was, of course, a peculiarity in some ways because lay participation in communion was, at least according to some research, uncommon at the time.[102] Thus, the juxtaposition represents something remarkable, if strange. But this, far from creating malaise or indifference regarding the

---

[101] Carlos Eire, *War Against the Idols: The Reformation of Worship from Erasmus to Calvin* (Cambridge: CUP, 1986), 17.

[102] My reflections on the significance of the eucharist have been influenced by Eire, *War Against the Idols*, 8–27. See also Sarah Beckwith, *Christ's Body: Identity, Culture, and Society in Late Medieval Writings* (London: Routledge, 1993), 21–40.

Eucharist among the people, seems to have strengthened the profound sense of wonder which was attached to the Eucharist by ordinary Christians at this time. The Mass, then, increasingly became a fundamental expression of the heart of the religious experience enjoyed by European Christians.

Prophets like Zwingli, Bullinger, and Bibliander felt enormous consternation over Romanist views and practices concerning the Eucharist, the Mass, and the numerous cultic exercises of the Roman Catholic Church—in short, a concern over idolatry.[103] Or, as "Bullinger writes, as Elijah called upon Israel to leave its baals and 'Jezebelism,' so contemporary prophets and preachers were now calling upon Christendom to leave idolatry and superstition."[104] This concern for idolatry manifested itself in a number of ways. It manifested itself in a mocking of common Eucharistic devotional practices. Individuals interrupted Corpus Christi processions which made their way through cities, towns, and villages and were accompanied with hymns and regalia. Some preached against it. They mocked the doctrine of transubstantiation, subjecting it to scathing criticism and detailed theological review. On a popular level, this tirade against the doctrine manifested itself in things such as the Affair of the Placards in France in 1534 as well as iconoclasm seen in places like the Swiss Confederation, the Netherlands, and throughout Europe. Europe was witnessing what Carlos Eire has called a "War Against the Idols." In scathing denouncements of the superstitious belief foisted upon all humankind by the Roman church concerning Christ's body and blood, these reformers wrote nuanced and incendiary treatises analyzing from theological, philological, and historical contexts the Roman doctrine and practice. They authored voluminous accounts of the theology of the Eucharist,[105] which became the subject of greatest concern for

---

[103] In addition to Carlos Eire's work, see the important study, Christopher Elwood, *The Body Broken: The Calvinist Doctrine of the Eucharist and the Symbolization of Power in Sixteenth-Century France* (New York: OUP, 1999).

[104] Rodney Petersen, "Bullinger's Prophets of the 'Restitutio'," in Mark S. Burrows and Paul Rorem (eds), *Biblical Hermeneutics in Historical Perspective* (Grand Rapids, Mich.: Eerdmans, 1991), 245–60, esp. 251. Carlos Eire contends that such concerns, at least as they relate to Reformed Protestantism, are the result of a "new Christian interpretation of the relationship between the spiritual and the material" (Eire, *War Against the Idols*, 28).

[105] One thinks of massive works like Vermigli's *Defensio Doctrinae veteris & Apostolicae de sacrosancto Eucharistiae Sacramento . . .* (Zurich: Froschouerus, 1562).

many of them. Their attacks manifest their belief that Europe was in the grip of a false religion.

Concerns about the Eucharist and idolatry were often expressed more generally by these reformers as a concern about the state of religion in Europe and the fear that Europe had succumbed to a false religion. These reformers saw Satan behind the rise of Antichrist, the Pope, and his influence over Christendom, and they feared for Europe. This fundamental concern is given voice in works such as Zwingli's *De Vera et Falsa Religione*... *Commentarius*[106] and in a most interesting way by the brief catechism produced by Leo Jud and published in 1539. In it, the interrogator leads the responder through an introduction in which the latter explains that humankind was created to know the infinite God and that eternal life is found in that God. The next question, still appearing on the first (quarto-sized) page of this catechism, reads:

> Interrog.: What can hold us back from this aim and from eternal life?
>
> Respon.: False religion (*Falsa religio*), or if you prefer, superstition, and a dishonorable life, and if I may say it in one word, not fearing God, or neglecting God.[107]

In fact, the very first doctrinal head to be treated in this catechism is *de vera religione*, the final paragraph of which expands upon the character of false religion. Jud's catechism exemplifies brilliantly a chief concern of the reformers.

This concern would profoundly shape thinking on the prophet's vocation as it is articulated by the collection of theologians upon whom I have been focusing attention here. The influence of this concern will become clearer in the next section of this chapter, where I will analyze in a constructive way the thinking of these theologians on prophecy and the prophetic vocation. There we will be able to see the idiosyncrasies which appear in their views on prophecy and, also, how these idiosyncrasies owe their existence to these reformers' intense concerns over idolatry.

---

[106] Ulrich Zwingli, *De Vera et Falsa Religione*... *Commentarius* (Zurich: Froschouerus, 1525).
[107] Leo Jud, *Catechismus brevissima Christianae religionis formula,*... *in communem omnium piorum utilitatem excusa* (Zurich, no date), A4^{r-v}. It was likely produced in 1538 or 1539.

The Confusion Caused by Anabaptism

Another concern, or frustration, would also leave its mark on these men's views on prophecy, namely, Anabaptism. My discussion of it might be helpfully introduced by citing a portion of a letter from Wolfgang Capito. He declares, in a missive to Nicolaus Prugner dated 10 June 1526, that "Today our weaver shouted at Matthew in the cathedral."[108] The Matthew he has in mind is Matthew Zell, who was preaching at the time of the incident. Capito relates the fact that after Zell had read a passage from Deuteronomy 28 and commented on the repercussions which await disobedience, the weaver, whose name was Hans Wolff, "Barked,"

> You are disobedient to the Holy Spirit. What you say goes against him and is a lie. In his name I command you to withdraw and permit me to say what the Spirit wishes to say.[109]

This experience—the experience of having to deal with Anabaptists who take the idea of prophecy to mean that they can, *inter alia*, speak the word of the Lord and can denounce the trained minister who is in the pulpit whenever they feel led to do so—is another encounter, indeed, trauma, which influences thinking on what prophecy is and how it ought to be understood and talked about.

I will, in what follows in the remainder of this section, attempt to demonstrate something of the impact this experience—which was associated particularly with Anabaptist appropriations of the *New* Testament prophetic office—had upon these theologians' work on prophecy. I will do this by exploring the character of the thinking of Zwingli, Gwalther, Vermigli, and others on the locus of prophecy, with a particular eye towards exposing the variety, novelty, and even apparent confusion that one finds within that thinking—confusion which is present because, in part, of the Anabaptists. I will take some time probing these matters since it will help provide us with the proper milieu from within which to consider Calvin's own views on prophecy, which as we have already seen in Chapter 1 also exhibit confusion. I contend that this confusion owes much to the presence of

---

[108] Wolfgang Capito, *The Correspondence of Wolfgang Capito*, ed. and tr. Erika Rummel, with Milton Kooistra, 2 vols (Toronto: University of Toronto Press, 2009), ii. 204.
[109] Capito, *Correspondence*, ii. 204.

Anabaptists, whose conduct was, in the eyes of many, so profoundly shocking, exasperating, and incendiary that it moved theologians to alter their understandings of prophecy in an effort to deal with the threat.

Such confusion, or at least peculiar variation, has already been found, by scholars, in the views on prophecy held by Heinrich Bullinger and, for that matter Martin Luther too.[110] Similar qualities are, likewise, found in Bullinger's teacher, Zwingli, and (to some degree, it would seem) Oecolampadius[111] as well. In Zwingli's *Der Hirt* and his *Von dem Predigtamt*, for instance, he articulates the position that the offices of pastor, bishop, evangelist, apostle, and prophet are, in effect, the same.[112] In discussing the office of "shepherd," he describes it as that "which we call bishop, pastor, people's priest, prophet, evangelist or preacher."[113] Elsewhere, he declares the "office of evangelist is none other than the prophetic office, as long as 'prophet' is understood to be one who plucks up and plants. He is really none other than a bishop or pastor."[114] Plucking up and planting is a reference to Jeremiah 1: 9–10, which we will come across again in due course. Later in *Von dem Predigtamt*, Zwingli attempts to describe qualities which are associated particularly strongly with

---

[110] I am specifically thinking of Daniel Bolliger, "Bullinger on Church Authority: The Transformation of the Prophetic Role in Christian Ministry," in Bruce Gordon and Emidio Campi (eds), *Architect of Reformation: An Introduction to Heinrich Bullinger, 1504–1575* (Grand Rapids, Mich.: Baker, 2004), 159–77, and also Peter Opitz, "Von prophetischer Existenz zur Prophetie als Pädagogik; Zu Bullingers Lehre vom munus propheticum," in Emidio Campi and Peter Opitz (eds), *Heinrich Bullinger: Life—Thought—Influence; Zurich, Aug. 25–29, 2004 International Congress Heinrich Bullinger (1504–1575)*, 2 vols (Zurich: TVZ, 2007), ii. 493–513; esp. 501–3. On Luther, see Thompson, *John Calvin and the Daughters of Sarah*, 196–202. Additional coverage of Luther and Lutheran views on prophecy is found in Robin Barnes, *Prophecy and Gnosis: Apocalypticism in the Wake of the Lutheran Reformation* (Stanford, Calif.: Stanford University Press, 1988); Philip M. Soergel, *Miracles and the Protestant Imagination: The Evangelical Wonder Book in Reformation Germany* (New York: OUP, 2012).
[111] Iohannes Oecolampadius, *In Epistolam B. Pauli Apost. Ad Rhomanos Adnotationes a Ioanne Oecolampadio Basileae praelectae, & denuo recognitae* (Basel: Andr. Cratandrum, 1526), 84[r–v]. Wolfgang Capito, *In Epistolam Apostoli Pauli ad Romanos, Commentarii* (Basel: Hervagius, 1555), 291, where he mentions his view on 1 Cor. 14: "Prophetia aliquando est praedicatio verbi dei in genere, quo sensu accipitur 1 Cor 14," cf. with one of Oecolampadius' letters to Gaspard Hedion Iohannes Oecolampadius, *D. D. Ioannis Oecolampadii et Huldrichii Zwinglii Epistolarum libri quatuor* (Basel: [R. Winter], 1536), 16[r].
[112] ZW 3: 52; ZW 4: 391–400.   [113] ZW 3: 13.
[114] ZW 3: 52; ZW 4: 391–400.

each office, which he manages to do with some success, though arguably at the expense of consistency. Interestingly, Zwingli, writing in the 1520s, is intent upon discussing the New Testament prophetic office in a positive manner as an authoritative biblical interpreter and reformer, though he has to fight hard against "the Anabaptist attempt to equate prophetic with lay exposition of scripture."[115] Other theologians writing on the topic in the 1530s, 1540s, and 1550s will find such a positive appraisal of the Pauline prophetic office increasingly difficult to produce.

Variety, disorder, and some novelty can also be seen if we consider the work of Conrad Pellican and Martin Bucer. Pellican's thoughts on passages like Romans 12: 6 and 1 Corinthians 14: 1 offer little of interest,[116] but his work on 1 Corinthians 12 raises a wider range of issues. Prophecy, he explains there, in a work published in 1539, can be taken variously. Teaching others and, in fact, even the simple act of being taught are, he contends, both legitimately called prophecy.[117] To prophesy, he continues, taking up a different angle on the topic, is an office which entails convicting others of their sin (*vitia arguere*) and threatening the wrath of God on the impious, while promising the mercy of God to the pious. Additionally, he adds, prophets predict the future either by revelation from the divine spirit or by conjecture from past events.[118] Pellican, still carrying on with his discussion, enters into a brief discourse on testing the spirits, which is introduced by a comment about how easy it is for people to be deceived. He concludes his treatment with comments on the necessity of having Hebrew and Greek in order to understand scripture. Much of what he has been saying appears to be taken from Zwingli's *Annotatiunculae . . . ex ore Zwinglij in utranq; Pauli ad Corinthios Epistolam.*[119] The emphasis on

---

[115] Bolliger, "Bullinger on Church Authority," 160. See Zwingli's complaint about Anabaptists in, for instance, his letter to Vadian (ZW 8: 332). Zwingli makes no mention of prophecy in his *In Cata Baptistarvm Strophas Elenchus Huldrichi Zuinglij* (Zurich: Froschouerus, 1527), which is mostly about baptism.

[116] Conrad Pellican, *In omnes apostolicas epistolas, Pauli, petri, Iacobi, Ioannis et Iudae D. Chuonradi Pellicani . . .* (Zurich: Froschouerus, 1539), 141 and 258.

[117] Pellican, *In omnes apostolicas epistolas*, 250.

[118] Pellican, *In omnes apostolicas epistolas*, 250.

[119] Pellican says this on 1 Cor. 12: 5 in his, *In omnes apostolicas epistolas*, 251. See, Ulrich Zwingli, *Annotatiunculae per Leonem Iudae, ex ore Zvinglij in utranq; Pauli ad Corinthios Epistolam publice exponentis conceptae* (Zurich: Froschouerus, 1528), 106, 115–17, 120–3. A rereading, after a long time, of a portion of Thompson's study has reminded me that Zwingli mentions the idea of prophecy as hearing prophecy in *Von dem Predigtamt* (ZW 4: 414); see *John Calvin and the Daughters of Sarah*, 189.

the languages was, of course, one of the points stressed by these theologians as a way to differentiate true prophets from Anabaptists (since the latter ordinarily did not have Hebrew or Greek).

A rather different kind of innovation can be seen if we turn from Pellican to Martin Bucer. In Bucer's thought, he aligns himself with a Tradition 1 view of prophecy, as can be seen, for instance, in his excursus on prophecy attached to his exposition of Matthew 11: 29. But even within that excursus, Bucer discusses different kinds of prophecy. Significantly, he treats prophecy as a phenomenon experienced within the first (*primori*) church; this is in relation to 1 Corinthians 14—here, then, he introduces a strongly historical perspective into his analysis of the locus, understanding this Pauline manifestation of the office as one in which the prophet was occupied with the interpretation of scripture but one which ought to be rightly understood as belonging solely to the early church era.[120] This would seem to be innovative in itself but also appears to serve a broader purpose in relation to the church of his own day. In fact, throughout his writings, he betrays a desire to remove prophecy (in any form) from the experience of the church of his own era. Willem van't Spijker, in his study of Bucer on the ecclesiastical offices, rightly contends on this point that Bucer's strategy here "is undoubtedly to be viewed against the background of the conduct of countless pseudo-prophets who claim divine authority for their teaching."[121] Though van't Spijker does not mention the Anabaptists by name here, it seems clear that that is who he has in mind. Thus, in Bucer's thought one can see both innovation and also the presence of frustration and pastoral concern in relation to those within his church who would seek to misuse the Pauline office of prophet.

Similar qualities can be found in Rudolph Gwalther's thinking on prophecy. Gwalther also, like Pellican, argues that the art of hearing

---

[120] Martin Bucer, *Enarrationes perpetuæ in Sacra Quatuor Evangelia, recognitæ nuper [et] locis compluribus auctæ* . . . (Argentorati: Georgius Ulricherus Andlanus, 1530), 113^v–115^v; he also speaks about prophets in 111^v–113^r. See also Bucer, *Epistola Epistola D. Pauli ad Ephesios,* . . . (Strasbourg: s.n., 1527), 84^v–85^r. This places Bucer's use of the distinction which Chrysostom and others make between a prophet and doctor—namely, that the latter must work to understand the scriptures whereas the former does not—into a distinctly historical light.

[121] Willem van't Spijker, *The Ecclesiastical Offices in the Thought of Martin Bucer,* tr. John Vriend and Lyle Bierma (Leiden: Brill, 1996), 41, 46-7; quotation is from 46.

prophecy is a kind of prophecy.[122] Further, he avers that prophets predict the future, explaining that there were many such prophets during the time of the apostles.[123] Such predictions concerned things which were necessary to know. Today, however, this office is finished; "we do not need them."[124] Thus here again the historical is introduced into considerations of the locus of prophecy. Gwalther also describes prophecy as interpreting the scriptures. He asserts, in fact, that it should not be understood simply as recitation or interpretation of scripture but, rather, it is the kind of expounding which brings consolation, penetrates the soul, etc.[125] In elaborating, he argues that prophecy should be understood not only as preaching (*donum vaticinandi*) as was common in the early church but also as writing about the scriptures (*scripturae tractationem*).[126] In this context, he comments on the ministry in his own day, and severely criticizes the Anabaptists whom he says, derisively, "all want to prophesy (*qui omnes prophetare volunt*)"[127]—clearly echoing the frustrations articulated by Capito and Bucer.

So then, in these three examples (Pellican, Bucer, and Gwalther), we see ingenuity, initiative, and some apparent confusion combined, in at least two of them and likely all three, with an apparent concern for the present circumstances of the church and, in particular, the danger the Anabaptists pose through their claim to the Pauline prophetic office. Two more examples will bring this section to a close. I begin with Peter Martyr Vermigli's reflections on prophecy, a sizeable portion of which—namely, two loci in his Genesis and Judges commentaries—focuses on prophecy as prognostication. This man, who spent time in Zurich, Strasbourg, and Oxford after fleeing Italy, was schooled in the Thomist tradition and so, perhaps not

---

[122] Gwalther (1 Cor.), 208ʳ (on 1 Cor. 11: 2–6). He argues this in comments on 1 Cor. 11: 2–6 ("every man who prays or prophesies . . .").

[123] Gwalther (1 Cor.), 243ʳ (on 1 Cor. 12: 8–12). He argues this in a homily on Rom. 12: 6–7, as well, see Gwalther, *In D. Pauli apostoli epistolam ad Romanos homiliae* (Zurich: Froschouerus, 1566), 169ʳ⁻ᵛ.

[124] Gwalther (1 Cor.), 243ʳ (on 1 Cor. 12: 8–12).

[125] Gwalther (1 Cor.), 285ʳ⁻ᵛ. See also *In D. Pauli apostoli epistolam ad Romanos homiliae*, 169ʳ⁻ᵛ.

[126] Gwalther (1 Cor.), 270ʳ.

[127] His discussion of preaching as God's word comes from Gwalther, *Isaias: in Isaiam prophetam Rodolphi Gvaltheri Tigurini homiliae CCCXXVII* (Zurich: Froschouerus, 1583), 303. For his censuring of Anabaptists, see Gwalther (1 Cor.), 251ʳ (on 1 Cor. 12: 37–40).

surprisingly, much of his work on the locus reads like a standard articulation of prophecy according to Tradition 1. That there is more to his thinking is hinted at by remarks such as this one on 1 Kings 13: "We also see here four duties (*officia*) of prophets which are set forth: first, fighting falsehood and teaching truth; second, predicting the future; third, doing miracles; and finally, praying on behalf of those who are afflicted."[128] Though perhaps not as odd as Pellican's and Gwalther's claim that hearing prophecy is prophecy, this is still a fascinating observation. Vermigli also distinguishes himself for treating prophecy from an overtly historical perspective, as we found in the work of others. For instance, he asserts that there is, with respect to prophecy, a discrimination of times (*discrimina temporum*).[129] Elaborating, Vermigli notes that there were prophets before the law, "Abraham, Noah, Enoch and Adam," prophets during the time of the law, "such as Moses and others," and prophets during the apostolic era, "such as the prophecies of many holy men during the time of the primitive church (*sanctorum virorum in primitiva Ecclesia*)."[130] So there is clearly more to his thought than meets the eye. This can be expanded upon further if we turn to his treatment of Paul on prophecy.

When commenting on the office of prophet in relation to the standard Pauline passages, Vermigli strikes several different notes. In treating 1 Corinthians 12: 10, he argues that "prophecy" refers to predicting the future.[131] Addressing other relevant Pauline texts, such as 1 Corinthians 14: 3, 26–32 and Romans 12: 6,[132] the Italian understands the Apostle to be referring simply to the ordinary ministry of the word (*ad verbi ministerium*), which Vermigli argues is *not* rightly associated with prophecy. In other words, these passages refer only to ordinary preaching.[133] But his reading of Romans 12: 6 is

---

[128] Peter Martyr Vermigli, *Est regum libri Duo posteriores cum commentariis Petri Martyris Vermilii* (Zurich: Froschouerus, 1566), 117b.

[129] PMV (1–2 Sam.), 112[r].

[130] PMV (1–2 Sam.), 112[r]. See a similar reading in his exposition of 1 Cor. 12: 28, PMV (1 Cor.), 82[v].

[131] PMV (1 Cor.), 82[v].

[132] On 1 Cor. 14: 3: "Prophetia vero maiorem afferebat utilitatem, quod ad verbi ministerium accederet maxime" (PMV (1 Cor.), 106[v]); see also his handling of 1 Cor. 14: 26–33, esp. 29–31 (PMV (1 Cor.), 205[r]–207[r]). On Romans, see PMV (Rom.), 1346.

[133] PMV (1 Cor.), 206[v]–207[r]. For more, see Jon Balserak, "'We Need Teachers Today, Not Prophets:' Peter Martyr Vermigli's Exposition of Prophecy," *Archiv für Reformationsgeschichte*, 103 (2012), 148–72. In fact, he attacks the link which is sometimes made between prophets and teachers, in his locus on prophecy from the

worthy of a bit more attention. On it, Vermigli notes that while in the primitive church era there were many who were gifted by God to foretell the future (i.e. prophets—Peter, Agabus, etc.), this is not what Paul has in mind here. Rather Paul, he says, is only discussing those offices which are perpetually and always necessary to the church (how he comes to that conclusion is unclear). What Paul seems to be doing, Vermigli contends, is setting out two general offices which the Apostle then divides into parts in the remainder of the verse.[134] So "prophecy" functions, as Vermigli sees it, in tandem with "ministry." Paul sets down these two general offices. He is doing this, Vermigli contends, because humankind consists of two parts. The human being is body and soul. The correspondence is intended to indicate that God is concerned for both human souls and human bodies. "Ministry" covers the body, "prophecy" the soul. In Vermigli's opinion, the word "prophecy" as it appears in Romans 12: 6, embraces the gifts, which are mentioned later in the verse, of teaching and exhortation. Accordingly, Paul is simply referring to the ordinary teaching office.[135] What this, and several of the observations considered in this paragraph, would seem to indicate is that Vermigli does not believe that the New Testament prophetic office continues into the post-apostolic church. In fact, he makes clear, in his locus on prophecy in his Genesis 20 commentary, that he believes the prophetic office ceased following the church's primitive era. There he asserts that "[w]e have no promise that Christ would adorn his church with such gifts [as prophecy] perpetually."[136] From the context, it is apparent that Vermigli clearly means "in our day."

Yet, this is not the end of the story. For turning to Vermigli's Old Testament commentaries, one finds a different sensibility. Vermigli, in his Genesis commentary, declared: "[i]n my judgment, it ought not to be denied that there are still prophets in the church."[137] On this idea, he further observes in his treatment of 1 Samuel: "If the ordinary

---

Genesis 20 commentary. There, he closes his brief remarks on the issue by asserting that the only way one can claim that a teacher is a prophet is if "you are willing to twist the words of Paul in 1 Corinthians" (PMV (Gen.), 81[r]; also: "interpretes divinarum literarum dicebantur prophetae" (PMV (1–2 Sam.), 111[r])).

[134] PMV (Rom.), 1346.

[135] Vermigli does, later on in his exposition of this text, refer to prophecy as a general office (*generale munus*), but again it is clear that he is not treating it as if Paul had in his mind a specific church office of prophet. PMV (Rom.), 1346.

[136] PMV (Gen.), 81[r].   [137] PMV (Gen.), 81[r].

ministry at any time does not fulfill their duty, God raises up prophets extraordinarily in order to restore things to order."[138] That he has Zwingli in mind seems quite likely, though I have yet to find a place in which he confirms this. But, whether he had someone particular in mind or not, he plainly asserts within the context of addressing Old Testament prophecy that that prophecy is not dead.

Having now looked briefly at Vermigli's thought on Old and New Testament prophecy, it will be interesting to query whether he comments on the Anabaptists and, if so, in what context. The Anabaptists do, in fact, receive criticism from him in his treatment of the Pauline prophetic office. Criticisms such as the ones I am finding are particularly noteworthy for the interests of the present study because men like Pellican, Bucer, Gwalther, and Vermigli were writing on the issue into the 1530s (mid-to-late), 1540s, and 1550s. In Zurich, by 1526, Conrad Grebel, Felix Mantz, George Blaurock, and the small group of dissenters who were with them had begun calling themselves prophets and denouncing Zwingli as a false prophet and Antichrist, which led to debates and a flurry of publications by Zwingli and others condemning the Anabaptists. Part of the Anabaptists' ability to do this rested on Pauline references to prophecy which they were using, or exploiting (if one adopts a Zwinglian perspective), to establish their authority. Similar troubles also appeared at the same time in Strasbourg,[139] as I have already noted via the citation from Capito's letter to Prugner and also through my brief discussion of the Strasbourg prophets and Melchior Hoffman, whose *Das XII. Capitel des propheten Danielis ausgelegt* was published in 1526. But we can now see that the reformers were still excoriating Anabaptists' appropriating of the Pauline prophetic office in the 1550s—which is important for my treatment of Calvin in Chapter 3 and which also nicely brings us back to Vermigli. In his lectures on 1 Corinthians 14: 29–32, addressing the questions of who can speak in church and how order can be maintained within the church, Vermigli condemns the Anabaptists for destroying all order within the church. They, Vermigli complains, use this Pauline text—specifically "For you can all

---

[138] PMV (1–2 Sam.), 113ʳ.

[139] See Miriam Chrisman, *Strasbourg and the Reform; A Study in the Process of Change* (New Haven: Yale University Press, 1967), 177–200; Chrisman, *Lay Culture, Learned Culture; Books and Social Change in Strasbourg, 1480–1599* (New Haven: Yale University Press, 1982), 144–50 *et passim*; Thomas A. Brady, Jr., *Ruling Class, Regime and Reformation at Strasbourg, 1520–1555* (Leiden: Brill, 1978), 236–58.

prophecy one by one" (1 Cor. 14: 31)—as grounds for their pursuits. They acknowledge no order in the church (*ordinem ... nullum*)[140] and would destroy the church if they were allowed to, Vermigli contends. Thus, once again we discover concerns about the Anabaptists linked with the issue of prophecy—concerns which, it would seem clear, affected Vermigli's handling of the locus of prophecy by moving him to push the authoritative office of prophet into an *Old* Testament arena and to claim that any prophets appearing in his day would have effectively been Old Testament messengers who had been raised up by God to reform the church—a position which I will expand upon in due course.[141] Thus, he was able to hold onto the prophetic status of reformers (whether he had Zwingli in mind, or not) while excluding the Anabaptists from any claim to prophetic authority.

The final example I will turn to in order to demonstrate the themes of variety, ingenuity, and confusion is Wolfgang Musculus, the reformer of Bern. On the face of it he betrays a good deal more consistency than Vermigli. He presents a particularly interesting case, in fact, because in him we find one who appears in many ways to be the clearest successor to Rhabanus Maurus. Musculus' judgments seem almost like an extrapolation of Maurus' position. He consistently sets out the view that there are two kinds of prophets (*duo prophetarum genera*), one which predicts the future and another which interprets the word of God and explains it to the people. This is set out in his *Loci Communes*, and commentaries on Genesis, Isaiah, Romans, 1 Corinthians, and 1 John (he does not assert this in his exposition of the Psalms or Ephesians 4: 11).[142] Yet, despite the apparent consistency and clarity of his coverage, inconsistencies can be found. The main problem one finds relates to the fact that Musculus does not appear to know what to do with the second kind of prophet—and, again, specifically the Pauline office of prophet—who expounds the scriptures. He handles this prophet in three ways.

The first way Musculus handles it is by dropping discussion of the prophet as interpreter in midstream (as it were). For instance, in the *Loci Communes*, after delineating the above-mentioned two kinds of

[140] PMV (1 Cor.), 207ʳ.   [141] PMV (1 Cor.), 206ᵛ–207ʳ.

[142] Wolfgang Musculus, *In Mosis Genesim plenissimi Commentarii* (Basel: Joannem hervagium, 1565), 488. The other passages will be referred to at later points in this discussion of Musculus.

prophets, he divides the Pauline offices into those which pertained to "the evangelical dispensation only" and those pertaining to "the ordinary ministry." Continuing, he places prophets (i.e. predictors of the future) together with apostles and evangelists and argues that they fall into the former category. They are not a part of the ordinary ministry of the church. (He says the same in his exposition of Romans 12: 6 and implies this in his treatment of Ephesians 4: 11, where he declares that prophets were promised for the commencement of the New Testament era.[143]) But Musculus seems to have neglected to take up the second kind of prophet. He simply makes no further comments on the prophet as interpreter and, specifically, on whether this kind of prophet still exists or is abrogated like the first kind.[144]

The second way Musculus handles the matter is essentially historical in character; that is, he switches from discussing prophecy to discussing the ordinary ministry of the word. When expounding 1 Corinthians, he again asserts the idea that there are two kinds of prophets. Accordingly, in 1 Corinthians 12: 6, Musculus thinks prophets who predict the future are indicated.[145] But in 1 Corinthians 14: 3, he believes that "prophets" refers to those who interpret and preach the scriptures. This time, he pays a considerable amount of attention to this second kind of prophet, referring to them as "ecclesiastical prophets (*ecclesiastici prophetae*)." He divides the roles of these prophets into three: edification, consolation, and exhortation. He discusses each in turn. Here two observations might briefly be inserted. First, it is slightly confusing to find Musculus explaining that "prophecy" in 1 Corinthians 14: 6—only three verses after 1 Corinthians 14: 3—refers to prediction of the future.[146] Second, it is surely even more curious to see how much attention he pays to the prophet as interpreter when he had entirely dropped this second kind of prophet in the *Loci Communes*. Following Musculus' treatment of edification, consolation, and exhortation, he adds a brief section in which he shifts attention seamlessly from discussing "prophets" to

---

[143] The phrase he uses is "Novi Testamenti primordiis," see Wolfgang Musculus, *In Epistolas Apostoli Pauli ad Galatas, et Ephesios Commentarii* (Basel: Hervagius, 1569), 106.

[144] Wolfgang Musculus, *Loci Communes* (Basel: Hervagius, 1564), 194–5. For Romans, see Wolfgang Musculus, *In Epistolam Apostoli Pauli ad Romanos, Commentarii* (Basel: Hervagius, 1555), 291–2.

[145] Musculus (1 Cor.), 486.   [146] Musculus (1 Cor.), 541.

discussing the ordinary "ministry of the word."[147] He does not explicitly acknowledge the shift; it could well be that he viewed these two terms as interchangeable. He simply does not say.

The third way Musculus handles the prophet as interpreter is perhaps the most perplexing. In his commentary on Isaiah, he sets out his common division of two kinds of prophets. The second kind is referred to by Paul in 1 Corinthians 14, he explains, according to which "as many people as interpret the scriptures are prophets." But, Musculus explains in the next sentence, it is less common that we call (*vocemus*) such individuals prophets. "And the Scripture itself uses this sense rarely (*hoc sensu raro utitur*)," he asserts. Musculus, having made this point, then adds the odd explanation that the scripture frequently (*frequenter*) calls "prophets," inserting the Hebrew word, those who prophesy or otherwise expound the divine will of God or extol God's greatness "by a peculiar inspiration of the Spirit (*ex peculiari afflatu spiritus*)." His use of the Hebrew word would seem to indicate a highlighting of the Old Testament prophetic office. With this sentence, he concludes the paragraph. Precisely what he means by all this is unclear.[148] He simply drops the whole discussion at this point.

There is more that could be said on Musculus' views on prophecy, for I have not treated his handling of the topic in his Psalms commentary, where he discusses the notion that *all* Christians are *prophetas*.[149] But it seems I have said enough, except that I should note that Musculus in discussing prophecy also complains about the Anabaptists. When treating 1 Corinthians 14: 29–33 ("Two or three prophets should speak . . . the spirit of the prophets are subject to the prophets"), he lambasts the Anabaptists for causing disorder in the church through their prophesying.[150] These comments were published in 1559. Not only do they plainly resemble the remarks made by those

[147] Musculus (1 Cor.), 535–7.

[148] Musculus, *In Esaiam Prophetam Commentarii . . .* (Basel: Hervagius, 1557), 2–3. All of this is stated, it is worth reiterating, in his preface to his Isaiah commentary. While this helps explain his concern for inserting the Hebrew word for prophet, it fails to assist us in understanding precisely what he means. Is he making a distinction between the ordinary interpretation of scripture, which is sometimes called prophecy, and the spirit-inspired interpretation? It is not clear.

[149] Wolfgang Musculus, *In Sacrosanctum Davidis Psalterium Commentarii: In Quibus Et Reliqua . . .* (Basel: Hervagius, 1556), 892.

[150] Musculus (1 Cor.), 577–8.

whom I looked at earlier, but they are also significant because they confirm that concerns about Anabaptists and prophecy were felt beyond the confines of Zurich and Strasbourg and were felt (again) in relation specifically to the *New* Testament office of prophet during the second half of the sixteenth century. With these matters treated, this chapter can now turn to a constructive analysis of the theology of prophecy espoused by the theologians upon which I am focusing.

THE EARLY MODERN PROPHET-REFORMER

Despite the perception among many that the Anabaptists misused the New Testament prophetic office, the place to begin this section is still undoubtedly with Zwingli's organizing of the Zurich *lectorium* known as the *Prophezei* meetings, which began on 19 June 1525 and were the outworking of his reading of 1 Corinthians 14: 26–33.[151] The *Prophezei* was, it should be noted, not the first such meeting of its kind. Prior to its beginning, Oswald Myconius lectured, in German, on the New Testament in the Fraumünster. Heinrich Bullinger held biblical lectures in Kappel (before the start of the *Prophezei*), also in German. Moving further afield, Strasbourg had its *christliche Übung*, Bern its *lectiones publicae*, and later Geneva followed with its *congrégation*.[152] But what was started by Zwingli, and his companions, in the Zurich

---

[151] ZW 4: 397–8; Zwingli, *Annotatiunculae per Leonem Iudae, . . . Pauli ad Corinthios Epistolam*, 115–17, 120–3.

[152] I am grateful to Peter Opitz for an email exchange about the *Prophezei* and about some of these other early Bible study ventures. Also see his "Von prophetischer Existenz zur Prophetie als Pädagogik," ii. 493–513. For the equivalent in Geneva, see Erik A. de Boer, *The Genevan School of the Prophets: The Congrégations of the Company of Pastors and their Influence in Sixteenth Century Europe* (Geneva: Droz, 2012); also de Boer, "The Presence and Participation of Laypeople in the *Congrégations* of the Company of Pastors in Geneva," *Sixteenth Century Journal*, 35/3 (2004), 651–70. On the *Prophezei* meetings, see, *inter alia*, Philippe Denis, "La Prophétie dans les Eglises de la Réforme au XVIe siècle," *Revue d'Histoire ecclésiastique*, 72 (1977), 289–316; Bruce Gordon, *The Swiss Reformation* (Manchester: University of Manchester Press, 2002), 232–8. The importance of the *Prophezei* has been signalled by a number of scholars. See, *inter alia*, Gottfried Locher, "In Spirit and in Truth: How Worship Changed at the Reformation," in *Zwingli's Thought; New Perspectives*, 28; Anja-Silvia Göing, "Die Ausbildung reformierter Prediger in Zürich 1531–1575: Vorstellung eines pädagogischen Projekts," in H. J. Selderhuis and Markus Wriedt (eds), *Bildung und Konfession: Theologenausbildung im Zeitalter der Konfessionalisierung* (Tübingen: Mohr Siebeck, 2006), 293–310.

Prophezei was unquestionably hugely significant to the Swiss Confederation and to Early Modern Europe. The pattern of its practice is described by scholars in a number of publications, and will not occupy us here. We know that it was conducted in Latin and that the participants worked with the original languages, reading from the Vulgate, the Hebrew text, and, then, the Septuagint, as they treated each passage of a given Old Testament biblical book. They abandoned the traditional pattern of following liturgical readings, replacing it with the *lectio continua* approach. The meetings issued in the *Prophetenbibel* of 1529 and had a lasting impact throughout Europe.[153]

Given the shadow Zwingli cast, it is not at all surprising to find the early Bullinger following his teacher. He asserts in various places, including his *De propheta libri duo*, commentary on Romans 12: 6, his handling of 1 Corinthians 14: 3, and his *De scripturae sanctae authoritate . . . perfectione, deque Episcoporum, . . . Libri duo* that Paul understands by prophecy here "not the prediction of the future but the interpretation of the Holy Scriptures."[154] Additionally, Rudolph Gwalther seems to fall in line with Zwingli and Bullinger, articulating a similar position.[155] Likewise, a Lutheran such as Melanchthon can be found articulating the same view in his remarks on 1 Corinthians 12: 28.[156] One may suspect the influence of Erasmus upon both the

<hr/>

[153] The pattern of their practice in the *Prophezei* is described in a number of places; see Heinrich Bullinger, *Reformationsgeschichte*, i, ed. J. J. Hottinger and H. H. Vögeli (repr. Zurich: Nova-Buchhandlung, 1984), 289–91; Locher, "In Spirit and in Truth," 27–8. The impact of the *Prophezei* extends throughout various parts of Europe and the New World; see Denis, "La Prophétie," 289–316. A recent study discusses John a Lasco's employment of the model and its spread among the English puritans; see Michael Springer, *Restoring Christ's Church: John Lasco and the Forma ac ratio* (Aldershot: Ashgate, 2007).

[154] Heinrich Bullinger, *In priorem d. Pauli ad Corinthios epistolam, Heinrychi Bullingeri commentarius* (Zurich: Froschouerus, 1534), 170ᵛ; Bullinger, *De prophetae officio, et quomodo digne administrari posit, oratio* (Zurich: Froschouerus, 1532), 3ʳ⁻ᵛ; Bullinger, *De scripturae sanctae authoritate . . . perfectione, deque Episcoporum, . . . Libri duo* (Zurich: Froschouerus, 1538), 79ʳ⁻ᵛ; see, Bolliger, "Bullinger on Church Authority," 161.

[155] Rudolph Gwalther, *In D. Pauli Apostoli Epistolam ad Romanos Homiliae*, 163ᵛ.

[156] For Melanchthon, see *Commentarius in epist. Ad Corinthios* 12: 28 in CR 15: 1133–4. Melanchthon expands slightly more on the subject of prophecy in comments on Rom. 12: 6 in which he explains that the right interpretation of scripture "requires some revelation (*opus est aliqua revelatione*)" (CR 15: 708 from his *Commentarii in epistolam Pauli ad Romanos*). Again, though by no means impossible, it nonetheless seems doubtful to me that these thinkers represent a conscious continuation of a medieval tradition.

Swiss and possibly Melanchthon too, though that point is perhaps debatable.[157] That one finds these thinkers supporting the Zwinglian endorsement of New Testament prophecy while also vehemently criticizing the Anabaptists for appropriating it provides a glimpse into something of the complexity surrounding thinking on the Pauline version of the prophetic office at this time.

So, a collection of Swiss theologians, led until his unfortunate death on a battlefield in Kappel by Zwingli, gathered together for what was essentially a Bible study according to what appears prima facie to be a Tradition 2 understanding of prophecy. One may legitimately inquire as to whether this can be called pioneering. But it was.

The prophet, according to this collection of theologians, is raised up by God as a kind of covenant prosecutor. The picture ultimately in view here is of someone like Isaiah, Jeremiah, or one of the other Old Testament prophets. That is to say, the covenant tends to be central to the thinking of these theologians on the true religion and, on this basis, the prophet is a servant of that covenant. In this innovative portrait of the prophet, he[158] is a fighter. His weapon is the scriptures and his principal enemy is rampant idolatry. He is raised up by God to interpret the scriptures authoritatively; with an authority which verges on infallibility. He does this interpreting within a context in which the right understanding of the word of God has been discarded in favor of human inventions and superstitions. Accordingly, this prophet is a kind of outsider; the established church does not want to hear what he has to say. He is raised up precisely because the priests of the church have failed in their duties, and it is his calling to clean house and return the church to the truth. The prophet knows himself to be the very mouthpiece of God. He speaks the truth; the pure word of God. Thus, he is called to reform the church from the idolatry which it has embraced and let nothing stand in his way of doing this. This reforming work does not involve predicting the future but rather speaking the word of God authoritatively in the church.

---

[157] The likely influence of Desiderius Erasmus on several of the Swiss is rightly suggested by Max Engammare. See Erasmus, *Novum instrumentum* (Basel: Johann Froben, 1516; repr. Stuttgart-Bad Cannstatt: Frommann-Holzboog, 1986), 477, as cited in Max Engammare, "Calvin: A Prophet," 92. See also Abraham Friesen, *Erasmus, the Anabaptists, and the Great Commission* (Grand Rapids, Mich.: Eerdmans, 1998).

[158] For careful analysis of what many of these theologians thought about women as prophets, see Thompson, *John Calvin and the Daughters of Sarah*, 184–202.

Examining these ideas more meticulously, I begin with a basic shift which has already been alluded briefly to earlier in this chapter but will now be clarified and expanded upon. Musculus, when writing on the prophet Isaiah, introduces this for us. In the preface to his treatment of this Old Testament prophet, Musculus sets out the familiar notion that there are two kinds of prophets (*duo prophetarum genera*), as we saw earlier (citing 1 Corinthians 14 along with other texts). Within his discussion, Musculus declares that generally (*plerumque*) these two kinds of prophesying are joined together, "as we see in the writings of the prophets."[159] This ascription of interpreting to the prophets of the *Old* Testament era is what catches my attention. It is tantalizing; and moving from Musculus to Gwalther, we find the point made unmistakably. At the beginning of his Isaiah homilies, Gwalther, speaking about the calling of (obviously *pre*-Christian) Old Testament prophets, observes: "For prophets are interpreters of the divine will," by which he seems plainly to mean the scriptures.[160] It is *this* innovation—namely, that these theologians focused their attention on the ministries of the *Old* Testament prophets, whom they believed to be interpreters of the scriptures and covenant prosecutors—that will be significant to what I extrapolate upon. While theologians like Gwalther or Bibliander do not reject the idea that Old Testament prophets received supernatural knowledge, yet they see them primarily as scriptural interpreters raised up to apply and defend the *Old* covenant strictures. To elaborate, in Tradition 1 and Tradition 2 the consistent implication has been that the latter related to the *New* Testament office of prophet while the former related to the *Old* Testament office. In fact, I have found no writer from either the ancient or the medieval period who described an Old Testament prophet as an interpreter of scripture.[161] But as the views of my collection of Early Modern theologians are examined, one discovers that many of them seem to believe Old Testament prophets are interpreters of God's Word, specifically of the Law of Moses. And, perhaps more importantly, they seem to be drawn to modeling their

---

[159] Musculus, *In Esaiam Prophetam Commentarii*, 2.

[160] Gwalther, *In Isaiam prophetam homiliae*, 1.

[161] There is arguably some possibility that Origen might have viewed Old Testament prophets as interpreters; see Hällström, *Charismatic Succession*, 10–21. Likewise, Aquinas, *Expositio in Epistolam I ad Corinthios* 14, in *Aquinas Opera*, xiii. 281–2. Though from my reading of Aquinas, the point could at best only be said to be *implied* by the Dominican.

own reforming ministries after the Old Testament prophetic ministry model rather than that of the New Testament model. Calvin, I will argue, follows the same pattern which, irrespective of who we are talking about, seems at least in part to have been motivated by the intense frustration produced by the Anabaptists' utilizing of the New Testament paradigm. This does not, I hasten to add, result in all these theologians completely jettisoning any interest in the New Testament prophetic office. Rather, it results in them having the kind of ambiguous attitude towards that office that I discussed in the previous section. This is true of Calvin as well, as I have shown in Chapter 1.

Examining these ideas further, it becomes clear that for theologians like Zwingli, Bullinger, Bibliander, Vermigli, and Musculus reforming means something discernibly different from what it meant for many medieval prophets and prophetesses. For these Early Modern prophets, their reforming authority is founded upon their God-sanctioned interpreting of scripture; the truth of God as expounded from the Bible is, in effect, their warrant. For them, also, the Old Testament prophets provide a kind of template for what it means to be a prophet. Both they and their old covenant predecessors occupy the same role as reformers of a church drowning in idolatry. Both exercise a ministry which focuses on exposition and application of scripture. Thus, our Early Modern prophet-reformers are keenly interested in the ministerial labors of prophets like Isaiah, Jeremiah, Amos, and Micah, because their work is effectively identical to it. These Early Modern prophets conceive of their own age as "mirroring"[162] that of the Old Testament prophets. Thus, they see the problems which they face as reflected in the Old Testament books and also understand the approach which the Old Testament prophets took to those problems to be the approach which they should take in their own era.[163] In

---

[162] See, for instance, Pellican, *In omnes apostolicas epistolas*, 250–1; Zwingli, ZW 3: 5–68; Zwingli, *Annotatiunculae per Leonem Iudae, ... Pauli ad Corinthios Epistolam*, 115–17, 120–3; Gwalther, *In prophetas duodecimo, quos vocant minores, Rodolphi Gualtheri ... homiliae* (Zurich: Froschouerus, 1577), 17ʳ. This mirroring idea is apparent throughout the thought (on prophecy) of individuals Zwingli, Bullinger, and Bibliander, as scholars have rightly noted; see Fritz Büsser, "Der Prophet-Gedanken zu Zwinglis Theologie," *Zwingliana*, 13 (1969), 7–18; esp. 7–8, and Petersen, *Preaching in the Last Day*, 139 n. 11.

[163] To be sure, the Old Testament prophets' callings involved declaring the kingdom of Christ. Zwingli, Bullinger, and these other thinkers spent plenty of time and energy on the predictions of Christ's appearance and salvific work, which they obviously saw as essential for all sorts of reasons. But this message (of Christ's

these Early Modern theologians' opinions, laboring against idolatry
was central to the Old Testament prophets' callings, as it also is for
their own callings within sixteenth-century Europe.

In this reimagining of the prophetic office, several qualities surface
as crucial. One of the more prominent qualities is that, as an interpreter of the law, the prophet "adds nothing"[164] to it. This, these
Reformation-era theologians believe, was true of the Old Testament
prophets as interpreters of the Law of Moses and it is true of themselves as interpreters of the scriptures. The Old Testament prophets,
these men believe, expounded and applied the Mosaic Law to the
ancient people of God, and all of what they preached was merely
extrapolation upon what is found in the Mosaic Law. They preached
nothing new. They, to put this idea in a different way which furthers
my discussion of it, produce "pure" exposition. This purity is normally set in contrast to the Roman Catholics, who added their own
accretions to the divine word with their praying to saints and for the
dead, imposed celibacy, veneration of images, Eucharistic adoration,
and so forth.[165] The true prophets of God, by contrast, do not
contaminate God's word with their own additions. This is apparent
in a number of Zwingli's writings in which he is at pains to insist that
no human ideas ought to be introduced into the prophets' speaking
for God.[166] These points are also set out nicely by Pellican in his
Praefatio in Libros Canonicos Prophetales. There Pellican explains,
through reference to the Hebrew and Greek words for prophet, what
the common understanding of a prophet is. This common understanding has to do with, he says, predicting the future. According to
this, he continues, certain thinkers divide the Old Testament in a
three-fold manner: the law, the prophets, and the histories. But
Pellican contends that this is not a satisfactory explanation, for
Moses and the other prophets all treat the same material. "Again,
prophets add nothing to what was handed down by Moses, but only
explain it more clearly (*exponunt dilucidius*), applying those things to

appearance and salvific death) was contextualized by these Swiss thinkers such that
time and time again they emphasized the fact of the diametrical opposition which
existed in the prophets' day between the purity of worship in God's kingdom and the
impurity of idolatry.

[164] ZW 3: 21, 34, 61.
[165] For thorough handling of the subject, see Bullinger, *De scripturae sanctae
authoritate ... perfectione, deque Episcoporum, ... Libri duo*, 39ᵛ–64ᵛ.
[166] ZW 3: 21–3, 33–4, 61; ZW 4: 397–8.

the capacities of those living in their own times." The same thing is expressed by Bibliander in his prefaces to Isaiah and Nahum.[167] This reimagining of the prophetic vocation also induces these theologians to discuss, in their treatments of prophecy, the matter of the interpreting of scripture. In point of fact, a large amount of space is often devoted by them in their discussions of prophecy to the question of proper exegesis. This is exemplified brilliantly in Bibliander's prefaces to Isaiah and to Nahum and in Bullinger's *De Prophetae Officio* and *De scripturae sanctae authoritate . . . perfectione, deque Episcoporum, . . . Libri duo.*[168] In these and other writings, one finds discussions of the importance of knowing the languages and of the crucial need for the Spirit's aid in the interpreting task. These qualities, for instance, are discussed as matters of great importance to prophecy by Zwingli in his *Von Dem Predigtamt*, particularly the crucial place of languages.[169] The same stress upon languages is made by Luther in relation to the prophet. Here is not the place to consider at length their individual treatments of the topic of biblical exegesis, as that would divert my attention away from the present subject.[170] Rather, the fact will simply be noted and underlined, that these

---

[167] Conrad Pellican, *In Prophetas Maiores et Minores, ut vulgo vocantur, hoc est, in Isaiam, Ieremiam, . . . Commentarii Conradi Pellicani . . .* (Zurich: Froschouerus, 1582), unnumbered preface. For Bibliander, see Theodor Bibliander, *Oratio Theodori Bibliandri ad enarrationem Esaiae prophetarum principis dicta . . .* (Zurich: Froschower, 1532), 12^{r-v}, and Bibliander, *Propheta Nahvm Ivxta Veritatem Hebraicam, Latine redditus per Theodorum Bibliandrum; adiecta exegesi, qua uersionis ratio redditur, & authoris diuini sententia explicatur. Tigvri: Apvd Christoph Froscho., Mense Ivl. Anno M. D. XXXIIII.* (Zurich: Froschouerus, 1534), 9^{v}. The standard bibliography for Bibliander is Christian Moser, *Theodor Bibliander (1505–1564): Annotierte Bibliographie der gedruckten Werke* (Zurich: TVZ, 2009).

[168] Bullinger, *De Prophetae officio . . . Oratio*, 3^{v}–10^{v}, et passim; also Bullinger, *De scripturae sanctae authoritate . . . perfectione, deque Episcoporum, . . . Libri duo*, 132^{v}–135^{v}; in the latter, it is difficult to choose one or two sections, as this treatise is, in some ways, all about scripture interpretation, though it ranges widely over other issues, polemics against Rome, etc. On Bibliander, see the excellent treatment, Bruce Gordon, "'Christo testimonium reddunt omnes scripturae:' Theodor Bibliander's Oration on Isaiah (1532) and Commentary on Nahum (1534)," in Bruce Gordon and Matthew McLean (eds), *Shaping the Bible in the Reformation; Books, Scholars and Their Readers in the Sixteenth Century* (Leiden: Brill, 2012), 107–41. I am grateful for Bruce Gordon allowing me access to this chapter prior to its publication.

[169] A similar sentiment is also found in the *ratio enarrandi prophetas* which appears at the beginning of Wolfgang Capito's Habakkuk commentary; see Wolfgang Capito, *In Habakuk prophetam* (Strasbourg: Vvolphium Cephalaeum 1526), 4^{r}. This he does not express with regards to the specific task of the prophet but with regard to the work of interpretation.

[170] See *Bible de Tous les Temps: Le Temps des Réformes et la Bible* and *Hebrew Bible; Old Testament,* 2 vols, ed. Magne Saebø (Göttingen: Vandenhoeck & Ruprecht, 2008).

theologians regularly link discussion of biblical interpretation with their views on the prophet and prophecy, and their reason for doing so would seem to be precisely because they see the prophet as an interpreter. The character of prophetic authority, as understood by these theologians, is also important to their conceptualization of prophecy. Precisely because these Early Modern prophets viewed prophets as pure expositors of God's word, they also would declare categorically that the prophet is God's mouthpiece.[171] These prophets believe that what they bring forth in their exegesis is nothing less than the word of God itself, as if God opened the clouds and spoke. There is a purity to their expositions which contains nothing human. This fact gives these prophets profound authority.

The prophet is called to be aggressor. Prominent here is Jeremiah 1: 9–10. "I have put my words in your mouth. See, I have appointed you this day over the nations and the kingdoms to pluck up and to break down, to destroy and to overthrow, to build and to plant."[172] The importance of Jeremiah's calling to Zwingli and Bullinger is rightly noted by Peter Opitz,[173] who draws attention to Zwingli's use of it in his *Der Hirt* and its influence upon his understudy as appears in Bullinger's *De Prophetae Officio*.[174] The importance of this biblical passage can also be seen in Zwingli's *Von dem Predigtamt* and Bullinger's Commentary on Jeremiah 1: 9. The passage—which is also of marked significance to Calvin, as shall be seen in the next chapter—sets down the notion that the prophet is a kind of covenant prosecutor, raised up in order to "pluck up and destroy (*abbreche und zerstöre*)"[175] anything set in opposition to God and God's kingdom. It also asserts that the prophet should replace opposition to God with submission to the divine will. Here, the prophet, who is given authority over the world and even kings, is enlisted to go on the

---

[171] See Bullinger, *De Prophetae officio . . . Oratio*, 3ʳ; Gottfried Locher, "'Praedicatio Verbi Dei est Verbum Dei'—Henry Bullinger between Luther and Zwingli. An Essay on his Theology," in *Zwingli's Thought; New Perspectives*, 277–87. For a brilliant example from Zwingli, see ZW 4: 394.

[172] See Jeremiah 1: 9b–10, *New American Standard Bible* (New York: CUP, 1977).

[173] Opitz, "Von prophetischer Existenz zur Prophetie als Pädagogik," ii. 493–513, esp. 501–3, Opitz's whole piece is a fine treatment of Bullinger's position on prophecy. See also Büsser, *Heinrich Bullinger*, i. 127–61.

[174] See Opitz, "Von prophetischer Existenz zur Prophetie als Pädagogik," ii. 494–8; also, Büsser, *Heinrich Bullinger*, i. 127–61.

[175] ZW 4: 397.

offensive, attacking fearlessly all powers whether ecclesiastical or civil, to bring everything under the authority of the word of God.[176] Such was the calling and authority not only of the Old Testament prophets but also of their Early Modern counterparts. That they believe *themselves* to possess such a calling and authority (i.e. that they themselves are prophets) is apparent in many of their writings, such as Zwingli's *Von dem Predigtamt* (and, arguably, in *Der Hirt* too) and throughout Bibliander's *Oratio . . . ad enarrationem Esaiae prophetarum principis.* The same can be said for Bullinger's *De officio prophetico.* Likewise, Bullinger declares, when speaking of Zwingli, that he is a "prophet" and that "God raised up this man to restore the glory of his church."[177] Bullinger also identified a "company of prophets" in one of his sermons on Revelation (preached in the early 1530s and published in 1537), listing "Mirandola, Reuchlin, Erasmus, Luther, Zwingli, Oecolampadius, and Melanchthon."[178] Additionally, one finds Philip Melanchthon identifying Martin Luther as a prophet, discussing those prophets mentioned by Paul in 1 Corinthians who are singularly gifted for the renewal of doctrine, "as Augustine was in his age and Luther is in ours."[179] Ulrich Zwingli identifies Martin Luther as Elijah, one of the two witnesses—Elijah and Enoch—promised in Revelation 11: 3.[180] Likewise the exchange

[176] ZW 3: 23–4; ZW 4: 394, 397; see also Zwingli, *Annontationes et satisfactiones complanationis Huld. Zuinglii in Jeremiam prophetam,* i. 5–17 (ZW 14: 514–15); Zwingli, *Annotatiunculae per Leonem Iudae, . . . Pauli ad Corinthios Epistolam,* 116; for Bullinger, see Bullinger, *De Prophetae officio . . . Oratio,* 3ʳ⁻ᵛ; Bullinger, *De scripturae sanctae authoritate . . . perfectione, deque Episcoporum, . . . Libri duo,* 66ʳ–67ʳ; Bullinger, *Heinrychi Bullingeri Jeremias fidelissimus et laboriosissimus Dei Propheta . . . concionibus CLXX* (Zurich: Froschoverus, 1575), 6ʳ⁻ᵛ.

[177] Bullinger, *De Prophetae officio,* 33ʳ.

[178] Heinrich Bullinger, *In Apocalypsim conciones centum* (Basel: Johannes Oporin 1557), 148, as cited by Petersen, *Preaching in the Last Days,* 149 n. 48.

[179] See Melanchthon's thoughts on Luther in *Commentarii in epist. Ad Corinthios* 12: 28 in CR 15: 1133–4; also generally on Rom. 12: 6 in *Commentarii in epistolam Pauli ad Romanos hoc anno M.D.XL. recogniti & locupletati* (Strasbourg: Apud Cratonem Mylium, 1540), 288. For a fuller exposition of Luther as prophet, see Hans Preuss, *Martin Luther. Der Prophet* (Gütersloh: C. Bertelsmann, 1933); Heiko Oberman, "Martin Luther: Vorläufer der Reformation," in Eberhard Jüngel, Johannes Wallmann, and Wilfrid Werbeck (eds), *Verifikationem: Festschrift für Gerhard Ebeling zum 70 Geburstag* (Tübingen: J. C. B. Mohr, 1982), 91–119.

[180] For Bibliander, see Bibliander, *Oratio Esaiae* 2ʳ⁻ᵛ, I owe this reference to Gordon, "Christo testimonium reddunt omnes scripturae," 16 (this is according to the pagination of the version which Gordon allowed me access to prior to the piece's publication). For Zwingli, see ZW 7: 218–22; I owe this reference to Petersen, *Preaching in the Last Days,* 117 n. 173.

of letters between Zwingli and Oecolampadius makes it clear that the two conceive of one another as prophets.[181] This collection of men is, they believe, raised up by God to interpret God's Word with divine authority and enforce its truth upon a church which had gone astray into idolatry. It will be argued in Chapter 3 that this same reimagined conception of the prophet is found in Calvin's theology and self-understanding.

* * *

This chapter plotted two trajectories (which I referred to as Tradition 1 and Tradition 2) which develop in Western Christian thought on prophecy. It discussed the relationship that developed between them and established that many thinkers within the patristic and medieval eras believed that prophets from both traditions existed in their own lifetimes.

Querying what happened to the prophet and these prophetic traditions in the sixteenth century, this chapter then demonstrated that for a number of Calvin's contemporaries, Zwingli, Bullinger, Bibliander, Pellican, Bucer, Gwalther, Vermigli, Musculus, and others, the prophet still exists, but that this existence takes a discernibly different form from what one finds in the Middle Ages. The difference comes largely, I argued, from the contours of a particular understanding of the Old Testament prophetic ministry which is developed and espoused by this collection of theologians. According to this understanding, prophets like Isaiah, Jeremiah, and Hosea are biblical interpreters who sought to reform a church which had become idolatrous by calling it back to the Mosaic Law. Here, the scriptures are of paramount importance; indeed, it was precisely in order to bring the church back to those scriptures that these prophets had been raised up. This, I showed, was what these Early Modern theologians believed about themselves and their own prophetic vocations, that is, they believed that they had been raised up by God to call the idolatrous church of their own day back to the divine covenant set forth in Holy Scripture.

In this chapter, I also identified two primary concerns or influences—apart (of course) from the traditions which would have been inherited from earlier periods in the church's thinking—which

---

[181] *D. D. Ioannis Oecolampadii et Huldrichii Zwinglii Epistolarum libri quatuor* (Basel: [R. Winter], 1536).

shaped the thinking of Zwingli, Pellican, Bibliander, and their colleagues on the locus of prophecy. One was the idolatry into which the
church (in their judgment) had fallen. The second was the Anabaptists and their habit of aggressively claiming prophetic authority based
upon Pauline texts such as 1 Corinthians 12: 28–32. The Anabaptists'
appropriation of the mantle of the New Testament prophet represented a significant frustration for all these theologians, I argued, and
seems to have resulted in confusion in relation to how to handle the
New Testament prophetic office. It also pushed a number of these
men towards the *Old* Testament prophetic vocation, which was
already a focal point because of these theologians' concerns about
idolatry. The same will be seen in Calvin's thinking on the locus.

3

Calvin, the Prophet

Calvin's contemporaries, Zwingli, Bullinger, Bibliander, Pellican, Bucer, Gwalther, Vermigli, Musculus, and others, articulate a powerful vision of the prophet. Aligning themselves with the Old Testament, they conceive of prophets as individuals raised up to interpret the scriptures authoritatively in order to call back from the brink a church which had fallen into idolatrous ruin. This authority seems to include within it an implied sense of infallibility. Prophets, they argue, are God's mouthpiece in the world, adding nothing to God's divine utterances but interpreting them purely and applying them to all, even the kings and priests over whom they have been given authority.

This chapter will take as a kind of working assumption the idea that Calvin adhered to this same vision of prophecy. We have, arguably, already been given some inkling that this might be true from what has been covered thus far. We know, as well, that his antipathy towards idolatry, the Mass, Roman cultic practice, and "papist" understanding of the Eucharist is similar to what one sees in the thought of Zwingli or Bullinger or Vermigli. Furthermore, and crucially, this assumption will be thoroughly demonstrated by the end of the chapter. But for now, it will be assumed, not so that I can avoid the work required to demonstrate its accuracy and truthfulness but so that I can do as much as possible in this chapter in as concise a way as possible (an aspiration which would, no doubt, have pleased Calvin).

With this assumption in place, I can focus on excavating Calvin's prophetic awareness. I will divide the chapter into three parts: (1) preference, (2) emulation, and (3) identity. First, I will identify a preference Calvin exhibits in his handling of the locus of prophecy; a preference for Old Testament prophecy. This is similar to the appeal which the Old Testament prophetic ministry held for some of Calvin's contemporaries, as I showed in Chapter 2. Once identified, this chapter will demonstrate that this is more than a preference; that Calvin actually emulates the Old Testament prophets in his own reforming ministry. Thirdly, the chapter will show that he not only emulates them, but identifies himself as one of them. That is to say, I will demonstrate that Calvin believed himself to be a prophet, such that what Vermigli[1] observed is an apt articulation of what Calvin believed both about Old Testament prophets like Isaiah or Jeremiah and about himself.

> If the ordinary ministry at any time does not fulfil their duty, God raises up prophets extraordinarily in order to restore things to order."[2]

This assertion from Vermigli offers a brilliant summary of the views of a number of Calvin's contemporaries, as discussed in Chapter 2, and also of what Calvin believed about himself—which is to say, that Calvin and, for instance, Jeremiah possessed essentially the same calling.

Having examined Calvin's context in the previous chapter, there are still some issues associated with establishing his prophetic awareness that I need to deal with, and the arrangement I have opted for in this chapter should allow me to do this in a fairly tidy manner. I have decided to separate Calvin's thinking on the Old Testament and New Testament prophets and to address details related to Calvin's understanding of each on their own terms. I am convinced that the variety and confusion exhibited by theologians like Zwingli, Pellican, Bucer, Gwalther, Vermigli, and Musculus towards the *New* Testament office of prophet (as I unearthed in the previous chapter) also appear in Calvin's thought on the office and that his thinking on it, like their thinking on it, was influenced by the Anabaptist claims to the Pauline office. Therefore, the present chapter will commence by addressing this issue. Having done so, it will be able to show that, while Calvin remains ambivalent towards the Pauline office (making a range of

---

[1] Incidentally, Melanchthon makes a similar remark, as does Calvin (as we shall see). Melanchthon's is by no means identical to Vermigli's assertion, but it does, nonetheless, speak about Augustine and Luther as prophets "singularly gifted for the renewal of doctrine," see *Commentarii in epist. Ad Corinthios* 12: 28 in CR 15: 1133–4.

[2] PMV (1–2 Sam.), 113[r]. Vermigli makes precisely the same point in expounding 1 Cor. 12: 28–31; see PMV (1 Cor.), 182[v]; see Balserak, "We Need Teachers Today, Not Prophets," 148–72.

different and apparently contradictory assertions about it) for his
entire adult life, he quite clearly is *not* ambivalent or uncertain
towards the Old Testament prophets. In fact, he identifies himself
with them. Thus, the Anabaptist "menace" helps explain the confusion which I found in Calvin's thought on the office of prophet in
Chapter 1.

IDENTIFYING CALVIN'S PREFERENCE FOR OLD TREATMENT PROPHECY

One of the less-apparent eccentricities that cleaves to Calvin's
thought on prophecy is a preference for Old Testament prophecy.
On the face of it, Calvin would seem to treat Old and New Testament
prophets in similar ways. Like other theologians, Calvin seems in
places to articulate the idea that within biblical literature there appear
to be two kinds of prophets (*duo prophetarum genera*).[3] Moreover,
with respect to both Old and New Testament prophets, he seems to
conceive of their labors as entailing prediction of the future and also
interpretation. He seems, therefore, prima facie to hold them to be
doing similar work in similar ways. Yet, there is more to Calvin's
handling of these two manifestations of prophecy than meets the eye,
as shall become clear in what follows.

---

[3] Calvin does not articulate this view explicitly in the way that someone like
Musculus does. To provide one brief instance of Calvin's reflections on the idea,
consider his commentary on Rom. 12: 6. There Calvin speaks of Christ having "put an
end to all the former prophecies and to all the oracles of God." This reference to
prophecies and the oracles of God could be seen to fit into Tradition 1. In the next
sentence, Calvin observes that "today in the Christian Church prophecy is almost
nothing except a correct understanding of the scriptures and a singular ability in
explaining it well" (Calvin, *Iohannis Calvini Commentarius in epistolam Pauli ad
Romanos*, 270). This is clearly Tradition 2. Also as noted in Ch. 1, Calvin asserts both
that prophecy has ceased and that it would continue. He declares "that the ministry of
the prophets was temporal" (CO 48: 149); also CO 41: 171–2 (on Dan. 9: 24); CO 44:
219–20 (on Zech. 7: 1–3); SC 8: 316 (Sermon on Acts 7: 35–7); CO 48: 75 (Commentary on Acts 3: 22); CO 27: 501 (Sermon on Deuteronomy 18: 9–15); CO 24: 271
(Commentary on Deuteronomy 18: 15–18) and also that "there will always be
prophets" (CO 27: 499 (Sermon on Deuteronomy 18: 9–15)).

Historical Distance and Ambiguity: Calvin on the New Testament Office of Prophet

Calvin's handling of the New Testament office of prophet is historically oriented and exhibits an ambiguity regarding his position on the office. On the whole, it manifests the same attitude towards the office I have found among other theological contemporaries writing after the 1530s, 1540s, and 1550s, with Anabaptist appeals to the New Testament prophetic office leaving theologians like Bucer, Gwalther, Musculus, or Vermigli rather uncertain about how to address it. Thus, their comments exhibit confusion, being sometimes positive, sometimes indefinite, sometimes historical and distant. This assessment of Calvin applies to his assertions on the topic found in all genres (sermons, commentaries, treatises like the *Institutio*, etc.). For Calvin, perhaps even more than other theologians, simply does not know with certainty how he should understand the office of New Testament prophet.[4]

This uncertainty can be seen in the variation which characterizes his thinking about the office. In expounding 1 Thessalonians 5: 20 ("do not despise prophecy"), he treats the word "prophecy" as referring to "the science of interpreting Scripture."[5] Accordingly, the passage offers, Calvin goes on to assert, a remarkable commendation of preaching. Here his comments are not unlike some of what was seen earlier from Vermigli and Musculus. According to these comments, it seems that Calvin believes that some New Testament references to prophecy refer to the ordinary ministry, as we saw with others in Chapter 2. Calvin seems here to transition from discussing prophecy straight into discussing the simple ministry of the word. Similar is Calvin's treatment of other texts: his exposition of Romans

---

[4] See Ch. 2 for discussion of the thought of figures other than Calvin on prophecy. It is worth remembering how hated the Anabaptists were by many in Early Modern Europe and particularly the (so-called) magisterial reformers. In addition to condemnations such as these found in biblical commentaries, one can discover material of a similar character elsewhere. A particularly pungent example is found in one of Melanchthon's missives. In a letter to Oswald Myconius, he says he desires that the magistrates use the "utmost severity" (i.e. put them to death) in dealing with the Anabaptists, and expresses regret that he and others had been so "stupidly lenient" towards them when they first arose (see CR 2: 17 as cited in Sachiko Kusukawa, *The Transformation of Natural Philosophy: The Case of Philip Melanchthon* (Cambridge: CUP, 1995), 78).

[5] CO 52: 176.

12: 6 and an allusion he makes to Ephesians 4: 11 in a sermon on Jeremiah 17: 13, 15–16.[6]

His exposition of Ephesians 4: 11, however, offers a different handling of the office. In his commentary on this Pauline passage, Calvin identifies the prophetic office as involving interpretation and spiritual application by means of a "remarkable gift of revelation" (this idea of revelation likely being associated with John Chrysostom[7]). Calvin concludes that the New Testament prophet no longer exists in the Christian church.[8] Like apostle and evangelist, the prophet was only a temporary part of the ecclesiastical leadership and is no longer needed. He asserts the same thing elsewhere, as has already been noted. Curiously, when preaching on Ephesians 4: 11 some ten years after the publication of his commentary on the epistle, Calvin sets out a similar exposition of the meaning of the office but contends that the prophetic office *does* still exist. It is, however, "less common" in his own day than in the times of the early church.[9] But here his emphasis on the gift of revelation remains.

This revelation is an issue upon which Calvin reflects but about which he seems unable to come to a settled conviction. In his commentary on 1 Corinthians 14: 29–33, Calvin's remarks touch on a number of themes. He mentions, for instance, historical qualities associated with the early church era. But within these comments, he must deal with the phrase "and let others judge" (1 Corinthians 14: 29). Calvin appears to feel some awkwardness about this bit of Pauline instruction. "How," he inquires, "can prophecy, which is given by the Holy Spirit, be judged of by mortals?"[10] In addressing the question, he qualifies the notion of "a gift of revelation." He explains that the gift of the Spirit is given in measure and not fully possessed by any one person. Thus, all, even the most gifted, must

---

[6] SC 6: 122. Examples such as these seem to be suggestive of what one finds in the years after Calvin's death, namely, that the idea of prophesying seems in some quarters to become, in effect, equivalent to preaching. This is, in my judgment, *not* the understanding which ought to be ascribed to Calvin. Accordingly, for instance, prophesying is mentioned among later French Reformed church discussions, see Robert Kingdon, *Geneva and the Consolidation of the French Protestant Movement, 1564–1572* (Geneva: Droz, 1967), 106, 109, 129.

[7] PG 61: 265.   [8] CO 51: 197–8.

[9] CO 51: 556. Calvin's commentary on Galatians, Ephesians, Philippians, and Colossians was published in 1548. He began preaching on Ephesians in the spring of 1558.

[10] CO 49: 519.

have their prophecies scrutinized. What measure is to be employed? It is the rule of faith to which Paul refers in Romans 12: 6. Here, then, Calvin seems to dilute the idea of revelation, or at least to present a less robust conception of it than one finds elsewhere in his corpus. Different, for example, is his earlier treatment of 1 Corinthians 14: 6 in which he is free to handle the idea of a gift of revelation without the encumbrance of a command to submit it to the judgment of others. The text mentions four different kinds of edification. These are "revelation, knowledge, prophesying, and doctrine."[11] After acknowledging that differences exist among interpreters, Calvin explains that he places the first two (revelation and prophesying) together into one class. He declares that these pairs are linked; that what someone has "obtained by revelation, he dispenses by prophesying."[12] Becoming more specific, he explains that a prophet is an interpreter and minister of revelation (*interpres . . . et minister revelationis*). Elaborating on this slightly cryptic definition, Calvin then observes that prophesying does not consist in the simple (*simplici aut nuda*) interpretation of scripture but at the same time includes knowledge (*scientiam*) for applying it to present use. This knowledge is not obtained "except by revelation and the special inspiration of God (*nonnisi ex revelatione et peculiari Dei impulsu habetur*)."[13] Of *this* kind of revelation it is difficult to imagine Calvin being willing to speak in the diluted tones I discussed a moment ago. Rather, here it seems that Calvin thinks prophets receive a very specific word of revelation. Knowledge of a supernatural character is, in other words, what he seems to have in mind.

Looking further at the topic of revelation, we can now turn to the idea of prophesying as prediction of the future. Calvin ascribes this to the New Testament prophet in his commentary on Acts. When expounding Acts 11: 27–30, in which Agabus prophesies a famine throughout the world, Calvin explains that Agabus was granted the Spirit of God, who was the author of his prediction. Here, matters related to interpretation appear to be wholly absent. Prophecy, in this instance, is prediction by means of the reception of supernatural knowledge of the future. Thus, the New Testament prophet, according to Calvin, also prophesies in this Tradition 1 manner.

---

[11] CO 49: 519.   [12] CO 49: 519.   [13] CO 49: 519.

Stepping back, it seems that much of what Calvin thinks about prophecy in the New Testament appears to be governed by the historical and also by a humanist interest in languages, in words and their meanings. Indeed, it is interesting to read in his commentary on 1 Corinthians 12: 28–31: "For it is difficult to form a judgment (*difficile iudicare*) about gifts and offices of which the church has been deprived for so long, except for some traces or shadows which still appear."[14] An assertion such as this gives one the distinct sense that, rather like Bucer or Vermigli perhaps, Calvin adopted a view that the only expression one finds of the Pauline prophetic office is among the primitive church. Interestingly, among Calvin's thoughts on Acts 11: 27–30 is the observation that "the word prophet is taken in different ways (*varie*) in the New Testament."[15] If this is what Calvin believes, one wonders what this tells us. Could it be that in his mind there simply did not exist a clear, strong, unambiguous conception of what it meant to be a New Testament prophet? This is, of course, speculation, but it seems, nonetheless, to be credible. It finds support, furthermore, from Calvin's handling of the New Testament office of prophet in the 1543 edition of his *Institutio*, in which he declares: "By prophets, he means not all interpreters of the divine will, but those who excelled by special revelation; none such now exist, or they are less manifest (*quales nunc vel nulli exstant, vel minus sunt conspicui*)."[16] Such ambiguity seems peculiar and yet seems to typify his feelings towards the New Testament version of the office.[17]

Calvin, therefore, presents a varied and confusing image of the New Testament prophet; an image which did not seem especially to appeal to him. No doubt the ideas of interpreting and preaching, which Calvin contends are significant aspects of the New Testament prophetic office, suggest to a degree the importance of that office to him. Comments such as those on Romans 12: 6, 1 Thessalonians 5: 20, and portions of his treatment of 1 Corinthians 14: 29–33 are illustrative of this. But one can find other remarks on texts like Ephesians 4: 11, 1 Corinthians 12 and 14: 3 in which Calvin exhibits a sense of distance from the office. Moreover, the fact that he not

---

[14] CO 49: 507.   [15] CO 48: 263.

[16] CO 2: 779 (this is *Institutio* 4.3.4 in the 1559 edn).

[17] "It is notable that neither Bucer nor Calvin completely excludes some particularly good interpreters of scripture, prophets, but neither considers this office permanently necessary in all churches." in McKee, *Elders and the Plural Ministry*, 157.

infrequently describes the New Testament prophet as a recipient of a gift of revelation would also seem to put a degree of distance between it and him.

It might be wondered, however, whether Calvin ever criticizes the Anabaptists' appeal to the Pauline office of prophet. Such a criticism appeared, I showed in Chapter 2, in the writings of contemporaries like Vermigli, Gwalther, and Musculus. Do we find the same thing in Calvin? The affirmative answer is discovered right where one might expect it to be, namely, his comments on 1 Corinthians 12: 28–31. Explaining that the Lord only appointed ministers when he had endowed them with the requisite gifts, Calvin avers:

> From this, we should gather that they are fanatics (*fanaticos*) who force their way into the Church, compelled by an evil spirit and destitute of the proper gifts; indeed, many boast that they are under the Spirit's influence and glory in their secret calling from God, meanwhile they are unlearned and thoroughly ignorant.[18]

Calvin's comment here is reminiscent of the grievances of Capito concerning "our weaver" leveled in his letter to Nicolaus Prugner, which I addressed in Chapter 2.[19] The conduct and demeanor of his Anabaptist adversaries, moreover, resembles precisely what we found earlier among the complaints of theologians like Gwalther, Vermigli, and Musculus. That Calvin often used the word *fanaticos* to refer to Anabaptists is well known. The words cited above appeared in a commentary published by Calvin in 1545.

Relevance and Familiarity: Calvin on the Old Testament Prophetic Office

By contrast, a sense of familiarity marks Calvin's consideration of the prophets of the Old Testament era. He clearly believes this office possesses a relevance to his own day which the office of New Testament prophet did not. Calvin does not ordinarily depict these Old

---

[18] CO 49: 506. Calvin does not complain about the same thing either in the *Psychopannychia*—published in 1542 as *Vivere apud Christum non dormire animis sanctos, qui in fide Christi decedunt* (CO 5: 165–232)—or in his 1544 treatise, *Briève instruction pour armer tous bons fidèles contre les erreurs de la secte commune des anabaptistes* (CO 7: 45–142).

[19] Capito, *Correspondence*, ii. 204.

covenant prophets in the way that many of his patristic and medieval predecessors did, namely, as recipients of supernatural knowledge. Naturally, on the occasions when the biblical text mentions visions and the like, Calvin might refer to such ideas. But even then, his handling of them is usually very brief; the lengthiest such example is almost certainly his treatment of Ezekiel's visions recorded in Ezekiel 1 and 2.[20] Calvin can, of course, also mention the idea that Old Testament predictions have now been fulfilled in Christ.[21] But that notwithstanding, Calvin's conception of Old Testament prophecy falls unmistakably in line with the novel conception of it found among theologians like Zwingli and Bibliander. To Calvin, these prophets were interpreters of God's word, specifically the Mosaic Law.

As our examination of Calvin's position on the Old Testament prophetic office commences, the question of sources, and the chronology of those sources, needs to be discussed. Calvin's familiarity with the Old Testament prophetic books will be made abundantly clear in the *next* chapter, which focuses on his training lectures for Huguenot pastors. The subject of these lectures was the prophetic books. Thus, an abundance of material *could* be culled from those lectures, but as these training lectures were not started until late 1555 or early 1556, they are slightly limited in their usefulness. It would be ideal for my efforts here to be able to explore Calvin's views on Old Testament prophecy from material *other than* these training lectures—in fact, from *earlier* material. This would be useful for at least two reasons. One is that if I want to make my point that Calvin exhibits a familiarity with Old Testament prophecy, then I need to canvas works written prior to 1556, since that is so late in his life. A second reason appears in the fact that Chapter 5 will argue that Calvin had specific intentions when lecturing to the French pastors who sat under his tutelage; that he (in fact) sought in these lectures to raise up an army of prophets whom he could send into France in order to win it for the gospel and that he crafted these lectures with these aims in mind. This being so, I must be able to show Calvin's appreciation for Old Testament prophecy from different material, since otherwise

---

[20] CO 40: 21–76; see also CO 43: 89–41 (on Amos 3: 7–8); CO 43: 179 (on Obadiah 1: 1); CO 43: 332–3 (on Zechariah 4: 1–6); and CO 44: 126–30 (on Zechariah 1: 1–3).

[21] See, for instance, his sermon on Acts 7: 35–7; SC 8 315–16. Additionally, Engammare points to sermon 86 on Gen. 18: 16–21 (see Engammare, "Calvin: A Prophet," 89).

it could be objected that Calvin merely crafted this apparent appreciation and familiarity for Old Testament prophecy with his aims for these Huguenot pastors in mind.

Given these two points, the present discussion will focus a significant amount of its attention on Calvin's articulation of his views on prophecy in his *Ioannis Calvini commentarii in Isaiam Prophetam* published in 1551, from the notes taken by Nicholas des Gallars, who had attended Calvin's lectures on Isaiah in 1549. Calvin, it is known, read through the material which des Gallars had worked over in order to make corrections (I will have more to say on this project to record Calvin's lectures in the next chapter). Calvin also added to it a dedication to King Edward VI of England. In addition to examining his Isaiah exposition, I will occasionally draw material from Calvin's sermons on Jeremiah and Micah, which were preached in 1549 and 1550.[22]

To begin with, Calvin declares often that his own day mirrored that of the prophets.[23] This important sentiment is commonplace with him; if anything, it appears more often in his writings than in the corpora of someone like Zwingli or Bullinger.[24] He holds that the Old Testament prophets ministered within a corrupt, idolatrous church like that in which Calvin and his contemporaries ministered. Their labors, he believes, focused not merely on the corruption of the priesthood and of the king and his nobles but particularly on idolatrous worship through which Israel and Judah had departed from God's covenant. On these grounds, Calvin clearly feels a sense of identity with his own work fighting against the Roman Catholic cultic regimen. This sense even appears in various seemingly insignificant

---

[22] On these sources, see Jean-François Gilmont, *Jean Calvin et le livre imprimé* (Geneva: Librairie Droz, 1997); ET: *John Calvin and the Printed Book*, tr. Karin Maag (Kirksville, Mo.: Truman State University Press, 2005), 51–3.

[23] Calvin, *Ioannis Calvini Commentarii in Isaiam prophetam* . . . (Geneva: Ioannis Crispini, 1551), 1–2 (preface), 24 (on Isa. 1: 30), 32 (on Isa. 2: 8), 166 (on Isa. 16: 12), 185 (on Isa. 19: 1), 200 (Isa. 20: 2), 353 (Isa. 37: 35), 460 (on Isa. 45: 20), 553–4 (on Isa. 57: 1–4). As indicated in the abbreviations, this will be referred to hereafter as Isaiah 1551; I wanted to make extremely clear to the reader that it was the 1551 we are dealing with here. SC 6: 66 (Sermon on Jeremiah 15: 19–21 preached on 29 June 1549). "Calvin considered the struggle against idolatry to be an unending task, and thought that the situation of sixteenth-century evangelicals paralleled that of the ancient Israelites" (Eire, *War Against the Idols*, 255).

[24] As a theme, it essentially undergirds the whole of Bullinger's *De origine erroris libri duo, Heinrychi Bullingeri . . . ab ipso authore nunc demum recogniti, & aliquot locis* (Zurich: Froschouerus, 1568).

ways. For example, Calvin seems to believe that the Old Testament prophets were rhetoricians who, in their discourses, employed standard rhetorical devices. He believes their books (particularly the books of the prophets, rather than the Psalms, though he saw also the latter as prophecy) constitute collected "heads of doctrine (*capita doctrinae*)," in other words, commonplace books, not at all unlike Calvin's own *Institutio* or the *Loci Communes* of Melanchthon, Musculus, and Vermigli.[25] All of this exhibits a sense of familiarity which Calvin feels towards the ministry of these old covenant prophets. Their times were like his and their ways familiar to his ways.

Calvin, as did a number of his theological colleagues, describes prophets as interpreters of the law. He makes this point extremely clearly in his exposition of Isaiah and elsewhere.[26] His clearest expressions of it are in his two prefaces from his exposition of Isaiah and his lectures on the Minor Prophets. In both, he explicitly addresses the nature of the prophetic office and his descriptions of that office in the two pieces are, effectively, identical. Calvin does not address the nature of the prophetic office at length in his Psalms commentary or his expositions of Genesis or the Pentateuch Harmony, despite the fact that he does regard David and Moses as prophets.

These prophets are, Calvin says, interpreters of the law of Moses, which he identifies as "the whole doctrine of God" (*totam dei doctrinam*).[27] The law was, Calvin insists, "a perpetual rule for the Church."[28] As this plainly implies, Calvin's conception of the prophets is perfectly in line with the thinking of his contemporaries— Zwingli, Bibliander, Pellican, and others, as canvassed in Chapter 2— namely, that the work of the prophet involves "adding nothing" to God's law. Calvin asserts this with crystal clarity. So, "when the prophets inculcate moral duties, they bring forward nothing new, but only explain those parts of the Law which had been misunderstood."[29] He argues the same for the predictions of Christ and for the threats and promises found within the prophetic corpus. These as

---

[25] Isaiah 1551, 1–2 (preface). Also CO 42: 510 (on Hos. 14: 10); CO 43: 524 (on Hab. 2: 2).

[26] Isaiah 1551, 1–2 (preface), 172 (on Isa. 17: 10); see also CO 42: 198 (Introduction to Minor Prophets) also CO 24: 86 (on Exod. 7: 1); CO 38: 41 (on Jer. 9: 13–14); CO 44: 228 (on Zech. 7:11–12); CO 44: 493 (on Mal. 4:4); CO 27: 499 (Sermon on Deut. 18: 9–15).

[27] Isaiah 1551, 28 (on Isa. 2: 3).   [28] Isaiah 1551, 1–2 (preface).

[29] Isaiah 1551, 1–2 (preface).

well are mere elaborations on the law. They add nothing to it. On this, Calvin is adamant. This insistence naturally raises the issue of the covenant. Calvin clearly holds that the covenant contains the gospel. His convictions on the continuity which exists between the two testaments are quite clear. While he may acknowledge that the brilliance of the New Testament outshines that of the Old, he still frequently asserts that the covenant is one, differing only in administration as the church matures into full adulthood (Gal. 4: 1–3).[30]

This interpreting work was focused on reforming. Calvin believes the Old Testament prophets were raised up by God to reform the church. To be sure, at times he explains the existence of the Old Testament prophets in a way which would give one the impression they were raised up simply as teachers. For example, God forbids his people, Calvin says, from consulting magicians or soothsayers and requires them to be satisfied with the law alone, but promises them prophets to make known with lucidity God's will. Yet it is still the case that Calvin holds prophets to be reformers and covenant prosecutors.[31] The prophet, he contends, was raised up precisely because the church had departed from the truths found in the Mosaic Law. It is for that reason that Calvin emphasizes the idea that they add nothing to the law, namely, because the church (specifically, the priests) *had* added to the law, particularly in the cultic sphere. Thus, the prophets were called to return the church to what it had departed from, to purify the church from her corruptions. Again, the similarities between the thought of Calvin and some of his contemporaries are apparent. For all of them, the prophetic ministry took its starting point from the covenant which defined the people's relationship with God. The prophets were brought in because the church had broken covenant.[32] They were granted authority commensurate with their

---

[30] Numerous works exist on Calvin and the covenant; see Peter A. Lillback, *The Binding of God: Calvin's Role in the Development of Covenant Theology* (Grand Rapids, Mich.: Baker, 2001). I will not enter into further reflections on the topic as it is not, strictly speaking, relevant to my topic. For superb analysis of the medieval background to the covenant, see William J. Courtenay, *Covenant and Causality in Medieval Thought: Studies in Philosophy, Theology and Economic Practice* (London: Variorum Reprints, 1984).

[31] SC 6: 122 (Sermon on Jer. 17: 13, 15–16; preached on 26 July 1549); SC 6: 181 (Sermon on Lam. 1: 1; preached on 6 Sept. 1550).

[32] See Ch. 2 for the idea of the prophet as covenant prosecutor.

position as church reformers. Their readings of the law were true and must be heeded.

Calvin's conception of the prophets' reforming ministry is sufficiently nuanced to warrant further scrutiny. For, more than simply describing the prophets as reformers and leaving it at that, he perceives the prophets as having specific aims in relation to their preaching. Though they preached to all without exception, the Old Testament prophets, Calvin contends, do not have the same intention for all their hearers. Indeed, the prophets were, he contends, to announce condemnation to the bulk of the church that was reprobate (see Isa. 1: 9; 10: 21; Hos. 1: 11) and the promise of salvation to the remnant (see Isa. 10: 21; 37: 31).

According to Calvin, the Old Testament prophets distinguished in their preaching between two groups. Now, at one level, Calvin is willing to say that the prophets offered promises of salvation to all, together with their harsh criticism of the prevailing idolatry. Anyone could hear and respond to these promises. The prophets embellished their preaching with rhetorical devices designed to move and turn the hearts of their hearers (Isa. 24: 19), and so forth. Yet at a deeper level, Calvin insists that the prophets distinguished between two groups. The prophets proclaimed "the general ruin of the whole nation" who were reprobate and would never repent, but out of that "God rescues his people, whom he justly compares to a very small remnant."[33] It is clear, then, that according to Calvin, the prophets conceived of the bulk of the church of their day as reprobate and beyond hope. The word of promise which they offered was only for the small remnant whom God appointed to believe it. These promises did not, Calvin insists, belong to the reprobate. They only belonged to the elect. He makes this explicit in many places within his treatment of the prophets. With respect to this pious remnant, the prophets continuously sought to comfort them, encouraging them to be patient and to understand that the true state of God's church must not be assessed by looking at the conditions currently prevailing in the church. In this regard, Calvin comments on the fact that the prophets would

---

[33] Isaiah 1551, 16 (on Isa. 1: 9), 32 (on Isa. 2: 9), 384 (on Isa. 40: 1). Calvin says the work of the prophet is to console the people of God; but that not all are capable of being consoled (*capaces sunt*), therefore he so names *populum suum*. For these (promises) are peculiarly for the elect. See also CO 43: 256–61 (on Hos. 3); CO 40: 66 (on Ezek. 2: 3); CO 43: 421 (on Mic. 7: 13).

repeat a word of promise, on the grounds that the conditions within which the pious lived and worshiped were so dismal that the promise seemed laughably impossible; thus, they repeated it for otherwise it would not be believed. Their times, he argues, were difficult in large measure because the church was dominated by a faction which sanctioned idolatrous worship and sought to persecute any who did not comply with their policies. It was to this dominant group, who were reprobate, that the prophets declared condemnation.

The prophets possessed unrivaled authority, according to Calvin. They denounced idolatry, immorality, bribery, social inadequacies, and a myriad of other problems. In their preaching, they inveighed against leaders, ecclesiastical and civil, without fear. Kings and their nobles, priests and the high priest, were all subject to the word of the prophet, to whom all, even the king, must submit. The prophets did not refrain from employing the harshest language in their preaching, as this was what their calling required. "[E]ven kings," Calvin stated, "are not exempted from the duty of learning what is commonly taught, if they wish to be counted members of the Church."[34]

The source of the prophets' authority was that they spoke God's word. Calvin calls them God's mouthpiece. The prophets produced pure expositions of the word of God,[35] adding nothing of human origin to their meaning (as I have said). Their authority is not ascribed to the reception of supernatural revelation, as was the case for many early and medieval theologians, but rather to their bringing forth the word of God. He did explain, occasionally, that the visions these prophets received were intended to confirm the doctrine which they preached.[36] But his focus was continually upon the prophets' interpretations of God's word. "It would be absurd to boast of attending to the word," Calvin insisted, "were we to disregard the divine interpretations of it; as many persons at the present day." These interpretations were themselves God's word, for which reason Calvin declared that "God has put words into [the prophet's] mouth."[37]

---

[34] Isaiah 1551, 77 (on Isa. 7: 7), 379 (on Isa. 39: 5).
[35] Isaiah 1551, 1–2 (preface); SC 6: 38 (Sermon on Jer. 15: 12–13, 15–17; preached on 27 June 1549); SC 6: 26 (Sermon on Jer. 15: 6–10; preached 25 June 1549); cf. Susan Schreiner, *Are You Alone Wise? The Search for Certainty in the Early Modern Era* (Oxford: OUP, 2011), 79–129.
[36] Isaiah 1551, 26 (on Isa. 2: 1).
[37] Isaiah 1551, 1–2 (preface); see also CO 27: 527 (Sermon on Deut. 18: 16–20). Millet, "Eloquence des prophètes bibliques," 70.

In this way, Calvin underlines the notion that the prophets added nothing to the law but only elaborated upon it.

* * *

Calvin, like a number of his reforming colleagues, spoke in a various and ambiguous manner about the Pauline prophetic office. According to him, prognostication has ceased,[38] and yet, although he was willing to describe the New Testament prophet as a scriptural interpreter, he still exhibited an aloofness towards the office—an aloofness which was surely influenced by his disapprobation of the Anabaptist appropriation of it. By contrast, Calvin consistently exhibited an interest in, and appreciation for, the Old Testament prophetic vocation, as can easily be seen in the frequency with which he speaks of his own era as mirrored in the era of the prophets—"for we see today as in a mirror (*velut in speculo*) what the prophet teaches here."[39] Indeed, Olivier Millet has already pointed to Calvin's penchant for considering prophecy from an Old Testament perspective, and Millet is precisely right in his assessment of this matter.[40] Thus, it may sound strange prima facie, but Calvin feels an acquaintance with the Old Testament prophets which he does not feel for their New Testament counterparts.

MAKING SENSE OF THIS PREFERENCE: CALVIN'S EMULATION OF THE OLD TESTAMENT PROPHETS

Discovering Calvin's sense of familiarity with (his particular reading of) Old Testament prophecy, our next step is to investigate it. Here one might well ask what explains it. One might note, along these lines, the difference which existed between Calvin and other individuals,

---

[38] Isaiah 1551, 26 (on Isa. 2: 1). He also explained that this Tradition 1 sense of prophecy has now ceased; see, for instance, sermon CO 27: 526 (Sermon on Deut. 18: 21–2).

[39] Isaiah 1551, 366 (on Isa. 38: 35), 609 (on Isa. 63: 17). See also CO 43: 552 (on Hab. 2: 15); CO 38: 237 (on Jer. 15: 20).

[40] Millet, "Eloquence des prophètes bibliques," 68–70. See also Peter, *Sermons sur les livres de Jérémie et des Lamentations*, XIV–XVI; Ganoczy, *Young Calvin*, 287–97; Ganoczy, "Calvin avait-il conscience de réformer l'Eglise?," 172–7; Millet, *Calvin*, 492–7.

such as Zwingli or Bulllinger, on this matter and wonder why it existed. One might raise, again, the issue of the Anabaptists or, perhaps, one might query Calvin's understanding of the covenant. Or one might ask a host of other questions in an attempt to make sense of this.

But in fact, irrespective of what helps to explain Calvin's preference for the Old Testament prophets, his attitude towards them actually makes a good deal of sense from at least one point of view. Considering this preference from the perspective of Calvin's ministry, one can see that that ministry bore impressive similarities to his own descriptions of the ministries of Jeremiah, Joel, Elijah, and the other Old Testament prophets. As was just demonstrated, their labors were focused on interpretation of God's word towards the end of reforming the church of their own age which had been plunged into idolatry; and precisely the same thing was true of Calvin. This, of course, can *not* be said about New Testament prophets, whose ministry is never conceived of by Calvin in these terms.

Let us probe this ministerial perspective in a more sustained manner, beginning with the setting down of an important distinction. In his ministry, Calvin performed many of the tasks common to an ordinary minister of the gospel. He married and baptized and visited parishioners. He preached and catechized. Much of his pastoral ministry has been examined in Alexandre Ganoczy's *Calvin, théologien de l'Église et du ministère* or Léopold Schummer's *Le Ministère pastoral dans l'Institution Chrétienne de Calvin à la lumière du troisième sacrement* and more recently by works like Randall Zachman's *John Calvin as Teacher, Pastor, and Theologian* and Karen Spierling, *Infant Baptism in Reformation Geneva: The Shaping of a Community, 1536–1564.*[41] But Calvin, quite clearly, did more than carry on an ordinary pastoral ministry. His ministry entailed a major element for which he is arguably better known, namely, that of reformer. The two ministries are not mutually exclusive enterprises, but they are different, with the character of Calvin's reforming ministry being at

---

[41] Alexandre Ganoczy, *Calvin, théologien de l'Église et du ministère* (Paris, Éditions du Cerf, 1964); Léopold Schummer's *Le Ministère pastoral dans l'Institution Chrétienne de Calvin à la lumière du troisième sacrement* (Wiesbaden: Franz Steiner Verlag, 1965); Randall Zachman, *John Calvin as Teacher, Pastor and Theologian: The Shape of his Writings and Thought* (Grand Rapids, Mich.: Baker Academic, 2006); Karen Spierling, *Infant Baptism in Reformation Geneva: The Shaping of a Community, 1536–1564* (Philadelphia: Westminster/John Knox, 2009).

once aggressive, revolutionary, and arguably seditious.[42] It is this reforming element that will be examined here, as we seek to understand his preference for the Old Testament prophets. Lest someone carp at the distinction being made here, it is worth noting that this very distinction has recently been drawn by Amy Nelson Burnett, in her 2006 study *Teaching the Reformation*. She notes that while much attention has been paid to the work of reformers like Martin Luther and Ulrich Zwingli, little has been paid to the ordinary pastoral ministries of those who followed the reformers and were responsible for implementing the changes which they sought to establish.[43] Likewise, Olivier Millet alludes to the same distinction in one of his essays, referring to "[Calvin's] reforming agenda and his duties in Geneva."[44] Thus, the distinction is legitimate. It is precisely this—not Calvin's pastor work but his reforming vocation—that I wish to draw attention to and explore here.

Calvin's reforming agenda exhibited a fundamental concern for the state of religion in Europe and, specifically, for the idolatry which he believed was pervasive throughout European Christendom. His ministry was a "War against the Idols" as Carlos Eire has rightly argued.[45] Calvin's mention of, and condemning of, idolatry is ubiquitous and reminds us of the point already made, that he saw his own age as mirrored in that of the prophets. In his judgment, the Roman Catholic Church of his day had fallen into a "grosser idolatry" than ancient Israel.[46] The citation is from *Institutio* 4.2, and part of a sustained comparison of the Roman Catholic Church with the church of Old Testament Israel, which is wholly indicative of how he conceived of Rome.

In point of fact, Calvin aligns his reforming program with that of the old covenant prophets, which he took as a kind of blueprint. So, for example, in the just-mentioned chapter of the *Institutio*, Calvin argues against the charge of schism by contending that he and his fellow reformers were following in the path of Isaiah, Ezekiel, and the other Old Testament prophets and that to accuse the sixteenth-century reformers of schism requires accusing their Old Testament

---

[42] This will be considered in detail in the next chapter.

[43] Amy Nelson Burnett, *Teaching the Reformation: Ministers and their Message in Basel, 1529–1629* (New York: OUP, 2006), 5–6.

[44] Olivier Millet, "Calvin's Self-Awareness as Author," 94.

[45] Eire, *War Against the Idols*, 195–275.   [46] CO 2: 773–4.

prophetic counterparts of the same. The two ministries stand or fall together, Calvin clearly believes. The likes of Jeremiah and Ezekiel did not continue to worship with the visible church of their day, Calvin argues (continuing his line of thought), as that would have involved them in idolatry. Thus, Calvin's verdict on the issue of schism: "And surely if those were churches, it follows that Elijah, Micah and others in Israel, and Isaiah, Jeremiah, Hosea and the remainder of those in Judah, whom the prophets, priests, and people of their day hated and execrated more than any of the uncircumcised, were aliens from the church of God."[47] To condemn Calvin is to condemn Elijah and the other prophets.

Continuing, we might investigate the character of Calvin's own reforming program in more detail. How did he pursue reformation? A major element in his pursuit of it was biblical interpretation. He insists time and time again that his reading of the scriptures was right and the church's reading was wrong. This may be seen in at least three ways. First, continuing the line of thought found in the last paragraph, Calvin identifies numerous practices propounded by the Roman church as extraneous to scripture and idolatrous—his belief being that the theologians, priests, and bishops of the Roman Catholic Church had wrongly understood the Bible.[48] Second, Calvin regularly asserts, in his own expositions of scripture, that other interpreters are wrong and he himself right.[49] Calvin, in other words, is correct and one must agree with him, or they are wrong. More will be said on these issues later, but suffice it to say for now that Calvin pursues his reforming agenda by appearing as a scriptural interpreter whose calling it was to enforce the true meaning of the Bible upon a church which had strayed from it.

Calvin believes that he added nothing to the word of God. The fact is, one of his greatest complaints against the church of his day is precisely that they had added to it. According to his reforming agenda, he inveighs against the human inventions foisted upon the church by the wolves who had taken control of it and, ultimately, by the Antichrist himself, the Pope. Calvin's list of additions does not make surprising reading. It included false sacraments, prayer to the

---

[47] CO 2: 774–5.
[48] Examples abound; one example is CO 42: 246 (on Hos. 2: 17–18).
[49] These instances are, likewise, quite common; see, for instance, CO 42: 432 (on Hos. 11: 1).

saints and for the dead, enforced oracular confession, use of holy water, incense, candles, and other humanly devised elements inserted into divine worship, and the like. Against these, Calvin offered the remedy of the right understanding of scripture to which nothing was added.

Calvin's reforming ministry employs harsh criticism of any who stand in his way, including ecclesiastical and civil authorities. One can very easily find within Calvin's corpus remarkably scathing remarks about the state of the church, the Pope, bishops, priests, and the civil authorities. Even against those who purported to embrace the gospel of the reformers, he could be so harsh that one Reformation scholar was moved to query: "Why was Calvin so Severe a Critic of Nicodemism?"[50] The issue with the Nicodemites was, of course, one related to idolatry, the Nicodemites wishing to be evangelical but to attend Roman Catholic Mass. It is a matter with respect to which Calvin maintains a zero-tolerance policy. He makes it crystal clear that he, ultimately, saw no distinction between Nicodemites and the Romanists; they both supported idolatry. He states explicitly: "Yet we fight not only with the papists but also with those wicked scoundrels who boast themselves Nicodemites."[51] He does not, in other words, consider them evangelicals. They were as good as "papists," in his eyes.

To dig deeper, I will consider the basic question of how Calvin conceives of, and addresses, the Roman church of his day. Calvin consistently adopts one of two stances in relation to it. These will be familiar because they were discussed earlier in relation to the ministry of the Old Testament prophets. One stance he takes is to hold that the Roman Catholic Church is simply a reprobate church. In other words, he does not merely criticize its immorality, corruption, or doctrinal infidelity, but he declares it to have broken covenant with God. This is the stance he adopted when speaking about the whole body, whose head is the Antichrist himself. Accordingly, Calvin could, particularly in sermons, declare that Rome is simply not a church. So, in his sermons on Acts, he makes such a declaration on a number of occasions.[52] Similarly, in his 1559 *Institutio* he added a new chapter title which identifies Rome as the "false church." I have

---

[50] Indeed, the honorandus of the present monograph was the scholar; see David Wright's chapter in David F. Wright, Anthony N. S. Lane, and Jon Balserak (eds), *Calvinus Evangelii Propugnator; Calvin, Champion of the Gospel: Papers from the International Congress on Calvin Research Seoul, 1998* (Grand Rapids, Mich.: CRC Production Services, 2006), 66–90.

[51] CO 42: 290.   [52] e.g. SC 8: 43 (Sermon on Acts 2: 41–2).

written on Calvin's view on the church elsewhere, in which I demonstrated that this new chapter title represents not a new view adopted by Calvin in the late 1550s but rather the clarifying of a position which he held as early as the late 1530s.[53]

The other stance Calvin adopts relates to a small remnant of pious believers which he says exists within the Romanist church. Even at his harshest, he always allows for the notion that small pockets of true Christians dwelled within the corrupt Roman Catholic body. He explains in *Institutio* 4.2.12 in relation to Rome that there is one way in which it is acceptable to call the Roman Catholic fellowship a church. "I call them churches, in that the Lord wondrously preserves some remnant of his people there, though miserably torn and scattered."[54] Calvin would identify this small group as a remnant of the faithful, as Old Testament prophets had done.[55] Not surprisingly, Calvin is not content to allow these believers to remain in a corrupt Roman Catholic fellowship, despite his willingness to acknowledge that Rome still possesses certain vestiges which relate to the covenant (such as baptism). Calvin urges these believers to leave the Roman church in order that they may worship God in purity. He, in fact, insists that they cannot stay in the Roman Catholic Church and remain faithful to the gospel. Many of the writings he produced in the 1530s and 1540s on the Nicodemite question—here one thinks specifically of *Duae Epistolae*, *Petit traicté*, and *Excuse à Messieurs les Nicodémites*—deal with this very issue.[56]

These two stances are, of course, the same two that were found in Calvin's assessment of the ministry of the Old Testament prophets several pages ago. The division between corrupt body and tiny remnant which Calvin found in the preaching of prophets like Isaiah and Ezekiel is discernible in his own handling of the Roman church. Moreover, it was his position that the faithful remnant had separated from the corrupt body in the days of Isaiah and Jeremiah just as he and his fellow evangelicals had done in their own day. "Show me," Calvin insists, "one prophet or pious man who once worshipped or offered sacrifice in Bethel. They knew that they could not do it

---

[53] See Balserak, *Establishing the Remnant Church in France*, 19–52.

[54] CO 1: 557 (this first appeared in the 1543 *Institutio*).

[55] He could even declare in expounding Mal. 3: 1–2 that "[w]e know that Christ appeared not for salvation to all, but only to the remnant (*non omnibus . . . sed reliquiis*)" (CO 44: 463).

[56] OS 1: 287–362; CO 6: 537–88; and CO 6: 589–614.

without defiling themselves with some kind of sacrilege."[57] Thus, the character and contours of the two reforming ministries—the Old Testament prophets' ministry and Calvin's own—share this important similarity. In this regard, Calvin constantly seeks to encourage the small body of true and pious believers to continue to cling to the promises of God. His sermons and lectures as well as letters, biblical commentaries, and treatises are full of such encouragement. He regularly acknowledges the difficulties which threaten the small church throughout Europe and the trials it encounters from Roman Catholics. Indeed, it is sufficiently burdensome to him that it manages to find its way into his thinking almost by accident. So when he is defending himself and his fellows against the charge of schism, in a passage which I cited a few pages ago, Calvin cannot help but allude to the persecution which the remnant church endures. "And surely if those were churches, it follows that Elijah, Micah and others in Israel, and Isaiah, Jeremiah, Hosea and the remainder of those in Judah, *whom the prophets, priests, and people of their day hated and execrated more than any of the uncircumcised,* were aliens from the church of God."[58] Here he mentions only the persecution suffered by the Old Testament prophets. That he believed himself, his fellow ministers, and their congregations to be subject to the same abuse at the hands of the church of *their* day should become apparent in due course and moved Calvin constantly to strive to administer hope, urging his hearers to wait on the promises of God and not to despair.[59]

As mentioned, Calvin fearlessly attacks ecclesiastical authorities as well as civil. He makes clear that those governing the Roman church in his day are not immune from rebuke. In comments on Isaiah 28: 7, for example, in which the prophet inveighs against the drunkenness of the priests, Calvin insists that the Roman Catholic authorities are foolish for thinking that they can avoid condemnation. They "always have in their mouth the title of church and use the names of priests, bishops, and pontiffs as a pretext to strengthen themselves against the word of God."[60] Following this example, Calvin subjects the priests, bishops, and popes to a steady diet of extremely harsh criticism. He regularly identified the Pope as Antichrist and the priests as dumb dogs.[61] Examples

---

[57]　CO 1: 557 (this first appeared in the 1543 *Institutio*).
[58]　CO 2: 774–5 (italics mine).　　　[59]　Isaiah 1551, 77 (on Isa. 7: 7).
[60]　Isaiah 1551, 267–8 (on Isa. 28: 7).
[61]　CO 43: 131–2. See also CO 43: 127 (on Amos 7: 10–13); CO 43: 333 (on Mic. 3: 11–12); CO 37: 472 (on Jer. 1: 1–3); CO 37: 503 (on Jer. 2: 8) and CO 40: 95 (on Ezek. 3: 19).

are replete in his sermons and lectures, not to mention treatises such as his antidote to the Tridentine documents or his reprimand of Pope Paul III.[62]

The same is true of Calvin's handling of civil authorities. Just as the Old Testament prophets allowed no one, not even the king, to stand above God's word, so Calvin adopts the same attitude. In his reforming efforts, he petitions, censures, harangues, and complains vehemently about royalty, using some of the harshest language found in his corpus to do so. This will be treated at some length in the next chapter, but a brief word might be said on it here. Calvin addresses Francis I at the beginning and end of his *Institutio*. While he refers to him as the "Most Christian king" (a customary salutation at the time), Calvin also warns him of the divine imperative that all obedience to earthly authority must conform to true obedience to God. He notes, in this context, the example recorded in Daniel 6: 22 in which "the king exceeded his limits."[63] The passage was clearly a favorite of Calvin's and encapsulated brilliantly the note he wished to strike as he brought his magnum opus to a close. In the same manner, Calvin writes to the Emperor, Charles V, urging him to keep his word to call a conference to deal with the troubles within the church. He wrote to the emperor that, "[f]inal destruction [of the church] cannot be far off unless you interpose with the utmost speed."[64] He also writes to the kings of Sweden, of Poland, of England, and other countries, urging them to work for reform within their realms.[65] He instructs Edward VI that it "is of the greatest importance, most noble king, that you should be moved to action through consideration of the duty which God has enjoined upon you." Isaiah "exhorts all kings and magistrates, through the person of Cyrus, to stretch forth their hand to the church" when she is in distress in order that they work to "restore her to her former condition."[66] Calvin believes he has authority to counsel kings and he believes that, when they do not listen, it is his duty to rebuke them and, even, to urge their citizens to resist them.[67] This is patently clear in his vehement condemning of the

[62] CO 7: 365–506 and CO 5: 461–508.
[63] For the *Institutio* 4.20.32 see CO 2: 1117.
[64] *Supplex exhortatio ad Caesarem* see CO 6: 525–34; see 532.
[65] CO 17: 445–8, 450–1; CO 20: 116–22; CO 17: 413–15; CO 14: 30–7.
[66] CO 13: 670.
[67] The character of Calvin's urging and of his understanding of resistance will be examined in Ch. 4 and Ch. 5.

Peace of Augsburg while preparations for its implementation via the authority of Charles V were still ongoing. He called it a "hellish corruption" and queried agonizingly, "does not the world see how idolatry is being set up again?"[68] Calvin does not accept the notion that the position of the king or emperor invested them with an authority which made them immune from criticism. He believes, moreover, that he, like Isaiah or the Apostle Paul, is called to speak the truth of God to kings and those in authority, irrespective of their office. I leave the subject now, to pick it up again in Chapters 4 and 5.

FROM EMULATION TO IDENTIFICATION: CALVIN AS (OLD TESTAMENT) PROPHET

Calvin's emulating of the Old Testament prophetic ministry (as he understood it) has been demonstrated. As before, my next step is to investigate this. Again, one might ask what explains it. What does it mean for him to emulate the Old Testament prophets or what possessed him to do such a thing? In endeavoring to probe this emulation further, one might observe that Calvin's executing of his reforming agenda would seem to suggest his sense of the station which he holds. In other words, it suggests that he believes himself to be someone who possesses divine authority.

This self-belief is brilliantly exemplified in his *Institutio*. Speaking in his prefatory letter to King Francis I about the Roman Catholic Church's response to the reformers, Calvin complains that Rome calls the reformed doctrine "new" and "doubtful and uncertain," such that it must be confirmed by miracles.[69] Addressing these charges, Calvin situates himself in very good company, namely, that of the Old Testament prophets. He says that when the Roman priests accuse the reformed doctrine of being new, they show their ignorance. "It is this very thing," Calvin insists, "that the Lord complains of through

---

[68] CO 26: 98. Likewise, in a sermon on Job 13: 11–15 preached in late 1554 or early 1555, Calvin enters into a long diatribe against "the Interim" (which is presumably the phrase he is using at this time to refer to what is known as the Peace of Augsburg) in which he shows that he considers it as nothing other than the practices of the Roman Catholic religion being forcefully imposed upon the realm (CO 33: 619–20).

[69] CO 2: 15.

his prophet, 'The ox knows its owner and the donkey its master's stall, but my people do not understand' (Isaiah 1: 3)."[70] Thus Calvin, far from asserting that he has no authority or that Rome has misunderstood him, accepts the Roman charge and says those who preceded him in reforming the church had to deal with the same difficulties. Therefore, on the evidence of this passage, it must be concluded that Calvin *does* believe himself to be one who has been invested with authority. In point of fact, the way he addresses kings, and also popes, betrays his conviction that he speaks with an authority which excels either (a point which will be examined in more detail in Chapter 5).[71] Again, it is worth noting, his contact in the letter to Francis I is precisely with the *Old* Testament prophets.

Probing this authority further, I return again to his handling of the Nicodemite situation. The Nicodemites, a thorn in Calvin's side and a group or movement over which he feels enormous frustration, are addressed by him in a manner which betrays both his self-consciousness as an author (what Stephen Greenblatt would call his self-fashioning and Millet calls Calvin's "authorial self-assertion"[72]) and his ministerial sense of *authoritas*. This is not only apparent in the body of the treatises which Calvin wrote against the Nicodemites, such as, for instance, his *Petit traité* and *Excuse à Messieurs les Nicodémites*,[73] but also in the epigraphs of these treatises. These epigraphs were not elements of the printer's signature and were almost certainly provided by Calvin himself.[74] In his *Excuse* the title page cites the Old Testament prophet, Amos 5: 10. "They have hated the one who delivers rebuke in the gate, and they have loathed the one who speaks what is right."[75] Here Calvin is undoubtedly responding to those Nicodemites who had complained bitterly about how harsh he had been towards them in his 1543 *Petit traité*.[76] He is comparing their protestations to the complaining which Amos received about his preaching. He is, moreover (it is impossible to

[70] CO 2: 15.   [71] See Engammare, "Calvin: A Prophet," 99–102.

[72] Stephen Greenblatt, *Renaissance Self-Fashioning from More to Shakespeare* (Chicago: University of Chicago Press, 1980); Millet, "Calvin's Self-Awareness as Author," 86–7.

[73] CO 6: 537–88; CO 6: 589–614.

[74] Millet, "Calvin's Self-Awareness as Author," 86–7.

[75] See *Bibliotheca Calviniana : Les œuvres de Jean Calvin publiées au XVIe siècle*, ed. Rodolphe Peter and Jean-François Gilmont, 3 vols (Geneva: Droz, 1991–2000), iii. 82/7.

[76] Wright, "Why was Calvin," 75–6.

miss), setting himself in the place of the prophet and claiming an authority corresponding to that of Amos. Calvin wants these French pseudo-evangelicals (in his judgment, that is what they were) to understand that they cannot complain with impunity; indeed, that they *dare* not complain about the treatment which they receive at his hands, for to do that is to complain against a prophet of God.[77] This is not the only epigraph in which Calvin communicated this message. The verso page of this same writing quotes Isaiah 30: 9–10: "This people is a rebellious people, they are hypocrites, folks who refuse to listen to the law of the Lord. They say to those who see, 'Don't see anything,' and to those who consider, 'Don't consider anything of what is right,' but speak of things which please us and see illusions."[78] Nor is it only in relation to the Nicodemites that Calvin employed the use of these epigraphs. One can also find epigraphs in some of his other writings, particularly those of a polemic character. In his 1537 *Duae Epistolae*, the words of 1 Kings 18: 21 "How long will you waver between two opinions? If the Lord is God, follow him, but if Baal is God, follow him" appear at the front of the printed version.[79] 1 Kings 18: 21 also appears as an epigraph in his *De Scandales, Articles de la Faculté de Paris, Brieve resolution*.[80] Thus, Calvin reveals not only his conviction concerning his own authority but identifies it more specifically as a prophetic authority.

The discoveries set down in the last several paragraphs only confirm what was becoming progressively clearer already. Calvin's depiction of himself as a prophet like Amos ought not, therefore, to come as a surprise. It had already been mooted in the common cause which he made with the Old Testament prophets and in his habit of calling his own age a "mirror" of the prophets' age (since, after all, such a portrayal raises the question of where Calvin sees himself in this mirror). Therefore, Calvin, it may be asserted, self-identifies with the old covenant messengers.[81]

---

[77] The work of Olivier Millet has been particularly helpful to my thinking on the material here; Millet, *Calvin*, 492–7, 503 and "Calvin's Self-Awareness as Author," 84–90.

[78] Cited from Wright, "Why was Calvin," 72.

[79] OS 1: 287.

[80] Again that Calvin would employ these means to assert his prophetic authority seems far from peculiar when one sees him from within the humanist tradition of which he was a part.

[81] On Calvin's association with the Old Testament prophets, see Peter, *Sermons sur les livres de Jérémie et des Lamentations*, XIV–XVI; Ganoczy, *Young Calvin*, 287–97;

One might query what it means for Calvin to see himself as an *Old Testament* prophet. But the previously cited remark from Vermigli, setting out the idea that God raises up prophets whenever the ordinary ministry had failed, explains things nicely.[82] The idea, here, is not so much that the Frenchman self-identifies as someone ministering under the terms of the old covenant but, rather, as someone with an authoritative ministerial calling to reform like that of Old Testament prophets like Jeremiah, Hosea, and Ezekiel. Calvin addresses the question specifically in material produced in the last decade of his life. He declares in a lecture on Jeremiah 32: 32, delivered probably in late 1562: "when, through either laziness or ignorance, the priests failed in the performing of their office, God raised up prophets in their place," in order to save the church from ruin.[83] Calvin makes the same point in lectures on Amos and Micah, delivered in the late 1550s.[84] The *extra ordinem* phrase employed by Vermigli is also employed by Calvin.[85] The underlying point, then, is that all of these prophets—Jeremiah, Amos, Micah, and Calvin—were raised up by God to reform the church because the priesthood of their own day had failed, this reforming being accomplished as a biblical interpreter.[86]

At this point, someone might object that when Calvin talks of God restoring the church from decay, he mentions "evangelists [who] are raised up in an extraordinary manner (*extra ordinem*) in order to

Ganoczy, "Calvin avait-il conscience de réformer l'Eglise?," 172–7; Millet, *Calvin*, 492–7; Millet, "Eloquence des prophètes bibliques," 68–70; Engammare, "Calvin: A Prophet," 90–2; Engammare, "Calvin lecteur de la Bible en chaire," in Wright et al., *Calvinus Evangelii Propugnator*, 147–60, esp. 158; Crouzet, *Jean Calvin: Vies parallèles*, 117–19; Balserak, "There Will Always Be Prophets," 92–112. Calvin's ambiguity towards the New Testament prophetic office has been hinted at by Millet ("Eloquence des prophètes bibliques," 68–70) and by myself (Balserak, "There Will Always Be Prophets," 89–91). Yet the following treatments would seem to argue that Calvin believed himself to be a prophet according to the New Testament manifestation of the office: Engammare, "Calvin: A Prophet," 92–3; Balserak, *Establishing the Remnant Church in France*, 84–7. Both works (I can speak with greater certainty about my own) asserted a fundamental continuity between Old and New Testament prophecy. I now believe I was wrong in this judgment.
[82] PMV (1–2 Sam.), 113[r].
[83] CO 39: 28.
[84] CO 43: 131–2 (on Amos 7: 10–13) and CO 43: 333–4 (on Mic. 3: 11–12).
[85] Calvin does add *quasi* (as if); see his comments on Mic. 3: 11–12, CO 43: 334.
[86] See *Aquinas Opera* ST II-II q. 174, a.6, ad3; section 924 in *S. Thomae Aquinatis . . . super Evangelium S. Matthaei Lectura*, ed. P. Raphaelis Cai OP (Taurini: Marietti, 1951), 145; Denis, *Commentariorum in Psalmos omnes Davidicos*, 2.

restore the pure doctrine which had been lost."[87] Or, in *Institutio* 4.3.4, he speaks of God raising up "apostles or evangelists to restore the Gospel as has happened in our own day."[88] This is further confirmed by his encomium of Luther as "a distinguished apostle of Christ by whose ministry the light of the gospel has shone."[89] Thus, Calvin does not, the objector would conclude, ascribe this restorative work to old covenant prophets but rather to New Testament offices like apostle and evangelist. Here, I can only say that some of Calvin's contemporaries were able to speak positively about the *New* Testament prophetic office and, indeed, Calvin himself (as I have already shown earlier) does the same. These just-cited instances are merely a few additional examples. If one wishes to complain that Calvin appears rather contradictory, I would not argue against the accusation. Many of Calvin's contemporaries examined in Chapter 2 also set out views which contain some conflicting elements. But in my judgment, the clarity of the argument set forth in this chapter for Calvin's self-identifying with the Old Testament prophets in relation to his own reforming ministry outweighs the force of the occasional passages one can find, such as these which I have just cited. I am inclined to see them as a part of that variety, ambiguity, and confusion which clings to the understanding of the New Testament office of prophet set forth by Calvin and a number of his colleagues.

So, Calvin self-identifies with the Old Testament prophets, who were (he believed) scriptural reformers. He *could*—it is, of course, within the realm of possibility—have believed himself to be a prophet who received revelation and was able to predict the future, like, for example, his countryman, Michel de Nostredame[90] or the German prognosticator, Johann Lichtenberger, who famously predicted the 1525 Peasants' War. And interestingly, Beza, in his reflections on Calvin's life, points to an occasion when (he believes) Calvin engaged in just such prophesying. In Calvin's lectures on Daniel, says Beza, he interpreted the prophet, "but, in the dedication, he also became a prophet, predicting impending storms at the very time when the

---

[87] CO 51: 197–8 (Commentary on Eph. 4: 11).   [88] CO 2: 779–80.
[89] CO 6: 250 (from *Defensio adversus Pighium*).
[90] On Nostradamus' prophetic claims (his Almanacs and quatrains, etc.) see Michel Chomarat, "De quelques dates clairement exprimées par Michel Nostradamus, dans ses 'Prophéties'," in *Prophètes et prophétie au XVIe siècle* (Paris: Presses de l'École Normale Supérieure, 1998), 83–93.

meeting of the bishops was held at Poissy."[91] Beza's remark notwith-standing, it can be stated with a fair degree of certainty that Calvin opposes the idea that anyone in his own day has the ability to predict the future. Calvin's opposition to such practices is apparent from his *Advertissement contre l'astrologie.*[92] This chapter, then, is *not* claiming that Calvin believes himself to be a Tradition 1-style prophet,[93] but rather that he conceives of himself as an authoritative scriptural reformer, self-identifying with the Old Testament prophets.

Calvin's sense of prophetic calling possesses a profoundly personal element—or certainly that is what Calvin would like the readers of his preface to his commentary on the Psalms to believe, namely, that his calling *is* like the one received by Jeremiah or Isaiah: personal, profound, and utterly life-changing. Of course, this was not unheard of in Calvin's day. John Knox claimed to have experienced such a calling when called to be the preacher for the small group with whom he was gathered in the castle in St Andrews. Calvin's preface to his commentary on the Psalms provides us with a glimpse into the Old Testament character of this calling. In writing in this preface concerning his encounter in Geneva in 1535 with Guillaume Farel, Calvin spoke in language which, irrespective of whether it reflects his true sentiments at the actual time of the encounter or, perhaps, his mature judgments of an event which he now looks back on, invites consideration.

> William Farel detained me at Geneva, not so much by counsel and exhortation, as by a dreadful imprecation, which I felt to be as if God had from heaven laid his mighty hand upon me to arrest me.... By this imprecation I was so stricken with fear, that I desisted from the journey which I had undertaken; but sensible of my natural bashfulness

---

[91] CO 21: 91.

[92] CO 7: 509–42. It is suggested by Sunshine that this work was, in effect, a polemic against Roman Catholicism in France (Glenn Sunshine, *Reforming French Protestantism: The Development of Huguenot Ecclesiastical Institutions, 1557–1572* (Kirksville, Mo.: Truman State University Press, 2003), 19). Whether it is or not (and it very well could be), it is clear that Calvin was wholly opposed to the kind of intense eschatological anxiety, interest in judicial astrology, production of almanacs, excitement over monstrous births, miracles, and the like that was so popular in his homeland; see Crouzet, *Les Guerriers de Dieu*, see esp. i. 103–236; ii. 330–60, 428–64, 464–539.

[93] Here I concur with Engammare, "Calvin: A Prophet," 89; Millet, "Eloquence des prophètes bibliques," 65–6; Crouzet, *Jean Calvin: Vies parallèles*, 117.

and timidity, I would not bring myself under obligation to discharge any particular office.[94]

Plainly, whether one is thinking of our own era or Calvin's, the event which the Frenchman recounts here is rather extraordinary. His language, furthermore, is neither random nor unrecognizable. Indeed, from a literary perspective, Calvin's language raises a number of very familiar images, and specifically, images which inspire reflection upon his thoughts on the nature of his calling to the ministry. His rehearsing of the incident, in addition to emphasizing the psychological, seems to recall God's visitations with and calling of various individuals as recorded in scripture. I might even go so far as to identify particular individuals (which I will do in a moment), though such identifications are best made only tentatively. Ganoczy, it might be noted, does not shy away from mentioning example passages, such as Isaiah 5: 25, 9: 12, 17, 21, Jeremiah 15: 6, Psalm 55: 1, and Psalm 138: 7,[95] in relation to Calvin's reference to the "mighty hand" of God. Clearly the metaphor is biblical and prophetic (remembering that Calvin held David and the writers of the Psalms to be prophets). Thus, one image is identified. I might also note the feeling of horror which Calvin mentions and the reluctance he exhibits to take up the divine calling given to him as bearing some similarities with Isaiah (namely, Isaiah 6) and with the reluctance expressed by Moses and Jeremiah. Thus, it does not seem a stretch to concur with Ganoczy in declaring: "The context of this passage is clearly prophetic."[96] That is to say, the literary images Calvin employs here are prophetic images. Continuing my analysis of Calvin's account, we find that he next relates his expulsion from Geneva in 1538, which he identifies as being "loosed from the tie of my vocation."[97] He briefly recounts his move to Strasbourg and, then, confesses that there he sought once more to live free from any "public charge." This leads us to Calvin informing his readers that, once again, he was forced to endure the horror of an imprecation like that one he had received from Farel. This time it is delivered to him by Martin Bucer. Here the work of comparison with a biblical prophet is done for us by Calvin himself. "Alarmed by the example of Jonah which he [Bucer] set before me," says Calvin,[98] he returns to the ministry. In his handling of the

---

[94] CO 31: 24.   [95] Ganoczy, *Young Calvin*, 397 n. 97.
[96] Ganoczy, *Young Calvin*, 305.   [97] CO 31: 26.   [98] CO 31: 26.

prophetic imagery, some subtle changes may be seen. What had previously been described as reluctance based on a simple claim to timidity has now become a kind of implied confession of disobedience; disobedience of the kind exhibited by Jonah. But despite the change, Calvin's trajectory is still clearly a prophetic one. The specific mention of Jonah here is most interesting, Jonah being, of course, the reluctant prophet. Ganoczy summarizes the Bucer intervention as follows: "Another intervention of the One who sees all, to trap the 'prophet' who is intent on slipping away."[99] This, in short, is a snapshot of how Calvin conceived of the origins and character of his prophetic calling. That snapshot is added to, sharpened, and defined by Calvin's remarks on David, which include the assertion that Calvin can behold in David, as in a mirror, "both the beginning of my calling and the continued course of my duty."[100]

Calvin also has recourse to the prophet Jonah in his responses to his friend Louis Du Tillet. Calvin had been very good friends with Du Tillet, the two of them fleeing Paris together. However, Calvin's friend became disenchanted with their flight from the Roman Catholic Church, eventually writing Calvin letters which probe his sense of calling and query whether he was not perhaps moved by human, rather than divine, impulses to jettison his true and rightful church home (namely, Rome). The batch of letters sent back and forth betray both genuine affection between the two and also a growing sense of frustration on Calvin's part at the persistence and impudence of Du Tillet. These letters covered the period directly following Calvin's abrupt expulsion from Geneva, along with Farel, in 1538. Du Tillet urges Calvin to see this as an evident sign of God's displeasure and an indication that he should return to Mother Church. His ordination, Du Tillet insists, was illegitimate and his search for spiritual truth outside of the Roman Catholic fellowship sinful. But Calvin demurs. In explaining his position, Calvin notes that he had spoken with individuals "whom you know" and received their confirmation as to the legitimacy of his calling and what he was doing. Concerning the idea of his returning to Geneva, he declares to Du Tillet, in a manner which suggests a sense of finality in regards to any further debate over the legitimacy of his vocation, "when the most moderate among them threatens that the Lord would find me out, as he did Jonah."[101] Once

[99] Ganoczy, *Young Calvin*, 306.   [100] CO 31: 21.
[101] Letter from Calvin to Du Tillet, dated 20 Oct. 1538 (CO 10b: 269–72).

again, then, Calvin's reflections on his own calling and sense of identity find expression in the experience of the Old Testament prophets.

Calvin's sense of authority can also be seen in his preaching. Calvin believed himself to be God's mouthpiece. This conviction recalls the belief of individuals like Zwingli, Bullinger, and Bibliander, and also aligns him with the long line of prophets whom God raised up to purify the church from her defilements and abuses, especially cultic abuses. It is subtly witnessed to in the preface to his exposition of Hosea in which Calvin describes the work of Isaiah, Micah, and the other prophets, pointing out that each of them "undertook what God had committed to his charge" and indeed confined himself within the limits of his particular calling and office. So Isaiah and Micah assailed Judah while Hosea and Amos turned their admonitions towards the kingdom of Israel. "For if we," Calvin states in the very next sentence, "who are called to instruct the church, close our eyes to the sins which prevail in it and neglect those whom the Lord has appointed to be taught by us, we confound all order." Here he not only links himself with the prophets but also underlines the imperative of his mission. Calvin does occasionally allude to this self-belief more explicitly in relation to his preaching ministry. We note one such allusion, for instance, in a sermon Calvin preached on 1 Timothy 4: 1–2:

> . . . let us note that the true prophets which were sent from God and performed their office faithfully, protested always that they spoke not in their own name, neither set their own fancies and dreams . . . but that it was the Spirit of God that spoke by their mouths. And there is good reason that we should make that protestation, if we will be heard. For who are we that men should obey us, . . .[102]

When Calvin preaches on Daniel 5 he declares: "For if one preaches in this city that God's vengeance will be felt, that people do not wish to receive what we announce in the name of God, and that it is in his name that we have spoken, that there is a prophet, they will ridicule all that."[103] And a sermon on Ezekiel contains the interesting exchange: "There are some today who say: 'There's Calvin who makes himself a prophet, when he says that one will know that there is a prophet among us. He's talking about himself.' Is he a prophet? Well,

---

[102] CO 53: 251.   [103] Engammare, "Calvin: A Prophet," 95.

since it is the doctrine of God that I am announcing, I have to use this language."[104]

Such explicit remarks are not especially common. It would, in fact, be rather surprising to discover that the man who famously noted his aversion to self-disclosure actually spoke about himself with great frequency. Accordingly, one discovers him alluding to, rather than explicitly confessing, his prophetic authority. It is, for instance, powerfully alluded to in another of his sermons on Psalm 16: 4 which he preached in 1549 and revised for publication, along with sermons on Hebrews 13: 13, and Psalms 27: 4 and 27: 8, under the name *Quatre Sermons* in 1552.[105] The prophetic tone which resonates in these sermons also appears outside of Calvin's sermonic corpus, as one can see by perusing a piece like his *Epistolae Duae*. As Millet notes "[t]he accusatory preface concludes with this quotation from Ezekiel 33: 33: 'When this comes—and come it will!—then they shall know that a prophet has been among them.'"[106] Likewise, his preface to his *praelectiones* on Daniel, which is dedicated to the Reformed churches in France, is a stellar example of the prophetic force and power with which Calvin writes.

To put matters another way, Calvin believes he is right. This is a conviction he ultimately ascribes to God, of course, but that fact takes nothing away from his own sense of being right. Accordingly, he disagrees quite frequently with the church's reading of particular passages of scripture, even when that reading has been held for centuries.[107] When it comes to specifically criticizing an ancient church authority, Jerome is probably his favorite target. "What he says is frivolous;"[108] his allegory on Zechariah 5: 1–4 is "puerile,"[109] and so forth. He even quips of Jerome that there was "no religion in the man."[110] He attacks Augustine for being "superstitious,"[111] Theodoret for being "ridiculous and puerile in what he says in the first

---

[104] Engammare, "Calvin: A Prophet," 95.   [105] CO 8: 377–452.

[106] Millet, "Calvin's Self-Awareness as Author," 86. For the *Epistolae Duae*, see OS 1: 284–362.

[107] See, for instance, the conclusions set out by Barbara Pitkin, "Prophecy and History in Calvin's Lectures on Daniel (1561)," in Katharina Bracht and David S. du Toit (eds), *Die Geschichte der Daniel-Auslegung in Judentum, Christentum und Islam: Studien zur Kommentierung des Danielbuches in Literatur und Kunst* (Berlin: de Gruyter, 2007), 323–47.

[108] CO 42: 493 (on Hos. 13: 14).   [109] CO 44: 195 (on Zech. 5: 1–4).

[110] CO 40: 128 (on Ezek. 5: 10).   [111] CO 43: 273 (on Jon. 4: 6).

book of his Ecclesiastical History,"[112] Hilary for being "frivolous" for "what he philosophies about the soul" in relation to Amos 6: 8,[113] and so forth. Origen receives similarly scathing treatment.[114] Calvin's handling of later fathers also includes lashing out against Bonaventure and Duns Scotus in a brief but pungent comment.[115] Peter Lombard and Gratian are not forgotten by him either.[116] Thus, Calvin does not hesitate to censure the greatest minds which the church had produced.

But more can be said. Many of the above-cited remarks had to do with readings of specific biblical texts. But in Calvin's comments on 1 Corinthians 3: 15, he moves into more alarming territory. His remark reads:

> It is clear that Paul speaks of those who always retain the foundation but mix hay with gold, stubble with silver, and wood with precious stones, namely, those who build upon Christ but, because of the weakness of their flesh, allow something of human origin to be mixed in as well or through ignorance deviate to some degree from the strict purity of God's word. Such were many of the saints, Cyprian, Ambrose, Augustine, and the like. Add to these, if you wish, some from more recent times, such as Gregory and Bernard and others of the same reputation, who, while they had it as their object to build upon Christ, often deviated from the right method of building. Such persons, Paul says, could be saved, but only on the condition that the Lord wiped away their ignorance and purged them from all dross. This is the sense of that phrase *as if by fire*.[117]

---

[112] CO 44: 388 (on Zech. 14: 20).   [113] CO 43: 111 (on Amos 6: 8).

[114] CO 38: 691 (on Jer. 31: 33); CO 23: 37 (on Gen. 1: 8).

[115] "But Paul urges Timothy to be satisfied simply to be a faithful minister of Christ. And surely we should view this as a far more honourable title than to be called a thousand times by the titles, seraphic and subtle doctors" (CO 52: 298 (1 Tim. 4: 6)).

[116] For references, see Lane's excellent concise treatment of Calvin's assessment of the corrupt Roman church, Lane, *John Calvin*, 42–6.

[117] CO 49: 357. Of course, I am not wishing to suggest that Calvin was not influenced in his own thinking by these writers, see Johannes Van Oort, "John Calvin and the Church Fathers," in Irena Backus (ed.), *The Reception of the Church Fathers in the West* (Leiden: Brill, 1997), 661–700; nor am I arguing that he had no regard for churchly tradition, see Ward Holder, "Calvin and Tradition: Tracing Expansion, Locating Development, Suggesting Authority," *Toronto Journal of Theology* 25/2 (2009), 215–26; Ward Holder, "Calvin's Theology: Tradition and Renewal," in Herman Selderhuis (ed.), *The Calvin Handbook* (Grand Rapids, Mich.: Eerdmans, 2009), 384–95.

Here Calvin sets down a striking observation, markedly different from merely criticizing an ancient writer for their exposition of a particular passage. On this occasion, Calvin collects together arguably the greatest theologians of the Western church and concludes that they all built with wood, hay, and stubble. While I am happy to acknowledge that Calvin's relation to the patristic authorities is complex,[118] I still feel justified in raising for discussion the question of whether Calvin did not perhaps believe that his *own* theology was superior to anything produced by any doctor of the church up to his day. Nor ought one to point to contemporaries of his as possible exceptions to this verdict. The only one with any legitimate possibility of holding that place would be Luther, for whom Calvin undoubtedly had immense respect. But he was certainly willing to criticize Luther. In fact, he did, on topics as important as the Eucharist. Of course, his problems with the theology of Zwingli are well known and have been noted already. The various Lutherans whom he fought with need not even be mentioned. Despite having respect for him, Calvin took Melanchthon to task for his theology (specifically views on predestination) and for particular decisions (like Melanchthon's signing of the Leipzig Interim). There was, in short, no one in Calvin's judgment who articulated right doctrine in the way that he himself had done.

Again, Calvin's aim is not to take the glory for being right. The glory belongs, he would argue vociferously, to God. But Calvin has, he contends, unreservedly given himself and his will over to God. His self-renunciation is not, of course, akin in any way to self-flagellation. It is, rather, a renouncing of self. Calvin's self—his life, will, and personal desires—do not matter any longer. God lives through Calvin, he wishes us to believe. The calling of Jeremiah comes particularly to mind here, whom Rodolphe Peter argued was Calvin's favorite prophet.[119] But irrespective of whether one thinks of a particular prophet or not, it seems clear that this notion of self-renunciation is part of his self-identify. It appears in letters and the *Institutio* and is part of what he wants us to understand about him. This self-renunciation is also witnessed in Calvin's deportment during his final years, when he would walk through the city of Geneva

---

[118] On the specific issue of complexity in this area, see the recent work of Esther Chung-Kim, *Inventing Authority: The Use of the Church Fathers in Reformation Debates over the Eucharist* (Waco, Tex.: Baylor University Press, 2011).

[119] Peter, *Sermons sur les livres de Jérémie et des Lamentations*, XIV–XVI.

leaning on a wall to keep himself upright and upon the shoulder of someone when he needed to cross the street because his frailty was such that he could not stand up by himself. This is a self-renunciation which one could marvel at, and it undergirds the notion that Calvin's claim to being right served something other than his own ego.

While it is a significant step to go from declaring that Calvin believes he is right to declaring that Calvin believes he could not err, it is a step which I am at least willing to consider. As the mouthpiece of God, did Calvin believe himself to be infallible in matters related to doctrine? The conclusion sits (I would suggest) more comfortably with the data than with our own individual feelings. The verdict is contributed to when one recalls that Calvin, on his death bed, declared "change nothing."[120] He, of course, writes no Augustin-ian-style retractions. Millet has argued that this was, at least in part, due to a humanist concern for "the internal consistency of his work."[121] This may well have been the case. But it also supports the conviction that, as a prophet, Calvin might have believed that he could *not* be wrong. I will not insist on this interpretation. I will, however, recall something Calvin writes regarding his conduct in personal (polemical) relationships.

> Insofar as I have enemies, they are all clearly enemies of Christ. I have never assumed a hostile stance out of a personal motive nor out of desire for strife. In fact, I have never been the cause of such. It is completely sufficient to me that I have an enemy for no other reason than that he ventured to oppose the pious teachings and the welfare of the church in a blasphemous manner.[122]

This comes from Calvin's *Responsio ad Balduini Convicia*, written in 1562. This fact is significant because, having been written so late, it covers all of his major encounters—with Bolsec, Castellio, Servetus, etc. It is a striking assertion. But is it any more striking than Calvin's disparaging of the pantheon of Christian theologians; his placing Augustine, Cyprian, Gregory, and Bernard among those who built with wood, hay, and stubble?

---

[120] *Discours d'adieu aux ministres* (CO 9: 893–4).
[121] Millet, "Calvin's Self-Awareness as Author," 95.   [122] CO 9: 570.

SUMMARY

This chapter took up and accomplished two goals: its primary goal was to explore Calvin's prophetic consciousness. Secondarily, it tried to provide some brief explanation for why he speaks in such an uncertain and, at times, confusing way about prophecy, particularly New Testament prophecy. This latter problem was answered by pointing to the Anabaptists and to the sense of profound concern and unease which he and many of his colleagues felt towards them. These considerations helped open a way for treating Calvin's self-identification with Old Testament prophets like Isaiah or Jeremiah.

Having examined Calvin's prophetic identity, his sense of authority needs now to be explored in greater detail. In the last few pages, this chapter pushed the notion that Calvin believed himself to be right and possibly infallible in matters related to doctrine. The next two chapters will analyze these ideas further, inspecting Calvin's ardent pursuit of what he believed to be God's will with respect to his homeland, France.

4

Calvin, the Prophets, and the French (Holy) Wars

Far from condemning the Schmalkaldic War, Calvin connects victory in that conflict with the spread of the gospel. In a letter to M. de Falais, dated 14 July 1547, he observes that God, in willing the defeat of the Schmalkaldic leaders, had dealt a blow to the progress of the gospel. "In the present state of affairs," he writes, "I recognize our God's intention utterly to deprive us of a triumphant gospel."[1] He goes on to muse rather philosophically about the Lord returning to his "early method of governing" the church. By early method, Calvin refers to God supporting the church through his "miraculous power" without "the help of an arm of flesh," that is, without an army winning victory over the forces of Charles V, who was so intent (in Calvin's judgment) upon crushing God's church. On this occasion, Calvin believed, it was God's intention not to see the gospel triumph but rather to "constrain us to fight under the cross of our Lord Jesus."[2]

Calvin's attitude towards the Schmalkaldic War places him broadly within a tradition which stretches back to conflicts like the Hussite

---

[1] CO 12: 552. Against this sentiment, see Daniel Pellerin, "Calvin: Militant or Man of Peace?," *Review of Politics* 65 (2003), 35–59. Pellerin refers to a letter, dated 16 Nov. 1546, from Calvin to M. De Falais in which, Pellerin states, "Calvin's reaction to the news of a great military victory by the Schmalkaldic League ... lacked enthusiasm" (Pellerin, "Calvin: Militant or Man of Peace?" 47). I could find nothing in the letter to validate Pellerin's observation. More will be said on Calvin's beliefs concerning war and the appropriateness of uprisings later. On the Schmalkaldic wars, see, Johann Gottlieb Jahn, *Geschichte des Schmalkaldischen Krieges: Eine reformationsgeschichtliche Denkschrift zur Erinnerung an das, für die ganze damalige protestantische Kirche verhängnisvolle Jahrzehend von 1537 bis 1547* (Leipzig: Reclam, 1837).

[2] CO 12: 551–3.

Wars and (arguably, in certain ways) the Crusades and forward to encounters such as the English Civil War.[3] It also raises questions about his attitude towards war in France and the possibility that such conflicts could help the spread of the gospel in his beloved homeland. Of course, France *did* enter into war in the early 1560s[4] and Calvin involved himself vigorously in that conflict.

The next two chapters will explore Calvin's attitudes towards war and the progress of the gospel. They will demonstrate how Calvin developed, probably beginning in the 1550s though perhaps earlier, a plan to win France for the gospel which included the possibility of armed conflict. They will show that Calvin trained "prophets" who were sent into the country to work intensely to undermine the king's authority on the grounds that he supported idolatry. These minister-prophets were also sent to prepare the French Reformed congregations for a possible military uprising, preparing them so that they would join with such an uprising. I will not be contending that Calvin wanted these pastors *themselves* to engage in armed conflict, as he was opposed to ministers bearing arms. But I will maintain that Calvin wanted to provide these ministers with a clear understanding of the godliness of such an uprising (when led by the right individual, namely, a Prince of the Blood), so that they could teach this to their congregations. These prophets were also dispatched into the country to be the voice of God, displacing the French Catholic priests. These chapters will also demonstrate that Calvin's plan saw him search for a French noble willing to support the evangelical religion, even if it meant initiating a coup. Ultimately, it is the argument of these

---

[3] See Michael Walzer, *The Revolution of the Saints: A Study in the Origins of Radical Politics* (Cambridge, Mass.: Harvard University Press, 1965), 12–13. Against Walzer's view of Calvin as fundamentally not a theologian but an "ideologist" (pp. 22–30), see Eire, *War Against the Idols*, 304–10. I concur with Eire but also find Walzer's blending, in Calvin, of the political and religious appealing.

[4] For excellent general treatments of the French Wars of Religion, see Mack Holt, *The French Wars of Religion, 1562–1629*, 2nd edn (Cambridge: CUP, 2005); Robert J. Knecht, *The French Wars of Religion 1559–1598*, 2nd edn (New York: Longman, 1996); Mark Greengrass, *The French Reformation* (Oxford: Blackwell, 1987). Interesting also, and relevant to the contents of the next two chapters, is this exchange: Mack Holt, "Putting Religion Back into the Wars of Religion," *French Historical Studies*, 18/2 (1993), 524–51; and Henry Heller, "Putting History Back into the Religious Wars: A Reply to Mack P. Holt," *French Historical Studies*, 19/3 (1996), 853–61; cf. Mack Holt, "Religion, Historical Method, and Historical Forces: A Rejoinder," *French Historical Studies*, 19/3 (1996), 863–73.

chapters that the war which commenced in the spring of 1562 represented the culmination of years of preparation by Calvin.

Central to my exploration of these matters will be the school of prophets (to speak somewhat imprecisely, as it was not called by this name, but nonetheless not incorrectly, as we shall see) which Calvin ran from late 1555 until his death in 1564. This school trained ministers and sent them into France. It was a bold endeavor on the part of Calvin and the Genevan pastors, and yet one which has received relatively little attention from Early Modernists.[5] Fundamental to this training was the theological lectures which Calvin delivered to an audience made up substantially, though not entirely, of ministerial trainees.[6]

The content of these training lectures will be the focus of the next chapter. In the present chapter, I will consider the equally important matter of the logistics of Calvin's sending of these ministerial trainees into France and his developing of relationships with French nobles and efforts to get them to use their position to the advantage of the Reformed witness within the country. As I move into the body of this chapter, I acknowledge that Calvin's attitude towards war in France and towards the huge number of questions associated with that topic was complex. I will, nevertheless, argue below that the attitude he exhibited towards war in his instruction to these soon-to-be Huguenot ministers was exceedingly positive. He did not urge them to start a war; in fact, he told them, as early as 1556, that they were already in one. The ultimate aim of the next two chapters will be to maintain

---

[5] Balserak, *Establishing the Remnant Church in France.* Other studies look at Calvin's expositions (i.e. these ministerial training lectures) from a theological or exegetical perspective, see Frederik A.V. Harms, *In God's Custody: The Church, a History of Divine Protection; A Study of John Calvin's Ecclesiology based on his Commentary on the Minor Prophets* (Göttingen: Vandenhoeck & Ruprecht, 2009); Pitkin, "Prophecy and History in Calvin's Lectures on Daniel (1561)," 323–47; Parker, *Calvin's Old Testament Commentaries*, 176–223. On the printing of these lectures and many aspects of their production, readership, and cost, see Gilmont, *John Calvin and the Printed Book*, 45–63 and 296–9. Though not focused on this school or lectures, for an important contribution on background, see Jeannine Olson, *Calvin and Social Welfare: Deacons and the Bourse française* (London and Toronto: Associated University Presses and Selinsgrove: Susquehanna University Press, 1989), 70–91, 168–82.

[6] Wilcox's analysis on the nature of the students is authoritative here; see, Peter Wilcox, "The lectures of John Calvin and the nature of his audience," in *Archiv für Reformationsgeschichte* 87 (1996), 136–48 cf. Parker, *Calvin's Old Testament Commentaries* (Edinburgh: T&T Clark, 1986), 13–24. More on the academy appears below.

that in this work Calvin reveals more of the character of his prophetic self-belief. Consideration of these issues will commence with a brief discussion of the background of these training lectures.

A HOLY ZEAL? CALVIN'S EFFORTS
TO REFORM FRANCE

Calvin's *praelectiones* on the prophets were first presented in the Auditorium and later in the Genevan Academy.[7] They were part of the training for ministers being sent into France to assist the Reformed churches in the country. This training was clearly different in certain ways from meetings like the Zurich *Prophezei* or the *christliche Übung* in Strasbourg. It was also different from the *congrégation* run by Calvin for Genevan ministers, on which Erik de Boer has recently written so superbly.[8]

Calvin lectured on biblical books from the beginning of his time in Geneva, but the *praelectiones* which interest us are those which he began in late 1555 or early 1556. Though more of the nature of these lectures will be set out soon, at present it may simply be noted that during this time Calvin began lecturing on the Minor Prophets.[9] He started with Hosea and proceeded through all of the Minor Prophets, after which he went on to lecture on Daniel, Jeremiah, and Lamentations, and died while lecturing on Ezekiel (his death was on 27 May

---

[7] See Wilcox, "Lectures of John Calvin," 141. There is some uncertainty about where these lectures were held; see Charles Borgeaud, *Histoire de l'Université de Genéve par Charles Borgeaud . . . Ouvrage publié sous les auspices du Sénat universitaire et de la Société académique*, i *L'Académie de Calvin, 1559–1798* (Geneva: George, 1900), 54. More recent work on the Genevan Academy includes W. Stanford Reid, "Calvin and the Founding of the Academy of Geneva," *Westminster Theological Journal*, 18/1 (1955), 1–33; T. H. L. Parker, *Calvin's Old Testament Commentaries*, 13–29; Karin Maag, *Seminary or University? The Genevan Academy and Reformed Higher Education, 1560–1620* (Aldershot: Ashgate, 1995). The founding documents can be found in *Ordonnances Ecclesiastiques et Autres* (CO 10: 5–150).

[8] See Erik de Boer, *The Genevan School of the Prophets*, which was published by Droz in 2012.

[9] Wilcox notes that Calvin began lecturing on the Psalms in 1552. Although he considered the Psalms to be a prophetic book, his lectures on them will not be examined here. My concern in this chapter is with the lectures which were begun as training instruction for the ministers sent into France. These training lectures were begun in late 1555 or early 1556; see Wilcox, "Lectures of John Calvin," 138–41.

1564). The details concerned with the recording of these lectures can be found in Parker, Wilcox, and Gilmont, who discuss the plan contrived and implemented largely by Jean Budé and Charles de Jonviller to record, also with the help of Nicholas des Gallars, "the entire text of these lectures."[10] The plan was concocted during the early 1550s and labored over, with Calvin feeling a considerable amount of pressure to edit and rework the notes prior to publication. Consequently, by the later 1550s and the lectures on the prophetic books, Calvin seems to have resigned himself to the publication of unpolished notes from these lectures. He clearly was not happy about this, but he also was cognizant of the fact that he could not stop their publication except by writing brand new commentaries on the prophets to replace these notes, and he did not have time to do that.[11]

Calvin began to lecture on the prophet Hosea during a time when Europe and Geneva were awash with change. The Perrinist faction, long-time adversaries to Calvin in Geneva, was no longer present in the city.[12] Achieving success in this tenacious struggle against the Perrinists helped him immensely in his efforts to consolidate his power within Geneva. This allowed him to look outward to other parts of Europe. The Peace of Augsburg, meanwhile, had brought substantial change to the religious landscape of much of Europe. The significance of this to Calvin was, *inter alia*, that a sizeable number of French evangelicals were beginning to turn more frequently to Geneva for aid[13] rather than to Strasbourg, as they had previously done, since Strasbourg was now Lutheran. The Council of Trent had recently prorogued for the second time. They would reconvene again

---

[10] Gilmont, *John Calvin and the Printed Book*, 53. See, Parker, *Calvin's Old Testament Commentaries*, 13–29; Wilcox, "Lectures of John Calvin," 136–48; Gilmont, *John Calvin and the Printed Book*, 45–63 and 296–9. See also *Ioannes Budaeus Christianis Lecturibus S.* (in CO 42, Prolegomena [unnumbered]), which will be made use of later on when I comment on the recording of Calvin's prayers; Gilmont, Parker, and Wilcox have little to say on the recording of Calvin's prayers.

[11] Gilmont, *John Calvin and the Printed Book*, 54.

[12] Some of *Les enfants de Genève*, as they were called, were put to death and some fled to Bernese territory. This occurred in the summer of 1555. For the politics of Calvin's Geneva, see Amédée Roget, *Histoire du peuple de Genève depuis la Réforme jusqu'à l'Escalade*, 7 vols (Geneva: Jullien, 1870–83); William Naphy, *Calvin and the Consolidation of the Genevan Reformation* (Manchester: University of Manchester Press, 1994).

[13] Among many studies, see Robert Kingdon, *Geneva and the Coming Wars of Religion in France, 1555–1563* (Geneva: Droz, 1956); Olson, *Calvin and Social Welfare*, 17–39, *et passim*; Sunshine, *Reforming French Protestantism*, 16–21.

ten years later. Calvin followed the council's progress, but was increasingly convinced of Rome's utter corruption.[14] Calvin kept abreast of all these and other developments, carrying on extensive correspondence with many throughout Europe.

The reason for beginning these lectures on the prophets was, as I have intimated, to prepare ministers for France. The lectures were attended by these ministerial trainees and were intended as their theological training. The lectures were attended, it should be said, by a variety of individuals and were not exclusively presented to these trainees. That being said, they were the primary audience and the lectures were aimed at preparing them for ministry in France. Examining the *Livre des Habitants de Genève*,[15] one can see that (for instance) three hundred refugees entered Geneva for each of the years 1554–6 and that in 1557 886 refugees entered the city and 632 in 1558. The majority of these were French, many of whom could be found among the attendees of Calvin's lectures. Wilcox has argued persuasively that this collection of individuals attended these lectures because they were associated with the efforts being made to advance the cause of the gospel in France and (for many of them) that association took the form of training to minister in the French Reformed churches.[16] We know, of course, that some churches were able to sponsor students to be trained in Geneva and return to future service.[17] We also know that Calvin had numerous requests from French churches. "My door is besieged like that of a king," he complained, so great was the clamor for pastors to be sent into

---

[14] Trent is mentioned in many letters, see CO 12: 246–9 (Hedio to Calvin); CO 12: 252–5 (Dazius to Calvin); CO 12: 265–6 (Theodoricus to Calvin); CO 12: 275–6 (Hedio to Calvin); CO 12: 325–7 (Farel to Viret); CO 12: 569–70 (Calvin to Viret); CO 12: 570–2 (Farel to Calvin); CO 12: 579 (Calvin to Viret); CO 12: 580–1 (Calvin to Farel); CO 12: 595–6 (Sulzer to Calvin); CO 12: 642–3 (Calvin to Farel); CO 13: 6–7 (Bullinger to Calvin); CO 13: 522–5 (Beza to Calvin); CO 13: 533 (Calvin to Farel); CO 13: 650–3 (Paceus to Calvin); CO 14: 17–18 (Bullinger to Calvin); CO 14: 100–1 (Calvin to Bullinger); CO 14: 149–51 (Bullinger to Calvin); CO 14: 154–5 (Bullinger to Calvin); CO 14: 165–8 (Paceus to Calvin); CO 14: 186–8 (Calvin to Bullinger); CO 14: 207–9 (Bullinger to Calvin); CO 14: 306–8 (Moibanus to Calvin); CO 14: 620 (Sleidanus to Calvin); CO 15: 49–52 (Bucer to Calvin).
[15] *Le Livre des Habitants de Genève*, i. *1555–1572*, ed. P. F. Giesendorf (Geneva: Droz, 1957), 54–218, as discussed in Wilcox, "Lectures of John Calvin," 136–48; also Kingdon, *Geneva and the Coming Wars*, 1–2.
[16] Wilcox, "Lectures of John Calvin," 142. See also Maag, *Seminary or University?*, 2–3, 8–9.
[17] On this, see Maag, *Seminary or University?*, 103–28.

France.[18] Estimates of the number dispatched from Geneva from 1555 until the commencement of the first of the civil wars vary, but tend to be higher than one hundred and sometimes more than two hundred.[19] Thus, a considerable number were sent in, which surely contributed to the Reformed churches growing as much as they did (which I will comment on in greater detail in due course).

Calvin trained and covertly sent many French refugees back into France to serve the small Reformed churches which had been appearing throughout the country from as early as the 1510s and 1520s, during the time of the Circle of Meaux. However, by the mid-1550s, French evangelicalism had grown but had splintered into different groups, some of whom—usually labelled "Nicodemites"[20]—were strongly opposed to Calvin's intervention into French evangelical affairs. The Nicodemites wanted to pursue a more moderate reforming of the French church and were willing to cooperate with Roman Catholicism and even attend Mass. Calvin was wholly opposed to such practices, believing the Mass to be idolatrous. Given this state of affairs, Calvin would have been sending these trained ministers to churches in France who aligned themselves with his theology. Indeed, as shall be seen, much within these lectures suggests that Calvin was using them as a way to fight against Nicodemites, whom he considered as no better than "papists."[21]

---

[18] CO 18: 467.
[19] See Kingdon, *Geneva and the Coming Wars of Religion in France*, appendices 1–3; Didier Boisson and Hugues Daussy, *Les Protestants dans la France moderne* (Paris: Éditions Belin, 2006), 61. See the very good summary in Ray Mentzer, "Calvin and France," in *Calvin Handbook*, 78–87. On the question of whether Geneva kept a list of French churches needing pastors, see Peter Wilcox, "L'Envoi des pasteurs aux Églises de France: Trois listes établies par Colladon (1561–1562)," *Bulletin de la Société de l'histoire du protestantisme français*, 139 (1993), 347–74. Of course, some churches were unable to get pastors from Geneva, on which see Karin Maag, "Recruiting and Training Pastors: The Genevan Model and Alternative Approaches," in *Revisiting Geneva: Robert Kingdon and the Coming of the French Wars of Religion* (St Andrews: Centre for French History and Culture of the University of St Andrews, 2012), 10–22. See also Maag, "Calvin and Students," in *Calvin Handbook*, 165–71.
[20] On Nicodemism, see Carlo Ginzburg, *Il Nicodemismo, Simulazione e dissimulazione religiosa nell' Europa del '500* (Turin: Einaudi Editore, 1970); Francis Higman, "The Question of Nicodemism," in *Calvinus Ecclesiae Genevensis Custos*, 165–70; Eire, *War Against the Idols*, 234–75; Perez Zagorin, *Ways of Lying: Dissimulation, Persecution, and Conformity in Early Modern Europe* (Cambridge, Mass.: Harvard University Press, 1990), 63–82; Wright, "Why was Calvin," 66–90.
[21] See CO 42: 273 (on Hos. 4: 5); CO 42: 290 (on Hos. 4: 15); CO 43: 289–90 (on Mic. 1: 5); CO 43: 73 (on Amos 5: 4–6); CO 43: 219 (on Jon. 1: 7); CO 41: 260 (on Dan.

These ministers would, of course, not have been welcome in France. Not only would the Nicodemites have been opposed to their arrival, but the French Catholics would have been especially incensed. French Catholic kings from Francis I onwards had sought to rid the country of these heretics, and although Henry II's reign may mark the "beginning of the decline of French heresy prosecution"[22] in the courts, he still promulgated the Edict of Châteaubriant in 1551 and followed it in the summer of 1557 with the Edict of Compiègne—both of which contained draconian measures aimed at ridding the country of expressions of Protestantism, particularly Calvinist expressions. But probably more significantly, scholars like Natalie Zemon Davis, G. Wylie Sypher, Denis Crouzet, and Barbara Diefendorf have demonstrated that religious hatred was intense among the French populace against these heretics and intensified during the 1550s up to 1562.[23] In point

11: 34). Also, see such studies as Denis Crouzet, *La Genése de la réforme francqise: 1520–1560* (Paris: Sedes, 1996) and Jonathan Reid, *King's Sister—Queen of Dissent: Marguerite of Navarre (1492–1549) and her Evangelical Network* (Leiden: Brill, 2009). Reid's analysis of French evangelicalism is thorough and extremely helpful—though I would possibly take issue with his thinking on Calvin and, to some extent, with his concluding section on the Wars of Religion. He writes in ii. 551, speaking of Calvin: "Surveying his published works to 1550, . . . Calvin wrote far more polemical tracts than anything else. After 1550, Calvin concentrated more fully on his biblical commentaries and other exegetical texts. In the majority of his pre-1550 controversialist works, he took aim at the members or former members of Marguerite's network, even if he does not name them overtly" (Reid, *King's Sister*, ii. 551). His capacity to pinpoint Calvin's attack on former members of Marguerite's network is excellent, but his remarks seem to suggest that Calvin, in turning to concentrate "more fully on his biblical commentaries and other exegetical texts," was setting aside that attack on her network. It is my contention that he did not set aside his attack, and that these lectures mark both a continuation of the attack and also an intensifying of his labors to win France for his version of the gospel over against any version which would cooperate with Roman Catholicism.

[22] William Monter, *Judging the French Reformation: Heresy Trials by Sixteenth-Century Parlements* (Cambridge, Mass.: Harvard University Press, 1999), 117.

[23] Natalie Zemon Davis, "The Rites of Violence: Religious Riots in Sixteenth-Century France," *Past and Present,* 59 (1973), 51–91; G. Wylie Sypher, "'Faisant ce qu'il leur vient a plaisir': The Image of Protestantism in French Catholic Polemic on the Eve of the Religious Wars," *Sixteenth Century Journal,* 11/2 (1980), 59–84; Barbara Diefendorf, "Prologue to a Massacre: Popular Unrest in Paris, 1557–1572," *American Historical Review,* 90/5 (1985), 1067–91; Crouzet, *Les Guerriers de Dieu,* see i. 103–236; ii. 330–60, 428–64; Barbara Diefendorf, *Beneath the Cross: Catholics and Huguenots in Sixteenth-Century Paris* (New York: OUP, 1991), 49–63. For more detailed coverage of some of the inflammatory Catholic preaching found in France during the 1560s and 1570s, see Barbara Diefendorf, "Simon Vigor: A Radical Preacher in Sixteenth-Century Paris," *Sixteenth Century Journal,* 18/3 (1987), 399–410.

of fact, it was precisely these harsh conditions that moved many holding Reformed views to flee France for Geneva—which explains the presence of the French refugees whom Calvin was training and sending back into the country.[24]

Sending illegal ministers into any country during this time would have been fraught with dangers, but the French situation presented a special case. Scholars like Marc Bloch, and a host of others, including more recently, Barbara Diefendorf and Nancy Lyman Roelker, have detailed the virtually divine position which French monarchs and the French nation believed themselves to hold in the Early Modern period.[25] French kings were deemed supremely favored by God; the French people the most Christian. Accordingly, for the French king "any attack on [his rights] or the independence and integrity of his kingdom is an attack on the faith. Conversely, any steps taken by the king to defend and strengthen his kingdom are for the good of the faith and the benefit of Christendom." Such convictions had been held since the Middle Ages. France and French Catholicism were interwoven into God's divine plan; Catholicism was as much a part of the political realm as the king, who was himself a type of Christ.[26] So, when King Henry II labored to see through parliament a bill which anathematized adherence to the Reformed religion as an offence punishable by death, he was doing so because the Reformed religion

---

[24] Again, see Wilcox, "Lectures of John Calvin," 136–48. It has, of course, been argued that Calvin's labors in France, particularly his harsh opposition to Nicodemism, were calculated to call French evangelicals out of the country to Geneva; see Eugénie Droz, *Chemins de l'hérésie: Textes et documents*, 4 vols (Geneva: Slatkine Reprints, 1970–6), i. 156–7. See also Eire, *War Against the Idols*, 260–4. The judgment seems speculative to the present author.

[25] Marc Bloch, *Les Rois thaumaturges: Étude sur le caractère surnaturel attribué à la puissance royale particulièrement en France et en Angleterre* (Oxford: OUP, 1924), 51–157, 460–77; Diefendorf, *Beneath the Cross*, 9–47; Nancy Lyman Roelker, *One King, One Faith: The Parlement of Paris and the Religious Reformations of the Sixteenth Century* (Berkeley, Calif.: University of California Press, 1996). See as well, Percy Schramm, *Der König von Frankreich: Das Wesen der Monarchie vom 9. zum 16. Jahrhundert, ein Kapitel aus der Geschichte des abendländischen Staates* (Weimar: H. Böhlaus Nachfolger, 1939); and Joseph R. Strayer, "France: The Holy Land, the Chosen People, and the Most Christian King," in Theodore Rabb and Jerrold Seigel (eds), *Action and Conviction in Early Modern Europe: Essays in Memory of E. H. Harbison* (Princeton: Princeton University Press, 1969), 3–16.

[26] Strayer, "France: The Holy Land," 8–9. Bloch mentions the application of the phrase "Christs du Seigneur" to kings, see Bloch, *Les Rois thaumaturges*, 51, 54, 70, 82; also, see Strayer, "France: The Holy Land," 8–9.

of Calvin and others was deemed by him an attack on the faith and on France herself. The same opinion would have been shared by the majority of the French establishment and people, who saw Calvin's religion as heretical and something which invited God's wrath upon the French nation if she did not rid herself of it.

Calvin would have known all this. Note, for instance, his practice of addressing the French king according to the traditional title of most Christian king, "*Francisco Francorum Regi Christianissimo.*"[27] Any attempt to challenge, let alone replace, French Catholicism would have been deemed by many within the country's government and populace to be outlandish and of apocalyptic significance (as Crouzet and others have shown), and Calvin would surely have been aware that this was so.[28] And, of course, Calvin did not curtail his efforts because of his awareness of how scandalous they would have seemed. Rather he worked tirelessly to make France Protestant at all levels of society.

Because Calvin knew the French authorities were wholly opposed to his plans for sending Reformed ministers into the country, he employed various measures in order to cloak his efforts. One finds pastors entering France under assumed names (*noms de guerre*). They apparently took obscure mountain passages in order to avoid the authorities along the border.[29] They were provided with false papers and ushered in secrecy to their eventual destination. Some idea of the intensity of the struggle and danger can be seen in a passage in these lectures in which Calvin refers to spies of the king (he calls them "persons lying in wait") whose job it is to ensure "that no one from the papacy may come over here."[30] Calvin also refers, when commenting on Zechariah 7, to those who trump up false criminal charges against "us" with a view towards tarnishing the reputation

---

[27] CO 1: 9–10; cf. Noel Valois, "Le Roi très chrétien," in *La France chretienne dans l'histoire* (Paris: SHF, 1896), 314–27, esp. 319–20. Nor, incidentally, does it seem accidental that Calvin conceived of the duty of the magistrate as involving the care of religion (see, for instance, CO 37: 210—this is an exposition of Isa. 49: 23). See also Calvin's dedicatory letter to his commentary on Paul's epistles to Timothy, written to the Duke of Somerset, CO 13: 16–18. See studies by Josef Bohatec, *Calvins Lehre von Staat und Kirche mit Besonderer Berücksichtigung des Organismusgedankens* (Breslau: M. & H. Marcus, 1937) and more recently Witte, *Reformation of Rights*, 39–80.

[28] Crouzet, *Les Guerriers de Dieu*, i. 103–236; ii. 330–60, 428–64, 464–539; see also Diefendorf, *Beneath the Cross*, 9–47; Heiko Oberman, *John Calvin and the Reformation of the Refugees*, 177–94; and Gordon, *Calvin*, 304–28.

[29] Kingdon, *Geneva and the Coming of the Wars*, 5.   [30] CO 42: 296.

of the evangelicals in the eyes of the common folk.[31] Kingdon describes those who could still identify the network of paths for pastors
coming into France used more recently by the Resistance during
World War II.[32] An alternative to using these paths was to attempt
to pass oneself off as a simple merchant when confronted by the
authorities through the use of forged documents. In whatever way
they travelled, these ministers made their way to the churches to
which they were assigned. Once there, Calvin had instructed at least
some of them to meet in secret, for fear that knowledge of a Protestant
cell would be too compromising to be safe.[33] This advice was not
always given. Indeed, by the time of his Daniel lectures (late 1559 or
early 1560), one can find Calvin urging his flocks to be bold in
confessing their faith, even with the attending dangers such boldness
posed.

Nor did Calvin and the Company of Pastors hide their work only
from the French authorities. They hid it from others as well. "In the
first years of the dispatches, the Company of Pastors told no one that
it was sending men to the churches of France—not even the governing Council of Geneva, which paternalistically ruled every other
aspect of the city's life as well as its relations with the outside
world."[34] Calvin did, eventually, speak to the Little Council and
request permission to continue this work of sending ministers in to
aid the French churches. Kingdon continues, in his explanation, to
remark that Geneva's ruling council understood that this act was
seditious and would, in effect, be considered as provocation to the
French government if discovered. Therefore strict secrecy was maintained. The account of how this work progressed includes the interesting story of France discovering at one point what was occurring.
On 27 January 1561, a special courier of the new king of France,
Charles IX, was sent to Geneva to inquire as to the dissension and
sedition which had been troubling France in the form of preachers
who had, for some time, been entering the land, having been sent by
either the ministers or the governors of Geneva. The king wanted all
these preachers to be recalled and no more to be sent. He also
requested a reply to his demands. The Genevan ruling council was

---

[31] CO 44: 226.
[32] Kingdon discusses the different ways these ministers managed to gain entrance
into France: Kingdon, *Geneva and the Coming of the Wars*, 38–40.
[33] CO 15: 754–56.   [34] Kingdon, *Geneva and the Coming of the Wars*, 33.

naturally keen to discuss the matter with Calvin and the Company of Pastors. The response communicated to France, which denied "having ever sent a single man to France,"[35] represents the kind of dissimulation which, though surely well-meaning, has not gone unnoticed by scholars, one of whom refers to Calvin's "superior powers of equivocation."[36] The whole episode is, in fact, quite instructive as to the character of what Calvin and his colleagues were doing. Nor is this the only morally questionable activity emerging from Geneva at this time; indeed, they conducted an illegal book trade into France as well.[37]

This dissimulation is instructive because it likely reveals something of Calvin's mind and intentions. It suggests very strongly that he knew the gravity and seriousness of what he was doing. If we imagine, for a moment, doing something similar in our own day and within our own country (that is, hiding from both our own and the government of a neighboring country something which was outlawed by the latter upon pain of death and severely compromised the security of the former), we are given some brief glimpse of the seriousness of what Calvin was doing. And yet he was unwilling to allow these facts to stop him. What drove him? How could he justify such a stance? Also fascinating, in this regard, is the fact that, when he was sending these ministers into France, he knew it was at a time when tensions between Catholics and Protestants were heated. As already noted, the mere presence of "Lutherans" (as they were often called) in France would have been seen by many to threaten the country with divine anger; that is, God would pour out his wrath upon France for failing to rid the country of such a heresy.[38] Thus, what Calvin was doing was provocative from this angle as well. For his rushing of ministers into France would have increased these tensions, pushing the country further towards the brink of civil war.

So why was Calvin willing to do this? What, in fact, *was* he doing? Why did it involve such risks and—more to the point—why did it elicit this duplicitous behavior from him? What were his ultimate aims and what plans did he pursue in order to achieve those aims?

---

[35] Kingdon, *Geneva and the Coming of the Wars*, 35.
[36] Walzer, *Revolution of the Saints*, 59. Cf. Crouzet, *Jean Calvin: Vies parallèles*, 416–24.
[37] See Olson, *Calvin and Social Welfare*, 51–69.
[38] See Diefendorf, *Beneath the Cross*, 9–47.

PREPARING FOR THE FUTURE: WAR AND
CALVIN'S PLANS FOR FRENCH REFORM

As already intimated, I believe Calvin's aim in sending ministers into France was, ultimately, focused upon preparing the Huguenots for the possibility of war within France. There were broader aims associated with his reforming efforts upon which I will comment in due course, but right now let us turn to this topic of war. In doing so, I will *not* address numerous issues which could be taken up: issues related to reasons why French nobles might be willing at this time to engage in violence, questions associated with factionalism (political, regional, etc.) within France, queries about whether a culture of violence existed at that time within the country, and other related matters.[39] Rather, I will focus on Calvin's reforming endeavors and their relationship to, or (rather) inclusion of, war. His actions, and those of the Company of Pastors, surveyed above raise deeper questions about the relationship between the Genevan-trained ministers and the religious wars in France. It is these deeper questions that I want to investigate now.

The subject of Calvin's relationship to war is complex. Hans von Schubert, Ernst Troeltsch, Michael Walzer, and others[40] have ascribed a progressive, war-like aggressiveness to Calvin and Calvinism. Meanwhile the commonality of the opposing position is testified to by Daniel H. Nexon who could, without any supporting footnote, refer to Calvin's commitment to "Pauline and Augustinian notions about the inviolability of rulers," meaning that Calvin was opposed in principle to the employment of, effectively, any form of aggressive,

---

[39] See Norbert Elias, *Über den Prozess der Zivilisation. Soziogenetische und psychogenetische Untersuchungen*, 2 vols (Basel: Haus zum Falken, 1939); Ellery Schalk, *From Valor to Pedigree: Ideas of Nobility in France in the Sixteenth and Seventeenth Centuries* (Princeton: University of Princeton Press, 1986); Arlette Jouanna, *Le Devoir de révolte: La Noblesse française et la gestation de l'État moderne (1559–1661)* ([Paris]: Fayard, 1989); Brian Sandberg, *Warrior Pursuits: Noble Culture and Civil Conflict in Early Modern France* (Baltimore, Md.: Johns Hopkins University Press, 2010).
[40] See Hans von Schubert, "Calvin," in Erich Marcks and Karl Alexander von Müller (eds), *Meister der Politik: Eine weltgeschichtliche Reihe von Bildnissen*, 2 vols (Berlin: Deutsche Verlags-Anstalt, 1923), 68–9 *et passim*; Ernst Troeltsch, *The Social Teachings of the Christian Churches*, ii, tr. Olive Wyon (London: Allen & Unwin, 1949), 576–688; esp. 590–602; these two works are discussed in Pellerin, "Calvin: Militant or Man of Peace?" 35–59; additionally, see Walzer, *Revolution of the Saints*, 21, 57–65.

military uprising.[41] It is, it may further be stated, quite easy to find material which seems to support either position. A portion from one of Calvin's sermons on 2 Samuel, for instance, preached on 5 June 1562 (soon after the first War of Religion began) serves, it might be thought, to support the latter viewpoint.

We have seen battles for such a long time. There is no end to them. And even apart from battles, we have seen how many people have been killed by wars. This has not been the case merely in one place and in a single army, but has gone on among princes who claim to be Christians and Catholics—and yet they are killing an infinite number of people.... One sees poor people dead among the bushes, and others who are left have to endure hunger and thirst, and heat and cold, and many deprivations—to such a degree that if you cut their throat, you would do them a favour. For they are suffering and will die ten times, so to speak, before death strikes the final blow.[42]

But quotations such as this one, with its lament over war and its effects, do not accurately—or, at least not thoroughly—encapsulate his attitude towards war and, specifically, towards the wars which began in France in the spring of 1562.

[41] Daniel H. Nexon, *The Struggle for Power in Early Modern Europe: Religious Conflict, Dynastic Empires, and International Change* (Princeon: Princeton University Press, 2009), 235–64; esp. 247. This assertion is made by way of comparison and has a supporting footnote related to Beza but not Calvin. Meanwhile, two pages earlier, Nexon asserts that Calvin staunchly opposed the Conspiracy of Amboise because it "clashed with his theological understanding of the inviolability of princely rule." Further, see Mellet, *Les Traités monarchomaques*, 58–61; Pellerin, "Calvin: Militant or Man of Peace?," 35–59; Judy Sproxton, *Violence and Religion: Attitudes towards Militancy in the French Civil Wars* (London: Routledge, 1995), 4–20; Raymond Blacketer, "The Moribund Moralist: Ethical Lessons in Calvin's Commentary on Joshua," in Wim Janse and Barbara Pitkin (eds), *The Formation of Clerical and Confessional Identities in Early Modern Europe* (Leiden: Brill, 2006), 149–68. I do, it should be said, concur, to a certain degree, with those who argue that Calvin loved peace and order. But, as will become apparent below, I also contend that he was willing to support, and even take steps intended to contribute to the commencement and continuation of, war—if the gospel would triumph as a result of that war. For an initial foray into some of these issues, see Jon Balserak, "Examining the Myth of Calvin as a Lover of Order," in Peter Opitz (ed.), *The Myth of the Reformation* (Göttingen: Vandenhoeck & Ruprecht, 2013), 160–75.
[42] Sermon on 2 Sam., cited in Bruce Gordon, "Toleration in the Early Swiss Reformation: The Art and Politics of Niklaus Manuel of Berne," in Ole Peter Grell, Bob Scribner, and Robert William Scribner (eds), *Tolerance and Intolerance in the European Reformation* (Cambridge: CUP, 1996), 128–44, esp. 128.

116   *Calvin as Sixteenth-Century Prophet*

Or, if such quotations communicate Calvin's deepest feelings about war, then we have to say that he managed to look, and *to work*, beyond those feelings. In other words, I want to suggest that, even if he deplored most wars and the devastation that they cause (and I have no doubt that he did), we can see if we attend to his actions that he was willing to countenance war, to prepare for it, and to perceive it as effecting good. He was, after all, driven by a motivation other than his personal feelings. Here it may be useful to remind ourselves that Calvin insisted frequently that he had renounced his own wishes and preferences when he took up God's commission.[43] Nor, I might add, was this a mere war; war considered in the abstract. Rather, this was a war against the Catholic regime which was smothering France with its unyielding support of idolatry. Thus, given his calling to "reduce the world to order," Calvin (I argue) sought to prepare for war even as he dreaded its approach.

His practical reasons for wanting to prepare the remnant church in France for war relate to a growing belief that war was a virtual necessity. He could write to Bullinger on 5 October 1559 of his fear that there would "be no end to the bloodshed,"[44] and again on 1 November 1560 lamenting that "[a] civil war in France is inevitable (*Ergo intestinum bellum in Gallia*)."[45] But his reasons and musings must also be unearthed through consideration of the fact that, in the face of the prospect of an inevitable war, he did not back down. Indeed, as we shall see more clearly in the next chapter, his training lectures through which he crafted ministers for service in France are *devoid* of the language of peace. Instead of urging peace, they—even as France descended into conflict—are full of vituperative and incendiary polemic against the "papists," the monarchy, and idolatry, and, moreover, riddled with talk of war. Their treatment of this topic is unequivocally positive; that is to say, war is depicted in these lectures as a legitimate, and even holy, calling in which one should pray for victory and which could, if God grants that victory, do enormous good for the kingdom of God in France.

---

[43] For instance, see letters CO 5: 386; CO 11: 30; CO 11: 91; CO 11: 113; CO 11: 96; all of which relate to his return to Geneva from Strasbourg and are discussed in T. H. L. Parker, *John Calvin: A Biography*, 79–81; 170. For intriguing thoughts on this self-renunciantion see Crouzet, *Jean Calvin: Vies parallèles*, 9–22, *et passim*.

[44] CO 17: 656 as cited in G. R. Potter and M. Greengrass (eds), *John Calvin* (New York: St Martin's Press, 1983), 163.

[45] CO 18: 230.

So, in other words, the attitude which we found earlier in relation to the Schmalkaldic Wars is one which I have also discovered in these lectures and in Calvin's conduct in relation to the French Wars of Religion. To be sure, Calvin despaired of the prospect of war coming to his beloved France. But be that as it may, no sense is given in these lectures that the church might still hold out some hope, in any way, for rapprochement with French kings; nor is any sense given that this inflexibility on the king's part means that the church should desist from its mission. Calvin does not call the French Reformed churches to engage in conflict resolution, but issues a clarion call to divide and conquer.

What do I mean by saying he sought to prepare his trainees for war? Clearly, I do not mean that these lectures read like Machiavelli's *The Art of War*. These lectures were, of course, designed to train his missionaries in order that they might enter and work for reform within the country,[46] preach to their congregations, and so forth. But that being granted, the lectures were also designed to equip his ministers with moral and theological reasons why the king and his government must be hated and why a revolt against him (by an individual with the proper authority[47] to lead such a revolt) must be supported. He does not set out sophisticated arguments. There is nothing philosophical in his coverage of the subject. Rather, Calvin

---

[46] A large amount of work has been done which examines the history of the reformation of particular cities of regions within France. For a small sample, see Natalie Zemon Davis, *Society and Culture in Early Modern France* (Stanford, Calif.: Stanford University Press, 1975); Janine Garrison-Estèbe, *Protestants du Midi, 1559–1598* (Toulouse: Privat, 1980); Philip Benedict, *Rouen during the Wars of Religion* (Cambridge: CUP, 1981); Raymond A. Mentzer, *Heresy Proceedings in Languedoc, 1500–1560* (Philadelphia: American Philosophical Society, 1984); Wolfgang Kaiser, *Marseille au temps des troubles, 1559–1596* (Paris: École des Hautes Études en Sciences Sociales, 1991); Marc Vénard, *Réforme protestante, réforme catholique dans la province d'Avignon, XVIe siècle* (Paris: Cerf, 1993); Penny Roberts, *A City in Conflict: Troyes during the French Wars of Religion* (Manchester: University of Manchester Press, 1996); Michel Cassan, *Le Temps des guerres de religion: Le Cas du Limousin, vers 1530–vers 1630* (Paris: Publisud, 1996); David Bryson, *Queen Jeanne and the Promised Land: Dynasty, Homeland, Religion and Violence in Sixteenth-Century France* (Leiden: Brill, 1999); Stéphane Gal, *Grenoble au temps de la Ligue: Étude politique, sociale et religieuse d'une cité en crise, vers 1562–vers 1598* (Grenoble: Presses Universitaires de Grenoble, 2000).

[47] As Willem Nijenhuis has shown, Calvin wrestled in the last years of his life with the question of active resistance engaged in by individuals, going back and forth as to its legitimacy, see Nijenhuis, "Limits of Civil Disobedience in Calvin's Last-Known Sermons," 73–94.

wanted to send to French Reformed churches ministers who understood and believed that a king bent upon supporting idolatry was so wholly at odds with the divine will that he must be resisted and must not be permitted to remain in office. These ministers would be able passionately and forcefully to articulate these reasons in the cities, towns, or villages in which they were sent to minister.

In order to explain Calvin's aims more properly, more contextual information will be helpful. Examining the 1550s, one finds Calvin growing increasingly interested in a politically oriented solution to the reforming of French Christianity. This was not a radical change for him since from the 1540s onwards he had actively sought conversions from among French nobles. And, in fact, he had argued as early as his 1536 *Institutio* that a lesser magistrate (found among the nobles) possessed the right legally and the duty before God to rise up against a king if that king had become tyrannical.[48] Nobles converted to the Reformed faith "offered protection to the nascent churches,"[49] which increased in number significantly during the 1540s and 1550s and into the 1560s.[50] This was surely one aspect of what Calvin was looking for from the nobility. But as his assertions in the *Institutio* suggest, he seems to have desired more.

Calvin plainly, in fact, hoped that the nobles would offer something in addition to protection, as his letters alone make clear.[51] We know that the mid-to-late 1550s saw the conversion to the Reformed religion of a number of very important high-ranking men, including

---

[48]   CO 1: 248 (from 1536 *Institutio*) which appears in *Institutio* 4.20.31 of the 1559. For astute interpretive work on the *Institutio* passage, see Ralph Hancock, *Calvin and the Foundations of Modern Politics* (Ithaca, NY, and London: Cornell University Press, 1989), 70–81; David Whitford, "Robbing Paul to Pay Peter: The Reception of Paul in Sixteenth Century Political Theology," in R. Ward Holder (ed.), *A Companion to Paul in the Reformation* (Leiden: Brill, 2009), 573–606, esp. 603–4.

[49]   Gordon, *Calvin*, 306.

[50]   A well-known passage in the *Histoire ecclésiastique des Églises réformées au royaume de France* relates the details of how Catherine de' Medici réquested that a count of all the Reformed churches in France be produced, determining that there were 2,150 by early 1562. This number has recently been reassessed; see Philip Benedict and Nicolas Fornerod, "Les 2,150 'églises' réformées de France de 1561–1562," *Revue historique,* 311/3 (2009), 559–60. I owe my knowledge of this article to Jeannine Olson. Benedict and Fornerod suggest that this number (2,150) may actually not have been excessively exaggerated.

[51]   I will refer to more letters very soon, but might simply draw attention to Calvin's earnest plea to Antoine of Navarre in Dec. 1557 (CO 16: 730–4) and in June 1558 (CO 17: 196–8).

Antoine of Navarre, who held the title of First Prince of the Blood or Prince of the French Blood Royal (that is, the most senior member of the royal house who was not a son of the monarch.[52]) In addition, François d'Andelot de Coligny was converted, as was his brother, Gaspard de Coligny, Admiral of France. The latter is addressed by Theodore Beza in the dedicatory letter to Calvin's lectures on Ezekiel.[53] All of these nobles would be seen by Geneva as enormously important converts. In particular, Antoine of Navarre and later his brother Louis of Condé, also a convert to the Reformed faith, were in positions to take leading roles in reforming Christianity within France and were urged throughout the later 1550s and into the 1560s, by Calvin and others, to do all they could to support the Reformed religion.

This was especially true of Antoine of Navarre. Calvin wrote to him (one can find letters as early as 1557) and sent him emissaries.[54] Calvin's efforts intensified following the death of King Henry II in the summer of 1559. Upon his passing away, the monarchy fell to Francis II who, being only 15, was under the control of his mother, Catherine de' Medici, but these events were accompanied with the usual jostling for power between the influential families within France. As Antoine was foremost among those who might assert his right to the regency, Calvin urged him earnestly to do so and complained vigorously to various friends and associates about Navarre's inactivity and unwillingness.[55]

---

[52] See Robert Kingdon, "Calvin's Socio-Political Legacy: Collective Government, Resistance to Tyranny, Discipline," in David Foxgrover (ed.), *The Legacy of John Calvin*, (Grand Rapids, Mich.: CRC Publication Services, 2000), 112–23.

[53] *Ioannis Calvini in Viginti prima Ezechielis Propheta capita praelectiones...* (Geneva: ex officina Francisci Perrini, 1565), ii^r–viii^v. The prefatory letter does not appear in the *Calvini Opera* edn of Calvin's Ezekiel lectures.

[54] The earliest reference I have found to Antoine is a letter dated 19 Sept. 1555 (CO 16: 770-1) from Piperinus to Blaurer. Calvin writes to Antoine from 1557 and, of course, knew Marguerite of Navarre from earlier; Marguerite was the mother of Antoine of Navarre's wife, Jeanne d'Albret. On Marguerite, who was an important figure in the Reformation, see Nancy Lyman Roelker, *Queen of Navarre: Jeanne d'Albret, 1528-1572* (Cambridge, Mass.: Harvard University Press, 1968) and Patricia Francis Cholakian, *Marguerite de Navarre: Mother of the Renaissance* (New York: Columbia University Press, 2006).

[55] See Calvin's letter to Sturm, 15 Aug. 1559, CO 17: 594-5; cited by Abraham Keller, "Calvin and the Question of War," *Modern Language Quarterly,* 11/3 (1950), 272–80, esp. 275.

What was Calvin's hope? Abraham Keller contends that it "is safe
to state" that Calvin "hope[d] that Antoine de Navarre would stage a
'peaceful demonstration' in Paris, assert his right as first prince of the
blood, and become the guardian or regent for the young François II,
ejecting the Guises from dominance and giving the government an
attitude favourable to the Huguenots."[56] While this reading of the
situation might appear plausible from a particular point of view, it
seems to overlook entirely the extraordinary acrimony that existed
between the French Catholics and the Reformed religion,[57] let
alone—in relation to this particular instance—between the various
rivals for the throne, Antoine of Navarre (head of the house of
Bourbon), Anne of Montmorency, and Francis, Duke of Guise.
Could Calvin have really thought it would be that simple? Could
this have been his plan?

It seems unlikely to me that Calvin, when contemplating ideas such
as this one—that is, the idea of a noble identified with the Huguenot
cause entering Paris to assert his right as Prince of the Blood—would
have seriously considered such a notion but would *not* have thought of
the eventuality that the noble's ambitions to become regent, or to
occupy the position of guardian to the young king, might well be met
with stout resistance and even violence from the French Catholic
nobles and population, who were convinced that as long as these
heretics remained in their land they ran the risk that God would
punish them.[58] Calvin surely would have contemplated this possibility
and allowed his plans to be shaped by it. His knowledge of the French
situation was sufficiently deep, nuanced, and thorough (his voluminous correspondences bear this out as do the contents of these training
lectures) to convince me that he would not have been unaware of the
seriousness of the situation in the country. To be sure, there were
Huguenot nobles in high positions in Paris during these years who
could have endeavored to support Antoine, but there were also Huguenots fleeing the country with harrowing tales of persecution. Surely
such knowledge would have influenced his planning.

[56] Keller, "Calvin and the Question of War," 275.
[57] This struggle is acknowledged by Calvin in letters; see, for instance, his Sept.
1558 missive to Zulegero, CO 17: 311–12. Crouzet, *Les Guerriers de Dieu*, see i.
103–236; ii. 330–60, 428–64, 464–539; Diefendorf, *Beneath the Cross*, 9–47.
[58] Crouzet, *Les Guerriers de Dieu*, see i. 103–236; ii. 330–60, 428–64, 464–539;
Diefendorf, *Beneath the Cross*, 9–47.

Returning to the summer of 1559, Calvin was clearly distraught by the outcome of affairs, insisting in a letter that the regency had been effectively stolen from Antoine by the Guises.[59] He does not, however, wholly give up on Antoine of Navarre, in the way that, for instance, Morel and Hotman do. Calvin is thoroughly disgusted with Antoine, but he still continues to entreat him to action, both writing to him and sending emissaries.[60] But this fact raises once again the question of Calvin's plans. What did he have in mind for Antoine or for any of the nobles who might be in a position to aid the Reformed religion, particularly those nobles who held high positions within the government? I am convinced that he developed a plan which, at least in the early stages, would have resembled a simple set of designs, which surely would have changed over time and which would likely have been multi-faceted in character. Calvin, in other words, would have likely formulated plans which were prepared to deal with various eventualities, so that if he witnessed failure (of the kind we have been discussing, where Antoine refused to pursue a claim to his place as First Prince of the Blood) in one area, he would still have other possibilities.

One of the eventualities which Calvin must have envisioned and prepared for was the possibility that the severity of the situation in France would increase and that, in particular, his hopes for any of the nobles with whom he made contact would be thwarted by the tensions and hostilities within the country. In other words, I think Calvin

---

[59] See Calvin's letter to Hotman and Sturm, 4 June 1560, CO 18: 97–100, at 98.

[60] CO 18: 608–10 (letter from Morel to Calvin dated 23 Aug. 1559) and CO 18: 621 (letter from Hotman to Calvin dated 2 Sept. 1559) both cited by Keller, "Calvin and the Question of War," 275. Keller rightly notes that Calvin's attitude towards Antoine differs from the attitudes of Hotman and Morel, citing a letter from Calvin to Vermigli dated 9 Oct. 1559 (CO 17: 652–3, cited in Keller, "Calvin and the Question of War," 275). In point of fact, Calvin complains about Antoine in a string of letters so frequently that he gives a clear indication that he retains some hope that Antoine might still be useful; see, to Bullinger (1 Nov. 1560, CO 18: 229–31); to Sturm (9 Nov. 1560, CO 18: 231–2); to Bullinger (9 Dec. 1560, CO 18: 254–6); to Sulcer (11 Dec. 1560, CO 18: 267–9) for a sampling. Calvin also continues to send emissaries to him. He writes in a letter to Sulzer dated 1 Oct. 1560 that the King of Navarre remains silent, but the churches of Gascony "enjoy a certain degree of peace," adding: "Our Beza is with him (*apud eum est*)" (CO 18: 202–4; specifically 204). A letter of Calvin to Sturm, written in Nov. 1560, alludes to the fact that François Hotman had gone to visit the King of Navarre to urge him to do more for the gospel in France (CO 18: 231–2). Additionally, writing to the King of Navarre on 16 Jan. 1561, Calvin urges him to use his influence to sway the regent, Catherine de' Medici (CO 18: 311–12).

would have seen that, unless he prepared for a situation in which the noble who was pushing for reform had an army at his disposal, his plans for reforming France would be doomed to failure. He had been calling the king a tyrant from as early as 1550[61] and he knew the character of French Catholicism. He was not naïve concerning the extraordinary complications which awaited anyone trying to reform French Christianity from within the country. Would he not have prepared for the idea of a "lesser magistrate"[62] requiring a ready army in order to do that reforming work? Would he not have foreseen the need to prepare within the country a body of believers who were ready to become soldiers and to respond to the call to fight under the leadership of a noble who was instigating a coup?

To pursue Calvin's thinking on this aspect of his plans further, I want to inquire into the question of the timing of Calvin's "conversion" to supporting a form of active resistance. Now, it is clear that he did not support the Conspiracy of Amboise[63] of 17 March 1560—though I will have more to say on this later. But, by the spring of 1562, Calvin would lend his strong support to Louis of Condé and his revolt against the French crown. Are we to assume, then, that his thinking changed in a fundamental way in 1562 and that prior to that date he was opposed to active resistance *ipso facto*? This seems to be what Robert Kingdon implied in a paper which he read in 1998 at the International Congress on Calvin Research, in Seoul. There he explains that Calvin generally taught passive resistance but that towards the end of his life he came to accept active resistance. Kingdon proceeds to argue that Calvin's "conversion to active resistance, in fact, can be dated with some precision."[64] Demonstrating his point, he notes that, as late as 1560, Calvin was "still discouraging proposals for overthrow of the French monarch by young Protestant noblemen like La Renaudie" (referring to the failed Conspiracy of Amboise), but in early 1562 he supported the plot of Louis of Condé. But, unless I have simply misunderstood Kingdon, this does not prove his point.

---

[61] Engammare, "Calvin monarchomaque? Du soupçon à l'argument," 207–26.

[62] CO 1: 248 (from 1536 *Institutio*) which appears in *Institutio* 4.20.31 of 1559.

[63] For some of the better literature on this conspiracy, see Arlette Jouanna *et al.*, *Histoire et dictionnaire des Guerres de Religion* (Paris: Robert Laffont, 1998), 52–69; Kingdon, *Geneva and the Coming of the Wars*, 68–78.

[64] Robert Kingdon, "Calvin and Calvinists on Resistance to Government," in *Calvinus Evangelii Propugnator*, 54–65, esp. 56.

For it could be that Calvin was in favor of, or at least accepting of the idea of, active resistance from an earlier stage in this thinking, but simply did not find a plot which he believed was viable, legal, and had a good chance of succeeding until 1562. Kingdon, in this paper, follows this observation by commenting on Calvin's "political shrewdness," namely, that he seemed to discourage plots that were doomed to failure, while supporting those which seemed to have a good chance of success. Here I am in complete agreement with Kingdon. That is to say, Calvin does not have to have gone through a "conversion to active resistance" in 1562 but merely to have finally found a plot which he felt on a practical level would be likely to succeed. In regard to the kinds of acts of iconoclasm and vandalism which some French Protestants pursued, Calvin insists, "I have never approved of them."[65] But that continued to be the case throughout his entire life. He *never* approved of approaches such as these, which rarely achieved anything except to inflame public opinion. This, however, tells us nothing about his position on the question of organized active resistance perpetrated by a lesser magistrate, who, Calvin believed, had the authority to engage in such resistance.[66] Indeed Alain Dufour[67] has shown that in the summer of 1560 Calvin and Beza were engaged in trying to raise money for troops which they would put at the disposal of Antoine of Navarre if he were willing to use them for the good of the Huguenot cause. So the idea that Calvin was disposed, despite his fear of war, to contemplate armed conflict prior to 1562 seems credible. Keller, in fact, finds evidence that Calvin's mind was opened to approve "'other means'—provided they were legitimate" following the events of the summer of 1559, when the Guise muscled out the weak-willed Antoine and took the

[65] He states this in a letter, dated 26 Feb. 1561, to the church of Paris, see CO 18: 376–8, esp. 378. Calvin also added an admonition against individuals taking up arms to the French *Institution de la religion chrestienne* 4.20.9–10; see CO 4: 1136–8, cited in Keller, "Calvin and the Question of War," 272.

[66] Kingdon, *Geneva and the Coming of the Wars*, 111–12.

[67] Alain Dufour, "L'Affaire de Maligny (Lyon, 4–5 septembre 1560) vue à travers la correspondance de Calvin et de Bèze," *Cahiers d'Histoire*, 8 (1963), 269–80 and Dufour, *Théodore de Bèze*, Histoire littéraire de la France publiée par l'Académie des Inscriptions et Belles-Lettres, 42 (Paris: Diffusion de Boccard, 2002), 315–470; esp. 359. I owe this reference to Philip Benedict, "Prophets in Arms? Ministers in War, Ministers on War: France 1562–74," *Past and Present*, Suppl. 7: *Ritual and Violence: Natalie Zemon Davis and Early Modern France* (2012), 163–96; esp. 171 n. 21.

throne. Keller points to letters between Morel, Sturm, Hotman, Bullinger, Beza, and Calvin in which a legal loophole related to the fact that the current king was a child (which allowed the Estates to be summoned and a privy council appointed which could be led by someone like Antoine) in order to make his case. Accordingly, Keller's analysis pushes the conversion of Calvin to an acceptance of "armed political uprising"[68] back to an earlier date, that is, late 1559— a date prior to the Amboise Conspiracy. It would seem, then, that the more we scrutinize this date of conversion, the earlier it keeps appearing to be.

It might be asked, then, what Calvin's thinking was in the mid-1550s, when things in Geneva had turned in his favor and he was beginning to win converts from among powerful French nobles and beginning to appeal to men like Antoine of Navarre to take up the Reformed cause within France. Specifically, one might wonder whether Calvin's stance on armed aggression against the French Catholic government was not softening during these years. What I will set out below constitutes evidence demonstrating that Calvin was actually willing to contemplate the idea of armed conflict as a way of introducing religious change into France—namely, an armed revolt led by a Prince of the Blood (i.e. lesser magistrate)—as early as 1556 or 1557. This is, as I will show, apparent from his lectures to his ministers whom he was preparing for the possibility of war and providing with robust theological and moral reasons for believing that the king may legitimately be removed from office because he had forfeited that office. So, I will argue, Calvin's conversion to active resistance cannot be dated with precision but was, rather, something which developed gradually during the second half of the 1550s in tandem with his developing relationships with powerful French nobles, whom he believed could help him turn the tide for the gospel in France.

We have yet to mention an idea lurking in the background of this discussion, namely, that of monarchomaque theory. The title is normally applied to the likes of Theodore Beza, François Hotman, Philippe de Mornay, and Nicolas Barnaud, not to Calvin. Max Engammare has mooted the possibility that Calvin held such a position in his "Calvin monarchomaque? Du soupçon à l'argument."[69] The

---

[68] Keller, "Calvin and the Question of War," 276.

[69] Engammare, "Calvin monarchomaque? Du soupçon à l'argument," 207–26.

next chapter will point to evidence from these training lectures which gently pushes scholarship to reflect again on this question, but will not comment on the specific issue in any detail, in part because more recent research, in particular the findings of Paul-Alexis Mellet's *Les Traités monarchomaques*, has raised serious questions about what is meant when someone speaks about monarchomaque theory.[70]

Before I begin to look more particularly at the lectures, in Chapter 5, I should reiterate the fact that scholarship on Calvin's lectures on the prophets does exist, though it is limited both in terms of the number of studies that have been produced and the scope of those studies. No one has, to my knowledge, asked the questions of these lectures that will be asked here. This is not my first venture into this field of study. I have written on a portion of these lectures, specifically on Calvin's exposition of the Minor Prophets. In that monograph, *Establishing the Remnant Church in France*,[71] the question of purpose was raised, but it was raised on a broader scale. That is to say, my study addressed Calvin's purpose in his lectures on the Minor Prophets (this monograph dealt only with Calvin's work on these prophets and not his later lectures on Daniel, Jeremiah, Lamentations, and Ezekiel) in terms of the question of how Calvin conceived of the church. It argued that he saw himself, through these *praelectiones*, as seeking to establish the remnant church, which existed over against and in direct conflict with, the "papist" church in France. Thus, Calvin had a two-church ecclesiology, which seems to have arisen gradually from the 1540s onwards in response, at least in part, to his appropriation of themes found in the prophetic books themselves and his reflections on various historical events occurring in the 1540s and 1550s. Here, however, the questions I am taking up are fundamentally different.

[70] Paul-Alexis Mellet, *Les Traités monarchomaques: Confusion des temps, résistance armée et monarchie parfaite (1560–1600)* (Geneva: Droz, 2007). See also the essays in Paul-Alexis Mellet (ed.), *Et de sa bouche sortait un glaive: Les Monarchomaques au XVIᵉ siècle* (Geneva: Droz, 2006).

[71] Jon Balserak, *Establishing the Remnant Church in France*. See also Parker, *Calvin's Old Testament Commentaries*, 176–223; Frederik A. V. Harms, *In God's Custody: The Church, a History of Divine Protection: A Study of John Calvin's Ecclesiology based on his Commentary on the Minor Prophets* (Göttingen: Vandenhoeck & Ruprecht, 2009); Pitkin, "Prophecy and History in Calvin's Lectures on Daniel (1561)," 323–47. These studies do not address the set of issues analyzed in the present monograph.

* * *

It may appear that we have drifted rather far from the matter of Calvin's prophetic awareness. But, as indicated at the commencement of this chapter, the material covered here, and below, aims to put flesh on the idea of this awareness—particularly in relation to the notion of authority. It investigates the shape and substance of this prophetic awareness by inquiring into Calvin's plans in relation to France which would appear to have been motivated by this sense of authority. Pursuing these matters further, the next chapter will examine the training lectures themselves. Here I have several things which I shall wish to explore, all of which relate to how Calvin sought to inculcate into his ministerial trainees certain convictions: Calvin's conception of the "papists" as the enemy in war; Calvin's intention to train a school of prophets to enter France and, effectively, assert their spiritual authority within the country; Calvin's teaching on the civil magistrate within these lectures; and Calvin's prayers about war. I will also, again, want to look at what these lectures and their aims reveal to us about Calvin and about the authority he believed he possessed.

5

War and Calvin's Purpose in his
Training Lectures

Scholars have paid little attention to the question of Calvin's purpose for his *praelectiones* on the prophetic books in relation to his immediate hearers, preferring instead to focus on issues related to Calvin's exegesis or his theology. Without specifically mentioning these lectures, Kingdon makes a general remark about the ministers being trained during these years needing to learn "Calvin's own painstaking technique of line-by-line exegesis."[1] It is very likely that Kingdon had in mind other aspects of the ministerial training program and not the theological lectures. However, I will contend, as has already been stated, that this was certainly *not* Calvin's primary purpose in these lectures. Meanwhile, Harms sees the lectures as broadly educational in their scope and focus (he does not see their purpose as being the training of ministers, but merely as a part of Calvin's general aim to educate the Genevan population).[2] Wilcox does not express an opinion on the purpose of the lectures, except to say that Calvin intended them to train ministers for the French Reformed churches.[3]

To be sure, as one approaches these lectures with the question of purpose in mind, one does not immediately see war as related to their purpose. Calvin mentions numerous themes and, as is characteristic of him, does a good job of sticking close to the prophetic text which he is expounding. That being said, when one examines these lectures (and the accompanying prayers) in relation to other portions of his corpus,

---

[1] Kingdon, *Geneva and the Coming of the Wars*, 14. See also, Maag, *Seminary or University?*, 2–3, 8–9.
[2] Harms, *In God's Custody*, 37–40.
[3] Wilcox, "Lectures of John Calvin," 136–48.

one finds a war-focused message which is not repeated in his other writings.[4] Now, the text of the prophets *does* mention war. But these are the prophetic books; Calvin was not lecturing on 1 Kings. That fact notwithstanding, Calvin addresses the idea of warfare frequently throughout these lectures in a way which should briefly be introduced. He does not discuss war primarily, or even much at all, when expounding a passage in which a prophet threatens devastation, such as, say, a coming attack by the Assyrians. His allusions to, and discussions of, war are more diffuse and, in this way, more penetrating.

Of course, it must be mentioned, before we go any further, that war has been a common theme for discussion within Christian circles since the days of the apostles. Calvin's contemporary, Erasmus, exemplified this perfectly in his *Enchiridion Militis Christiani*, in which he explained that the Christian life consisted in constant warfare. Thus, there was absolutely nothing new *per se* in Calvin's handling of the motif. But in these lectures, Calvin, conceiving of warfare as at once spiritual and earthly in character, had something more in mind in his discussion than did Erasmus.[5]

More specifically, Calvin described a war in which his trainees faced a present, this-worldly enemy—not merely Satan or the ungodly in a general sense but the "papists." The Catholics were unmistakably the enemy in this conflict. Nor should it be forgotten that the character of the French king's relationship with Christianity in France meant invariably that any idea of a two-kingdoms style of division being found in these lectures needs to be discarded. As Witte has rightly observed, Calvin's mature thought betrays the quality of "blur [ring] the lines between the earthly kingdom and heavenly kingdom, between spiritual and political life, law, and liberty."[6] In point of fact, we have in Calvin's conception of war in these training lectures an

---

[4] In the *Institutio*, for instance, his treatment of spiritual trials as part and parcel of the Christian life does *not* include discussion of warfare or the theme of war. For the rare references to the theme in the *Institutio*, see, for instance, *Institutio* 2.15.4 which speaks of "war under the cross" (CO 2: 364). It would be impossible in my judgment to conclude that warfare is a theme of any significance in a work like the *Institutio*.

[5] Here Pellerin's consideration of Calvin's use of military language, though thoughtful in many ways, is significantly weakened by his unawareness of Calvin's more aggressive language. In particular, Pellerin focuses his analysis on Calvin's New Testament expositions and letters, referring only very rarely (three times in total) to Calvin's expositions on the prophet. See Pellerin, "Calvin: Militant or Man of Peace?," 35–59.

[6] Witte, *Reformation of Rights*, 56; also Wolin, "Calvin and the Reformation," 429.

understanding very much like that found in the Old Testament.[7] Here, as we shall see, war is treated as an act of spiritual service and that includes the idea of military conflict. Victory in war is multifaceted and includes within it both the ultimate victory which awaits the church in heaven as well as victory in armed conflict, something for which one can pray and about which one can sing praises. In this latter sense, defeat of the enemy—be it Egypt, the Philistines, or Roman Catholics—is triumph for God.

Calvin introduces the idea of warfare very early in these lectures. In his handling of Hosea 6: 3, he explains: "Since, then, so heavy a trial awaited the godly, the prophet wished here to prepare them for the laborious warfare (*laboriosam militiam*)."[8] And the prayer that he prays at the end of this lecture turns to the same theme:

> Grant, almighty God, when we do not respond with appropriate gratitude to your favors and, having tasted of your mercy, we have wilfully sought our own destruction, that we,... [being renewed, we may fear your name and continue to advance] ... so that being armed with your invincible power,... we may pursue our warfare to the end (*hanc nostrum militiam*),... through Jesus Christ our Lord. Amen.[9]

This brief foray into the topic does not reveal to us the nuances of Calvin's thinking on it, but provides us, nonetheless, with a sampling of his general discussion of the theme. As I mentioned earlier, these training lectures began with Hosea. Thus, these remarks on war and this prayer about war were uttered by Calvin in mid-1556. They were, then, already at war.

This early date is noteworthy. One might well have expected Calvin to begin discussing war in 1562, when the first civil war began, or perhaps a little while previous, say in 1561, when war may have appeared imminent. But Calvin begins considerably earlier. Why?

---

[7] See evidence discussed later in this chapter which confirms this. It is also discussed, in relation to the Huguenots and (in varying degrees) Calvin, in Kingdon, *Geneva and the Coming of the Wars*, 110–13; Davis, "Rites of Violence," 51–91; Jouanna *et al.*, *Histoire et dictionnaire*, 205–12; Benedict, "Prophets in Arms?," 163–96; and Charles H. Parker, "French Calvinists as the Children of Israel: An Old Testament Self-Consciousness in Jean Crespin's Histoire des Martyrs Before the Wars of Religion," *Sixteenth Century Journal*, 24/2 (1993), 227–36.

[8] CO 42: 323. See also CO 43: 377 (Mic. 5: 9); CO 43: 435 (Nahum 1: 1). Other references to war will be found below.

[9] Calvin, *Praelectiones in duodecim Prophetas minores* ... (Geneva: Jean Crespin, 1567), 74.

In my judgment, the most plausible reason why he speaks about war to his trainees from virtually the beginning of these training lectures is because he wants to prepare them for it and help them to prepare French Protestants for its eventuality as part of his designs to bring reformation to the country. Again, this does not mean that he was wholly pleased with the idea. He may have feared and despised the thought of war in France. But, he mentions it in these training lectures from a very early date and is convinced that they are, in fact, already in a war with the Romanist church.

The early date is a harbinger for what is to come in these lectures. But such a proposition requires further examination. Did Calvin really have military conflict in mind when preparing these ministerial trainees who would soon be sent into France to assist struggling churches in Rouen, Lyons, or La Rochelle? To continue my analysis of this and related questions, I shall examine Calvin's treatment of the "enemy" whom his ministerial trainees would meet in this war—that enemy, as has been said, being the idolatrous "papists."

THE ORIGINS OF WARFARE: PAPISTS, IDOLATRY, AND EARLY MODERN FRANCE

It will be noticed that Calvin does not discuss just war theory or anything of the sort in these lectures. Such theoretical issues do not seem to have interested him here. Rather, as I have stated, an Old Testament perspective dominates his approach to war. He simply assumes in these lectures that war is permissible given certain circumstances. Calvin's conception of those circumstances is set out succinctly by Kingdon, who states that Calvin's rationale for resistance can be explained with the single word: idolatry.[10] A government

---

[10] Here I concur entirely with Kingdon, "Calvin and Calvinists on Resistance to Government," 56. Interestingly, Calvin's Old Testament orientation to war is not unlike what one finds in other writings of the time. One such writing is the pamphlet, *La defense civile & militaire des innocens & de l'Eglise de Christ*, which was published anonymously in 1563, probably in Lyon, following the first War of Religion. Though more radical than anything produced by Calvin, its presence provides one with a sense of the ideas which were in the air in France in the early 1560s. I owe this reference to Robert Kingdon, *Geneva and the Consolidation of the French Protestant Movement*, 153–6.

which permits, or commands, it must be resisted. This is what Calvin set before his trainees in this course of instruction. This was the reason, he insisted, why war was justified, though again he did not speak in terms of just war theory; perhaps therefore, it might be better to state the point in an alternative manner, namely, that this was why he believed that war was God-approved. Calvin did not explain anything in these lectures about the need for war to be perpetrated by constituted authorities, such as a Prince of the Blood. Nor did he enter into details about the background and history of papal idolatry in these lectures. One finds nothing akin to Bullinger's *De origine erroris libri duo* here.[11] Rather, he treats conditions as they existed at the time. It might briefly be noted, before I proceed, that the specific conditions which existed at the time within Europe, particularly France, were, in his judgment, spiritually appalling. Calvin seemed, arguably around the time of the Regensburg Colloquy, to come to the conclusion, simply, that all hope was lost for the Roman Catholic Church.[12] Having seen the events of the 1540s and 1550s, with the Augsburg Interim and Peace of Augsburg, the initial convening of the Council of Trent and its opening publication, and various occurrences such as the Massacre of Mérindol, one could plausibly argue that Calvin became convinced that the massive decline (indeed, near disappearance!) of the visible church which he had predicted in his *Supplex exhortatio ad invictissimum Caesarem* to the emperor, Charles V, in the early 1540s had in fact come to fruition.[13] Thus Calvin, by the mid-to-late 1550s, had several reasons to be convinced that "idolatry" was so intrinsic to the Romanist form of worship and, in addition, was sanctioned by the government, the French monarchy, that it was virtually beyond hope. Further evidence for this conclusion will appear soon. But for now it might simply be said that this belief had a controlling influence over much of his thinking.

Accordingly, an intense animosity towards the powerful "papist" church appears throughout these training lectures. Calvin often spoke derisively about representatives of the Catholic Church, such as the Pope, priests, or king, and on some occasions his animosity seems

[11] Bullinger, *De origine erroris libri duo* (Zurich: Froschouerus, 1539).

[12] See my *Establishing the Remnant Church in France*, 19–52.

[13] Calvin had, in his *Supplex exhortatio ad Caesarem*, expressed this concern to Charles V; see CO 6: 532. See also Heiko A. Oberman, "Europa afflicta: The Reformation of the Refugees," *Archiv für Reformationsgeschichte*, 83 (1992), 91–111; Balserak, *Establishing the Remnant Church in France*, 23–5, 80–3.

to have almost boiled over into vitriol: "We, therefore, are able boldly to overthrow the whole of the papacy."[14] He often does not identify the papacy explicitly as the adversary, but refers simply to the enemy. Discussing the trials with which the church is harassed, for example, Calvin remarks (in comments on Lamentations 1: 17) that it is a difficult thing to see the church afflicted with "the ungodly exulting over its calamities," while God's children are treated as the garbage of the world. But, he continues, "let us bear patiently our condition; and when we are treated so contemptuously by our enemies (*ab hostibus*), let us know that God exercises us with punishment and that the impious do nothing except through the providence of God."[15] The same can often be found in Calvin's prayers at the end of these lectures. This one, which comes at the end of his lecture on Micah 7: 10 is indicative of the kind of concerns Calvin addresses:

> Grant almighty God, as today we are surrounded by so many miseries so that wherever we turn our eyes, innumerable evils meet us every-where, . . . and while our enemies rage, having been fully armed and rise up ferociously against us on a daily basis, may we not doubt that you will be our protection, since you know that we are unjustly troubled by them . . . through your Son our Lord. Amen.[16]

For Calvin to speak here—before an audience made up predomin-antly of Frenchmen who had fled their homeland because of the brutal sanctions which they, as reformed Christians, faced from a government which they considered bloodthirsty—of the enemy as "fully armed" and raging and rising ferociously "on a daily basis" suggests that he has more than a spiritual adversary, like the devil, in mind. The same kind of language can be found in his letters.[17] We will spend more time with Calvin's prayers later in this chapter.

I might also note that in these lectures Calvin often identifies and expands upon the fundamental sense of conflict that existed between true followers of God (the "remnant") and "the papists"—identifying it as a kind of permanent conflict.

> The prophet, therefore, although he was alone, had to contend with the many false prophets. And today we have the same contest with the papists.[18]

<hr />

[14] CO 44: 433.   [15] CO 39: 528 (on Lam. 1: 17).
[16] Calvin, *Praelectiones in duodecim Prophetas minores*, 441.
[17] CO 17: 570–4; CO 17: 575–6; CO 17: 710–16; CO 19: 383–4 represents a sampling.
[18] CO 38: 548 (on Jer. 27: 9).

The comparison made in the above quotation (from his remarks on Jeremiah 27: 9) underlines this, and illumines his belief in the whole-sale corruption which now characterized the Roman Catholic Church in France. Accordingly, the claim of the "papists" to be children of God was simply false. They were, in Calvin's judgment, bastards. "So, as God sees it, all papists are bastards. It is in vain, then, that they boast that they are God's children."[19] For this reason, Calvin labeled the Roman Catholics with different terms and described them in a number of ways, in an effort to communicate to his hearers how utterly reprobate the "papists" were. A common way for him to describe them was as covenant-breakers. He spoke quite often of Israel as covenant-breakers, depicting them as hypocrites who turned the true worship of God into idolatry.[20] And, having done so, he would turn to accuse the Roman priests of the same breaking of God's covenant.[21] In keeping with this, Calvin rejoiced that God had saved him and his hearers from such covenant-breaking. For as he tells his hearers, "we were covenant-breakers under the papacy."[22] But his analysis of Rome went far deeper than this.

The Madness of the Idolaters

More than merely labeling them as covenant-breakers, Calvin seeks to analyze the mindset of the French Catholics whom his trainees would confront. He vigorously pursues a line of criticism in relation to idolatry and idolaters which is impressive in both its severity and its detail. As will come as little surprise by now, his remarks are equally applicable to those who lived at the time of Jeremiah and those who were Calvin's contemporaries. He plainly believes that there was a kind of disposition or orientation which is found in all idolaters and could be commented upon as if it were universal and timeless. He clearly also believes that knowing something of the idolater's mindset was important for the ministry these trainees would have in France.

---

[19] CO 42: 229–30 (on Hos. 2: 4).
[20] CO 42: 251 (on Hos. 2: 19–20); CO 43: 116–17 (on Amos 4: 12–13); CO 38: 318–19 (on Jer. 19: 1); CO 40: 354 (on Ezek. 16: 20); CO 41: 259–62 (on Dan. 11: 33–4) represents a sampling.
[21] Mal. 2 is the *locus classicus* for Calvin; see CO 44: 452–6.
[22] CO 42: 251 (on Hos. 2: 19).

Calvin states that idolaters suffer from a kind of madness. They are, in fact, delirious or frenzied (*phreneticis* or *insanus*). He argues that his Catholic opponents are possessed by "a mad zeal which possesses idolaters." For they are like men who are frantic. The superstitious, he continues, "know no bounds, nor any moderation, but a mad zeal at times lays hold on them." Idolaters are perverse. When God tries to chasten them, they "struggle against his scourges" because they are perverse and do not know what they are doing.[23] Likewise, he refers three times in his dedicatory epistle to his lectures on Daniel to the "madness of the impious."[24]

Probing, Calvin makes a range of observations which seek to explain the inner psychology of idolaters. In explaining the reaction of the king, in Daniel 2, to the fact that his wise men could not interpret his dream, Calvin explained "when superstition fails, madness immediately succeeds, and when those who are thought and spoken of as remarkably devout, perceive their fictitious worship to be of no avail, then they burst forth into the madness which I have mentioned, and curse their idols, and detest what they had hitherto followed."[25] Additionally, in one section, Calvin explains to his hearers that the idols worshiped by idolaters are actually the source of their madness. He makes remarks of this nature in his exposition of Ezekiel 6: 6.

> *And your idols*, says he, *shall be cut off.* I have said that this word is derived from heat. It signifies that the idols were the cause of their madness (*materiam ... insaniae*), since the Israelites were so corrupted with frenzied love, that they departed from God and looked only at their idols. But he compares the zeal with which idolaters are maddened to impure and brute lust.[26]

Further, in an earlier portion of his handling of Ezekiel (specifically, 4: 4–8), Calvin observes that "by idolatry, the prophet here points out the other sins of the people; for from this fountain flowed all other

[23] CO 42: 232 (on Hos. 2: 7).
[24] Calvin, *Praelectiones ioannis calvini in librum prophetiarum danielis, ...* (s.l.: apud Bartholomaeum Vincentium, 1571), *iii^v–*iv^r (the dedicatory epistle is not included in the *Calvini Opera* edn of the Daniel lectures, but it is included in CO 18: 614–24; I, however, have tended to use older versions for both Calvin's prayers and for his dedicatory epistles). These same qualities, he finds as well in Israelite idolaters. See, for instance, Dan. 2: 1–2 (CO 40: 557); Dan. 2: 7–9 (CO 40: 565–6); also Dan. 5: 4 (CO 40: 697–8).
[25] CO 40: 569–70 (on Dan. 2: 12).   [26] CO 40: 142 (on Ezek. 6: 6).

iniquities." Idolatry, then, was not merely one sin among many, nor simply an especially egregious sin, but it was the fountain from which all other sins flow. It was the source of sinfulness.

In the final analysis, these idolaters were driven and possessed by Satan, who is the ultimate source of idolatry. Calvin pursues this line of argument in comments on the origin of idolatry. As one might expect, he conceived of those who made images and idols for worship as particularly mad. A characteristic comment on this is found in his remarks on Jeremiah 51: 17. "What madness can be imagined greater than this? . . . when a smelter casts an idol, how can it be that a piece of gold or silver becomes a god?"[27] But Calvin's analysis penetrated behind the prophetic text to unearth what he takes to be the real source of this madness, namely, the devil. Calvin knows that the Catholics seek to distinguish themselves from those who are condemned by Jeremiah for making and then worshiping a piece of gold or silver. He is familiar, of course, with the argument set out most famously by Gregory that images are the "books of the unlearned." He opposes this argument, and insists that those who turn to idols and images for the purpose of teaching godliness are deceived by Satan. "When people seek to represent God under any visible form, they give way to the delusions and impostures of Satan."[28]

The Incurable Condition of Idolaters (including Nicodemites)

In the same way, Calvin also describes the "papist" enemy as incurable in their idolatry. This is often done in line with comments he makes on passages in the prophets which, in effect, offer the hearers no hope at all. One such is Hosea 5: 4, on which Calvin comments: "God here declares that the people were incurable. Never, then, will they apply themselves. Why is this so? Because they are sunk, as it were, into a deep gulf and their obstinacy is like the abyss. Inasmuch, then, as they are fixed in their superstitions, they will never apply their efforts to turn to their God."[29] This relates to Calvin's habit of distinguishing between the corrupt mass of people and the remnant

---

[27] CO 39: 456. Some other example, include CO 38: 344; CO 38: 428; CO 38: 486; CO 38: 497, 601; CO 39: 81; CO 40: 28; CO 40: 558; CO 40: 610; CO 43: 187; CO 44: 167–70.
[28] CO 38: 68.   [29] CO 42: 301.

(treated in Chapter 3).[30] The former were fairly regularly referred to as "reprobate" by Calvin. Of them, he says, "the reprobate are more and more hardened against God, and are continually stirred up and excited to madness."[31] Silence, mentioned in Zechariah 2: 13, refers to submission when related to the elect, "but the ungodly are also said to be silent, when God restrains their madness."[32] This is all God can do, for they are a "hopeless people."[33] "They are willfully blind, for they refused to be taught. Now this is the extremity of wicked perverseness that is, when people become so degenerate that they deliberately assimulate themselves to brute beasts by rejecting God's yoke."[34]

Whether speaking of Old Testament Israel or Early Modern Catholics, Calvin's estimation is that they would simply never leave their idolatry. "Their wickedness is wholly incurable."[35] This needs to be underlined as it relates directly to the theme of war which I am arguing is fundamental to Calvin's purpose in these lectures. Calvin told his hearers that the Roman Catholics were incurable.[36] In point of fact, they were so possessed by a kind of insanity that they ought to be feared by God-fearing believers. "We ought to perceive how the singular protection of God preserves us in daily safety amidst the ferocity and madness of our foes."[37] In describing the Catholics as incurably insane idolaters, Calvin depicted an enemy essentially implacable in its opposition.

Interestingly, he described the Nicodemites in similar terms. "Yet we fight not only with the papists but also with those wicked scoundrels who boast themselves Nicodemites."[38] Here Calvin provides us with a glimpse of his thoughts, at least at this late stage of his life,[39] on the Nicodemites and also how he conceived of them in relation to the war which he and his fellow evangelicals were in with Romanism. The Nicodemites were siding with the enemy and were, therefore, considered part of it. Thus, not only is Catholicism presented in these lectures as an incurable disease, but for all intents and purposes

---

[30] Also treated in my *Establishing the Remnant Church in France*, 154–64.
[31] CO 40: 682 (on Dan. 4: 32).   [32] CO 44: 166.   [33] CO 42: 235.
[34] CO 37: 699 (on Jer. 7: 28).   [35] CO 44: 302 (on Zech. 11: 4).
[36] CO 42: 229; CO 42: 235; CO 42: 254; CO 42: 280; CO 42: 281; CO 42: 498; CO 43: 167–8; CO 44: 465; CO 38: 429; CO 38: 471–2; CO 38: 555.
[37] CO 41: 23 (on Dan. 6: 21–2).   [38] CO 42: 290 (on Hos. 4: 15).
[39] George Tavard is correct to say that Calvin's attitude towards the Nicodemites hardened after the 1540s; see his "Calvin and the Nicodemites," in Randall C. Zachman (ed.), *John Calvin and Roman Catholicism; Critique and Engagement, Then and Now* (Grand Rapids, Mich.: Baker Book House, 2008), 59–78; see also Wright, "Why was Calvin," 66–90.

Nicodemism was as well. Recall, of course, that, in Calvin's judgment, the prophetic books identify and condemn Nicodemism. This is brilliantly displayed in his lecture on Micah 1: 5[40] and also in his reading of Ezekiel 20: 39. On the latter, he begins by commenting, as he not-infrequently does, on how "remarkable" this passage is. He then continues to explain that many in Calvin's and his trainees' own day were deceived. They think, he explained, that they could "partially obey [God's] commandments, and then pile up a great heap of superstitions." Scarcely one in a hundred can be found, Calvin continues, "who does not think it better partially to worship God than entirely to devote themselves to idols."[41] The intriguing thing about these comments is that they are made in early 1564. Calvin would die only a few months later. The first of the French Wars of Religion had already reached its sharpest point with the battle of Dreux in late 1562 and drawn to a close (of sorts). Thus, something of the ramifications of this fiercely unyielding position on worship had, arguably, been revealed and set before Calvin's nose, and yet he was *still* as insistent as he had been prior to the commencement of the military conflict on the impossibility of accepting, or cooperating with, those who hold a Nicodemite position. Continuing his assertion, Calvin explained to his trainees that, while such mixtures may please human beings, they are detested by God. He even urges that "monstrous indecision" of the kind exhibited by Nicodemites is "in God's sight worse than the papacy" since at least the Catholics are honest and upfront about their views on worship, whereas the inventions of those wishing to adhere to Nicodemite policies "mingled darkness with light and infected the pure doctrine with its leaven." It is, Calvin insists, "the result of hypocrisy."[42] Calvin was, then, keen to convince his trainees that all idolaters—including it would seem, even Nicodemites—were in an incurable condition.

We Shall Overcome

God stands on our side to defend our cause and to protect our safety.[43]

---

[40] CO 43: 289–90.
[41] CO 40: 507. Though I have cited these already, a reminder here is appropriate: CO 42: 273 (on Hos. 4: 5); CO 42: 290 (on Hos. 4: 15); CO 43: 73 (on Amos 5: 4–6); CO 43: 219 (on Jon. 1: 7); CO 41: 260 (on Dan. 11: 34).
[42] CO 40: 507.   [43] CO 38: 348 (on Jer. 20: 11).

Before leaving the topic of Calvin's analysis of the enemy in these lectures, we need to identify one last point, which is that Calvin did not shy away from commenting on God's assessment of—indeed, engagement in—the battle which raged between the evangelicals and the Roman "idolaters." Calvin made it crystal clear that God took sides in this war. God was, more precisely, on the side of the French Reformed churches. Calvin set down this position and adhered to it throughout these lectures. We have already seen it articulated in his assertion about boldly overthrowing the whole of the papacy[44] and it is articulated, as well, in the just-cited remarks on Jeremiah 20: 11.

It is absolutely clear that Calvin's God is with the Huguenots. Calvin is not at all averse to declaring that God and God's word were wholly on his side and the side of the French Reformed church. Such sentiments appear in early, as well as later, lectures on these prophetic books. One discovers them as early as 1556, when Calvin declared "today we may safely take the name of God in opposition to the papists." They have, he continues, nothing in common with the true God. "God's word stands on our side," Calvin is utterly assured. "We may then lawfully reprove the papists, and say that God is opposed to them, for we fight under his banner."[45] The reference to "fight[ing] under his banner or standard" is fairly common. Calvin's language, then, bristles with vituperative aggressiveness. The same appears supremely in Calvin's dedicatory letter to his Daniel lectures (which will be discussed later).

This confidence is, it should be said, asserted squarely alongside Calvin's encouragements to his hearers that their lives will be difficult and that the appropriate stance for them to take in the midst of these difficulties is to bear trials with patience, understanding that a sure and certain hope awaits them. Calvin repeats such sentiments continually. They act like a kind of refrain in some of his lectures. Calvin could, in these lectures, express with real thoughtfulness, even tenderness, the feelings of those who suffer and urged them, in the midst of such trials, to await what was to come. He was aware that hope is something which fades quickly. Thus, he regularly analyzed the prophets as preachers who sought to encourage their hearers with news specifically designed to allay their frustrations and aid them in their endeavors to be patient. This is apparent throughout these

---

[44] CO 44: 433 (on Mal. 2: 4).   [45] CO 42: 407–8 (on Hos. 9: 17).

lectures (one might consider his treatments of Jeremiah 10: 15, 31: 8, and 50: 7), and one could proliferate examples with ease.[46] The same can be seen, as well, in Calvin's comments on portions of the prophets which relay narrative history. Calvin declares in a lecture on Daniel 2 and the dream which the king had (which is recorded in that chapter), that he has already shown that the dream was not so much for the king's sake as for the consolation and support of "the remnant of the faithful" in those very severe troubles which awaited them, and were close at hand. What one finds on almost every page of these lectures is a pious church described as weary, existing "in those very severe troubles,"[47] and tempted to lose hope. Yet, despite this, there is confidence.

This confidence is also asserted in concert with a strong concern for the godliness of these ministers. They must, Calvin is regularly at pains to warn them, obey God's word.[48] In other words, Calvin is extremely concerned to make clear that God would not simply support these ministers while they proceeded to sin and defy God's commands. Rather, Calvin reminds them that God often chastens his own and that they should learn to understand God's chastening, for God would not withhold it from those who disobeyed him. Calvin often includes in his prayers requests that God "grant that we should not turn aside either to the right or to the left, but that we may depend completely upon your word, and so cleave to you that no worldly errors may lead us astray; may we continually persevere in that faith which we have learned from your law and prophets."[49] Moreover, Calvin urges his hearers to learn to benefit from divine chastening, and also to understand it. He seeks to explain to his trainees what is happening when God chastens his church, occasionally using the

---

[46] CO 38: 80 (on Jer. 10: 15); 38: 652–3 (on Jer. 31: 8); CO 39: 398–9 (on Jer. 50: 7). On the demoralization of French Reformed churches, see Penny Roberts, "The Most Crucial Battle of the Wars of Religion? The Conflict over Sites of Reformed Worship in Sixteenth-Century France," *Archiv für Reformationsgeschichte,* 89 (1998), 247–67; on Calvin's personal anguish in relation to life as an exile from his French homeland, see Max Engammare, "Une certaine idée de la France chez Jean Calvin l'exilé," *Société de l'Histoire du Protestantisme Français,* 155 (2009), 15–27.

[47] CO 40: 595. Also: CO 41: 122 (on Dan. 8: 25); CO 41; 151 (on Dan. 9: 14); CO 41: 297 (on Dan. 12: 7).

[48] CO 38: 97–104 (on Jer. 11: 1–5).

[49] See e.g. Calvin, *Praelectiones in Librum prophetiarum Jeremiae, et Lamenta-tiones . . .* (Geneva: Héritiers d'Eustache Vignon, 1589), 83[v] (at the conclusion of a lecture on Jer. 10: 16).

image of God fighting with both hands in the affair. God exercises his children, Calvin would insist, for their good. "God fights against us with his left hand and defends us with his right," Calvin likes to say, assailing his people in a weak manner (*informo*), and at the same time protecting and defending his people so they would ultimately be victorious.[50] Such understanding, Calvin plainly believes, is beneficial; it enables his trainees to be wise in the midst of struggles which have the potential to tempt one to despair.

This confidence that God is on the side of the Huguenots expresses itself in practical ways as well. Calvin, for example, clearly and repeatedly asserts that God's promises belong solely to the faithful and specifically, "us," i.e. Calvin, his hearers, the Calvinist churches in France. The Frenchman's common mode of speaking can be seen in his remarks on Micah 4: 1ff. (the text reads: "It shall happen in the last days that the mountain of the house of the Lord shall be established on the top of the mountains").[51] This text contains wonderful consolation, Calvin argues. Because it does, he insists that it must be directed by Micah only to the faithful, "for others were not capable of receiving this consolation."[52] Having made this point, Calvin continues his exposition. "We know," he avers, "that we find the same thing occurring throughout the prophets," namely, that they add consolations to threatening not for the sake of the whole people but to sustain the faithful in their hope. Calvin elaborates on the psychological reactions of the pious and the wicked to tokens of God's anger. Since the pious tremble at God's threatening, it is always necessary that God console them. Calvin therefore reasons that Micah, "up to this point," has directed his discourse to the wicked, but now turns to speak a word to the pious. Again, his point is that Micah addressed *only* the pious with this promise. The wicked are left out. Moreover, Micah addresses the faithful in such a way, Calvin reasons, that his doctrine especially belongs to us now (*ut haec doctrina maxime nunc ad nos pertineat*).[53] For, Calvin follows his logic to its conclusion, "how has it been that the kingdom of God has been propagated throughout the whole earth? How has it been that the truth of the gospel has come to us and that we are made partakers with the

---

[50] CO 42: 458 (on Hos. 12: 4).
[51] This is my translation of the Latin biblical verse cited in Calvin's corpus (see CO 43: 338).
[52] CO 43: 339.   [53] CO 43: 339.

ancient people of the same adoption, except that this prophecy has been fulfilled?"[54]

The just-noted practice of directly applying the promises to the faithful remnant and the curses to Roman Catholics is apparent throughout these training lectures. This fact raises an issue tangentially related to the promises of the prophetic books on which I shall set out a provisional suggestion. Several scholars, such as Richard Muller and perhaps especially Barbara Pitkin, have noted Calvin's historically oriented reading of prophecy (prophecy is, it may be said, a kind of historically oriented promise). Calvin, these scholars rightly argue, consistently does *not* read prophecies as pointing to the eschaton but rather sees them as promising an historical occurrence which had not happened at the time the prophecy was made but had already occurred prior to his own lifetime (the destruction of the temple in AD 70). This is the approach Calvin adopts even with passages which had for centuries been read eschatologically (such as Joel 3: 1–3). As Pitkin comments in her essay on Calvin's reading of Daniel:

> For Calvin, Daniel is not useful for calculating the end times, because in his view the book's prophecies are intended, in the first place, for the consolation of the ancient faithful.[55]

This fact is intriguing and raises an idea. Pitkin notes that Calvin believed that the prophetic text (in this case, Daniel) was intended to console the faithful. This was a crucial reason for interpreting the prophets in the way that he did. Thus, I would like to propose the idea that Calvin's historical (non-eschatological) reading of the prophets was governed by his overriding concern to use these lectures to prepare his trainees and through them the French Reformed churches;

---

[54] CO 43: 339. For a sampling see CO 42: 229 (on Hos. 2: 4); CO 42: 251 (on Hos. 2: 19–20); CO 42: 256, 260, 261 (on Hos. 3: 1, 2, and 3); CO 42: 289 (on Hos. 4: 15); CO 43: 45 (on Amos 3: 8); CO 43: 167–9 (on Amos 9: 10–11); CO 42: 553 (in Joel 2: 17); CO 42: 578 (on Joel 2; 32); CO 43: 182 (Obad. 5); CO 43: 339 (on Mic. 4: 1); CO 43: 364 (on Mic. 5: 1); CO 43: 376 (on Mic. 5: 7); CO 43: 421 (on Mic. 7: 13); CO 43: 566 (on Hab. 3: 2); CO 44: 272 (on Zech. 9: 9); CO 44: 463–5 (on Mal. 3: 3–4); CO 38: 72–3 (Jer. 10: 12–13); CO 41: 222 (on Dan. 9: 4); CO 41: 247 (on Dan. 9: 25); and my *Establishing the Remnant Church in France*, 164–72.

[55] Barbara Pitkin, "Prophecy and History in Calvin's Lectures on Daniel (1561)," 323–47, esp. 343. Also, Richard Muller, "The Hermeneutic of Promise and Fulfilment in Calvin's Exegesis of the Old Testament Prophecies of the Kingdom," in David Steinmetz (ed.), *The Bible in the Sixteenth Century* (Durham, NC: Duke University Press, 1990), 68–82.

that when he mentions "the faithful," he has in mind these trainees and the faithful Huguenots. Calvin wanted to console them and insists that the text must apply to them. Would it not make sense, then, that he would choose to employ an exegetical strategy which served this aim? His ministerial trainees did not need to know about the eschaton (one could argue). Rather, they needed to know how the text helped them as they entered France and the extremely dangerous circumstances they would encounter there. Calvin tailored his exegesis of the prophetic text accordingly.

Returning to and summarizing the main lines of my argument thus far, Calvin taught his ministerial charges that God would defend them, that God's promises belonged to them, and assured them that God was on their side. Calvin not only spoke of the "papists" as the enemy, but also of defeating them. He taught that the Catholics with whom his trainees would have dealings in France were, irrespective of their appearance and outward customs, incurable devils. They were reprobate and, as such, not recipients of the divine promises. God was, after all (Calvin constantly urged), not with them but with "us." Calvin also instructed these trainees that patience was essential. While it could be thought that his aims in saying such things were entirely towards heaven and categorically excluded this-worldly concerns, the judgment of the present author is that such a view is erroneous. Calvin did, to be sure, point his hopes and those of his hearers heavenwards, not only in these lectures but in many other writings as well, but his aims in these training lectures were earthly and this-worldly—which is to say, that they were focused on establishing the kingdom of God in France in his own day through the ministry of those whom he was sending into the country. We shall see that Calvin's reflections on victory included the war into which the Huguenots and French Catholics entered in 1562. He did not categorically promise victory in the war, but he prayed for it and seemed to believe that God would grant it. He was confident that "God stands on our side to defend our cause." This included God being on their side in all aspects of this war, including military conflict.

RAISING UP PROPHETS FOR WAR

So, these trainees and the Calvinist-linked French Reformed churches were already at war with the Catholics. How were they supposed to conduct themselves upon entry into France? Calvin, it should be made very clear, did not speak of their calling as involving the taking up of arms (a point which has already been made but should be underlined). He was opposed to ministers taking up arms, and nothing I have found in these lectures suggests such a role for his trainees. They were soldiers but not in that sense. Nor, as has been stated but should be reiterated here, did he encourage ministers to enter France and seek to initiate military engagement. He never explicitly discourages it, but neither does he encourage it—though once the first war begins, he certainly gives these trainees every reason through his prayers and his own conduct to enthusiastically support it.

What Calvin expected these trainees to do was perform the functions of ministers and prophets (the character of the latter having been discussed in the last chapter). Their callings were, in that sense, like Calvin's in that they had both pastoral and prophetic duties—though his emphasis in these lectures is decidedly upon the latter. For this reason, I shall spend some time addressing Calvin's conception of these ministers' calling to be prophets.

Calvin's School for the Prophets

Although Calvin sets in front of his trainees the example of the prophets' behavior, the force of their teaching, and many other things, he also insists that they are called to do more than merely imitate the prophets. Basic to what Calvin is doing in these lectures is instructing these men that they *are* prophets. It is clear, to be sure, that the format of these lectures differs from that adopted by the Zurichers in their *Prophezei* meetings. It also differs from the format of the *congrégation*, which Calvin ran in Geneva for pastors.[56] In the *praelectiones*, Calvin teaches trainees with limited, but growing, capacity with language (specifically, in this case, Hebrew). He is teaching individuals who would be sent away in a relatively short amount of time. Kingdon discusses how decisions were made about when to send a trainee into France, when they were actually ready to enter the fray. Kingdon also makes clear that, at various times, shortcuts were taken in order to prepare individuals more rapidly than, probably,

---

[56] On that format, de Boer, *Genevan School of the Prophets*, 35–69.

was wise.[57] These decisions were required due to the needs of the moment, as French churches clamored for assistance. There is simply no way that the apprentices with whom Calvin is working here could be expected to behave like Conrad Pellican or Rudoph Gwalther. For most of them, that is a bridge too far. The leisure for the implementation of such a program simply does not exist.

But despite these differences, it is clear that Calvin communicates to his trainees that he is sending them into France as prophets raised up by God; prophets not in the sense of millenarian prognosticator but in the sense of covenant prosecutor discussed in Chapter 2. Calvin believes, and wants these trainees to believe, that they were invested with divine authority for bringing change to France. He does not aim to send into France mere Bible teachers or pastors, but wants to fill the country with prophets invested with authority to work for radical change. Calvin, one can see, does not merely speak in a general way of "teachers and prophets" or merely discuss their offices together—"the prophet (*propheta*) was called to the office of a teacher (*docendi munus*)"[58]—but he elevates his trainees to the prophetic

[57] See Kingdon, *Geneva and the Coming of the Wars*, 14–24, 31–42.

[58] See e.g. CO 40: 21 or CO 40: 25. The phrase "teachers and prophets" is quite common in these lectures. So, for instance, when Calvin is discussing Joel 2: 28 in his exposition of Jer. 31: 34, he declares that God promises through Joel that "prophets and teachers would be everywhere," because God's grace would be so abundant (CO 38: 694). Similarly, he observes (on Jer. 32: 33 in commenting on Deut. 18: 18) that "[p]rophets and teachers are nothing other than the instruments of the Holy Spirit" (CO 39: 30). Along similar lines, Calvin employs a number of terms, such as teacher, prophet, pastor, bishop, interchangeably. A perfect example of this is his comments on Ezek. 3: 16–17 (CO 40: 89–91; see also CO 40: 616 (on Dan. 2: 48); CO 43: 339 (on Mic. 4: 1–2)). Calvin can appear at times to equate the office of prophet and the office of teacher when lecturing to his ministerial charges. This is apparent, for instance, in passages where he discusses the calling of Ezekiel, and declares that "the prophet (*propheta*) was called to the office of a teacher (*docendi munus*)" (CO 40: 21; see also CO 40: 25). In discussing Jer. 31: 32, he remarks that "the prophets, who performed the office of teaching after the restoration," urged the notion that their hearers should hope for something better than what they could currently see (CO 38: 687, on Jer. 31: 31–2). Likewise, in comments on Zech. 1: 1–3, Calvin notes that God sends "his word especially to his prophets, to whom he commits the office of teaching." He follows this point, a few sentences later, with the observation that Zechariah, "of whom we now speak, performed the office of a prophet after the return of the people from exile." CO 44: 126, 127 (on Zech. 1: 1–3); see also CO 44: 196 (on Zech. 5: 1–3); CO 43: 137 (on Amos 7: 16–17); CO 37: 475 (on Jer. 1: 1–3); CO 39: 23 (on Jer. 32: 16–18); CO 40: 309–11 (on Ezek. 14: 9). These demonstrate that Calvin spoke of the offices of prophet (*munus propheticum*) and of teacher (*docendi munus*) as effectively the same; i.e. these offices possess the same authority and the same divine calling—the authority of the prophet.

office.[59] He declares to them, for instance, when expounding Ezekiel 2: 6, that this passage "teaches us that none are fit to undertake the prophetic office, except (*nullos esse idoneos ad obeundum munus propheticum, nisi...*) those who are armed with fortitude and perseverance whatever may happen" such that they do not fear any threats, nor vacillate when confronted by troubles. Continuing, Calvin elicits the experience of God's servants, who persevered through good times and bad.[60] Likewise, in commenting on Jeremiah 20: 3, Calvin instructs his trainees that "we rightly and faithfully discharge the prophetic office (*rite et probe fungemur munere prophetico*), when we show no respect of persons, and disregard those external masks by which the ungodly deceive the simple, and are haughty towards God while they falsely pretend his name."[61] This calling to exercise this authoritative office can also be seen in Calvin's lecture to these trainees on Jeremiah 1: 9–10 which I will discuss momentarily, but the point to underline here is that the notion of prophetic authority is fundamental to what Calvin believed he was calling these ministers to exercise.[62]

Prophetic Authority and Calling

Calvin, then, conceives of these trainees as being equipped with authority and sent into France to perform a prophetic ministry similar to that of the Old Testament prophets. Concerning the authority which they are supplied with, Calvin has already (as we have

---

[59] All this relates, as I have said, to a conception of life shaped profoundly by the Old Testament (again, consider Kingdon, *Geneva and the Coming of the Wars*, 110–13; Jouanna *et al.*, *Histoire et dictionnaire*, 205–12; Davis, "Rites of Violence," 51–91; Benedict, "Prophets in Arms?," 163–96; Parker, "French Calvinists as the Children of Israel," 227–36). Calvin led these ministers to believe they were entering an environment in which they would meet idolaters essentially identical to those encountered by Amos, Jeremiah, or Ezekiel; an environment in which they would face a king like Nebuchadnezzar and would be required to worship idols or be put to death.

[60] CO 40: 71.   [61] CO 38: 337.

[62] Given this, I disagree with Harro Höpfl when he writes that "the office of the prophet is described by Calvin in a way which assimilates it to that of the pastor and theologian" (Höpfl, *Christian Polity of John Calvin*, 146). In my judgment, the opposite is closer to the truth. For the whole question of the character of ministerial authority as it is discussed in these lectures needs to be considered within the specific context in which these lectures were given and, more specifically, keeping Calvin's aims with respect to his ministerial trainees in mind.

just seen) noted that it is intended to equip them for fighting. That is to say, Calvin defines this prophetic calling with which his trainees are called by setting it over against all forces which might cause the prophet to fear and by insisting that nothing on earth is over God's prophet. One of the places in these lectures where Calvin makes this even clearer is his remarks on Jeremiah 1: 9–10. In a portion of this passage, one finds the assertion that prophets have authority over "the whole world, and even above kings," but in fact, Calvin's reading of the text offers what is in many ways an even stronger assertion of prophetic authority.

In interpreting Jeremiah's language, Calvin decides to raise a basic question about the purpose of prophets and teachers. His answer to the question is illuminating (and served, as will be apparent, as the inspiration for the title of Chapter 6).

> Why are prophets and teachers sent? That they may reduce (*cogant*) the world to order.[63]

So the kind of authority prophets and teachers possess—the kind of authority Calvin tells his trainees that they possess—is, if you will, unrivalled. The verb he uses is *cogant*: to force or compel. They are called to *make* the world submit. He declares within this same lecture that if the prophet finds teachable people, then he need not fight with them. Calvin's point here is made quickly, even curtly. The remainder of his comment suggests quite strongly that this curtness is due to the fact that he does not expect that to be the case at the present time, and this prompts him to muse further on the authority which prophets possess. So he continues: "but when there is no fear of God and no regard for him; when people are led away by the violence of their lusts, no godly teacher can exercise his duty without being prepared for war (*praelium*)."[64] *This* is the authority and the duty placed upon the prophets who carry God's word. They are not simply called to utter God's word and then to let people obey it or not obey it, depending on their preference. Rather, their calling is to reduce the world to order, which—given the state of humankind—means "regime change" (to use a modern military/political term). Calvin's prophets must be prepared to wage war. I shall, now, explore more

---

[63] CO 37: 480.
[64] CO 37: 478. Calvin sets out precisely the same requirement in his sermon on Jer. 15: 6b–10 (SC 6: 28).

deeply a different aspect of that authority, returning to the questions
of the prophet's authority in the civil realm and the question of war
(i.e. armed aggression) later.

This authority comes from, or finds (in a certain sense) as its
source, the fact that they speak for God, adding nothing of their
own. This, it will be recalled, is like the accents found among theologians like Zwingli, Bibliander, and Pellikan. Calvin can, for instance,
explain to these students, when speaking on Ezekiel 3: 16–17 ("you
will hear words from my mouth and will announce them to the
people from me"), that this passage presents to them a general rule
that they should "hear the word from the mouth of God."[65] God,
Calvin explains, "wishes to exclude whatever people fabricate or
invent for themselves." Not content with what he has said, Calvin
reiterates the point in several different ways, declaring that God
wishes all to be silent, not to offer anything of their own, God puts
a bridle on people so that they should not invent anything for
themselves, God wishes that no one should contrive their own devices, "nor dare to conceive either more or less than the word." God
alone wishes to be heard. God does not wish to mingle his word with
the words of others. God takes to himself, "what we should ascribe to
his supreme command over all things, namely, that we ought to hang
upon his lips."[66] This is Calvin's emphasis in these lectures.

With this authority, Calvin's prophets are called to do several
things. One of their duties is to labor to bring about conversion.
Concerning this, Calvin states, for instance, that "God considers
nothing more important than uniting miserable human beings in
the hope of eternal life."[67] Such an emphasis can be found in various
places in these lectures. In relation to the question of how one seeks
conversions among those (the Roman Catholics) whom he consistently describes as reprobate, Calvin makes the point not infrequently
that "we need to remember that some individuals will always be
curable, even though the whole body of the people seems to be
desperate."[68] Thus, although these ministers are being sent by Calvin
and the Company of Pastors into France to confront a corrupt church
body, they are to understand that there is always a tiny remnant
present within that mass who could hear the message of the Evangel

---

[65] CO 40: 89.   [66] CO 40: 89–91.
[67] CO 40: 93 (on Ezek. 3: 18).   [68] CO 40: 93.

and be cured. Moreover, it is their calling to guide and be watchmen for the congregations of the faithful to which they are assigned. That this shepherding would be performed within a hostile environment is apparent throughout his exposition, underscoring again the sense of divine authority imparted to these ministers.

But of greater prominence in these lectures is the calling to contend against all that stands in God's way. This can already be seen in Calvin's vivid remarks on Jeremiah 1: 9–10 cited earlier, and it can be found elsewhere as well. In his lecture on Ezekiel 13: 17–18, particularly the command found there, "son of man, set your face against the daughters of your people, who prophesy from their own hearts," Calvin reveals the intensity of his desire that his trainees learn to contend and defend the truth against all its enemies. Reflecting on the command to Ezekiel, Calvin proposes that it would have been "almost a matter of shame" for the prophet to do what he is commanded. It would, Calvin muses, have been considered by the prophet to have been beneath him to rebuke and dispute with women. "Hence it appears," Calvin reasons, "that God's servants cannot faithfully discharge the duties assigned to them, unless they strive to remove all impediments."[69] Calvin, one can imagine, reflects in his thinking on this passage upon the fact that many of his trainees would not end up in great cities like Paris disputing with the brightest theological minds in the Romanist church. They would, rather, wind up in small towns and villages, ministering to handfuls of unlearned men and women. He would, it seems likely, have been concerned that his trainees would scoff at the opponents whom they met and against whom they were required to defend the true religion. Whether he reasons in this manner or not, Calvin plainly seeks to inculcate into his trainees the idea that no opponent is insignificant. They must not, Calvin warns them, seek for great praise in their ministries but labor faithfully against any and all who contend against the truth of God. He reminds them that Paul strove with a workman named Demetrius (recorded in Acts 19: 24), and this would have likely felt a ridiculous thing for him. Paul had been given insight into secret things and been carried up to the third heaven, and here he was disputing with a craftsman. But, Calvin urges, this was his calling, as it also is the calling of his charges who would soon be sent off to serve in France.

<hr/>

[69] CO 40: 289.

Thus, he urges them that it is their duty to be God's "avengers and defenders of the doctrine of which they are heralds."[70]

Calvin's Prophets Raised up by God to Replace the Catholic Priests

A more specific word from Calvin on this authority and on the calling of his French missionaries relates to the Roman Catholic priests. That God, in Calvin's judgment, is entirely opposed to the Catholic ecclesiastical establishment in France, and for that matter the whole of Europe, is neither surprising nor something which Calvin feels he needs to prove, though he does comment on it in various places. In lecturing to his charges on Ezekiel 7: 26, for example, Calvin adds as a kind of addendum to what he has said thus far: "I omit to notice that this priesthood is not from God, since priests are created for sacrificing Christ, and that without any command."[71] "This priesthood" is, of course, the Roman Catholic priesthood. He makes similarly harsh and condemnatory criticisms in his handling of Ezekiel 3: 16–17, at which we were looking just a moment ago.

Calvin often instructs his trainees that the Roman priests are grossly disobedient covenant-breakers who exercise tyranny over God's people and are forsaken of God. The passage to which he frequently turns when speaking to the question of the complete failure of the Catholic priests, bishops, and the Pope is Malachi 2: 6–7. Malachi 2: 5–9 reads:

> My covenant with him was one of life and peace. I gave it to him as an object of fear; so he feared me and stood in awe of my name. The law of truth was in his mouth, and unrighteousness did not come from his lips;

---

[70] To further reinforce his point, Calvin then—perhaps drawing on another portion of Ezekiel's text which mentions garments which have holes in them and which these women sew—makes a rather astonishing remark concerning fleas. "Hence if fleas were to emerge from the earth (so to speak) and rail against sound doctrine, whoever were influenced by a desire for edification would not hesitate to contend even with those fleas. Thus the prophet's modesty is clear, because by God's command he turns to these weak women in order that he may refute even them" (CO 40: 289). Though a curious assertion, his point is crystal clear. Calvin wants his prophets to enter France and reduce it to order, allowing nothing to embarrass them or move them to set down their tools (so to speak) while there is work to be done. But such disputing is not all he demanded from them.

[71] CO 40: 174.

he walked with me in peace and uprightness, and he turned many back
from iniquity. For the lips of a priest should preserve knowledge, and
people should seek instruction from his mouth. For he is the messenger
of the Lord of hosts. "But you have turned aside from the way; you have
caused many to stumble by instruction; you have corrupted the covenant of Levi (*corrupistis foedus Levi*)," says the Lord of hosts. So I also
have made you despised and abased before all the people, just as you
have not kept my ways but have shown partiality in the law.[72]

The primary task of the priests, Calvin explained to his trainees, is to
teach the word of God. "These two things are, as they say,
inseparable—the office of the priesthood and teaching."[73] This, he
believes, is taught unequivocally in Malachi 2: 6–7. God, Calvin
explains, has by a "mutual pact between God and them (*mutua pactio
inter Deum et ipsos*)"[74] set the priests over the church "to this end,
that they should retain the people in true religion."[75] They were to do
this by teaching God's word. Yet, Calvin insists, they have not done
this. Rather they have taught their own ideas in place of God's word.
They are "dumb dogs."[76] They have broken the covenant established
between God and themselves.[77] In point of fact, Calvin argues that
these priests wished "to be exempt from all law, and yet to regard God
and the whole church bound to them."[78]

So far are the priests from teaching God's word that they are
described by Calvin as tyrannical. This is a commonplace in these
lectures, and Calvin applies the label to the Pope himself. "As the Pope
at this day declares that he is the vicar of Christ and the successor of
Peter, while he exercises tyranny (*tyrannidem*) over the Church."[79]
Calvin declares the same of the priests and bishops. The point which
Calvin focuses on in these lectures amounts to the notion that these
ministers of God hold the consciences of the ordinary people hostage
to their own ideas. The point is that they are not only godless and
corrupt, but they abuse their power and mistreat and enslave those
whom they are supposed to be helping. But Calvin clarifies (and in the
process, intensifies) this accusation of tyranny. The Catholic ecclesiastical authorities in France want to extinguish the gospel from the

---

[72] Tr. from the biblical text found in Calvin's lecture, CO 44: 435, 436, 437.
[73] CO 44: 435.   [74] CO 44: 434.   [75] CO 44: 434.
[76] CO 43: 131–2. See also CO 43: 127 (on Amos 7: 10–13); CO 43: 333 (on Mic. 3:
11–12); CO 37: 472 (on Jer. 1: 1–3); CO 37: 503 (on Jer. 2: 8); and CO 40: 95 (on Ezek.
3: 19).
[77] CO 44: 437.   [78] CO 44: 437.   [79] CO 38: 440 (on Jer. 23: 25).

face of the earth, he declares. He sets this down as a charge, but also seems to argue for it on the basis that the Roman Catholics realize that, as Calvin says, "their tyranny cannot stand unless the gospel be abolished."[80] To this end, Calvin avers, they will employ whatever means they require and have at their disposal.

This being the case, Calvin insists to his trainees that Catholic priests are wrong to claim the title of priests. They have, in fact, forfeited that title. "The prophet," Calvin asserts on Malachi 2: 9, "concludes that the priests in vain glorified in their office, for they had ceased to be (*desierint esse*) the priests of God."[81] Calvin is adamant on this, insisting that it is not these Catholics' title by right. Rather, it is a gift. Therefore, it is a sign of their wickedness that they claim this title while failing to do what God requires of those who hold it. Calvin emphasizes this in a number of places, including his lectures on Ezekiel 7: 26: "Let us learn from this passage, then, that the gift of prophecy and of all teaching is God's peculiar gift. Let us, also, learn that this gift is withdrawn" by God for various reasons—but it is his to give and his to withdraw.[82] Thus, as it was the priests' calling to teach God's word and they failed to do this, their claim to the title is falsified. Calvin does not subvert the teaching office (he insists), but rather merely the Catholics' claim to that office. They are prompted by Satan brashly to declare that their teaching is from God, when it actually is not.[83]

Calvin contends, therefore, that the ministers sitting under his tutelage in Geneva and about to be sent into France are raised up in order to replace the reprobate priests as the spiritual authorities of the country. This, Calvin explains, is the reason why God raises up prophets. He raises them up precisely because the priests have failed and need to be replaced (as I already alluded to in Chapter 3).[84] Calvin explains this to his charges on a number of occasions, clarifying the character of their mission and the context within which it is to be understood. Commenting on these issues on one occasion, he notes that Jeremiah was more suitable for the prophetic office because he came from the priesthood, unlike Amos or Isaiah.[85] Even here, though, Calvin clearly explains that God transferred the honor of the priests to the prophets because the former had become "dumb dogs."

---

[80] CO 43: 127 (on Amos 7: 10).   [81] CO 44: 437.   [82] CO 40: 174.
[83] CO 40: 174.   [84] See CO 39: 30 (on Jer. 32: 32).
[85] CO 37: 475 (on Jer. 1: 1–3).

When commenting on Amos 7: 10–13, he produces a humorous exchange between the "mitred bishops" and prophets who are contemporary with Calvin and his colleagues in which the bishop concedes his teaching authority to the prophets.[86] When commenting on Micah 3: 11–12, Calvin explains, once again, that the authority of teaching belonged to the priests but "through [their] idleness" and their "neglect of the teaching office," prophets were added by God. Elaborating, he explains that "in the papacy" the priestly office is exceedingly busied "with trifles and histrionics" and meanwhile Catholic priests neglect the most important thing, which is the teaching of godly doctrine. Given this, "it was necessary that prophets be raised up outside of the normal order of things (*quasi extra ordinem prophetas excitari*) while nonetheless the regular form of things remained."[87]

The force and simplicity of Calvin's paradigm would likely have impressed itself quite deeply upon Calvin's trainees. But what is also true is that Calvin's stress upon the authority of his prophets, at which we have already looked, would have communicated to them already the idea that they were raised up by God for the specific purpose of replacing the priests. Thus, the passages discussed in the previous paragraph essentially just make explicit and formal what Calvin clearly taught throughout these lectures. Calvin, therefore, trained his ministers to enter France and authoritatively declare themselves the voice of God in the country. They possessed, according to Calvin, the God-given right to pronounce divine condemnation upon the priests and upon the established ecclesiastical hierarchy within France, who were God's enemies and occupied their stations in direct violation of God's will. But this is not all; I need to say more about the callings which Calvin assigned to his trainees in regard to warfare.

TRAINING FOR WARFARE: CALVIN ON THE FRENCH MONARCHY AND CIVIL AUTHORITIES

Stepping back, one can start to see a vague sketch of some of the contours of Calvin's thinking on the character of this war and how he wanted to approach it—and how he wanted his trainees to understand

---

[86] CO 43: 131–2.   [87] CO 43: 333–4.

it. My sketch of these contours will be added to now by considering Calvin's instructions to his trainees concerning the French king and government.

The question of Calvin's attitude towards the monarchy, civil government more broadly, and a range of questions associated with this locus, including the matter of the legitimacy of active resistance, has been extensively researched. While it might be fair to say that scholarship has moved us away from some of the more conservative conclusions found in earlier works like Josef Bohatec's *Calvins Lehre von Staat und Kirche* and Marc-Edouard Chenevière's *La Pensée politique de Calvin*, it would be wrong to assert this universally.[88] Fairly conservative lines have recently been taken, for instance, by John Witte and Paul-Alexis Mellet.[89] It would also be wrong to suggest that anything like a consensus has been reached on any of these areas.

My own findings here will, broadly speaking, run along the lines laid down by scholars like Michael Walzer, Vittorio de Caprariis, Robert Kingdon, Willem Nijenhuis, Max Engammare, Carlos Eire, Philip Benedict, Denis Crouzet, and David Whitford, at least in regard to setting out a more progressive and more pragmatic Calvin.

"Calvin always had an acute sense of political realities,"[90] Kingdon rightly contends. This acute sense leads Calvin down increasingly more extreme paths. My analysis here finds a Calvin who, though oscillating back and forth on the question of armed resistance initiated by individuals,[91] is tirelessly working to find a lesser magistrate to do effectively whatever is required in order to reform France, including (I contend) initiating armed resistance. In line with this, Calvin focuses his ministerial training efforts on preparing heralds who will enter France and inculcate into those sitting in Reformed churches two things in particular: first, as I have already shown, that

---

[88] See Marc-Edouard Chenevière, *La Pensée politique de Calvin* (Paris: Éditions Je Sers, 1937), 327. See also, Josef Bohatec, *Calvins Lehre von Staat und Kirche*, (Breslau: M. & H. Marcus, 1937). Others, like Heiko Oberman and William Stephenson, adhere to conservative readings: Heiko Oberman, *John Calvin and the Reformation of the Refugees*, 72; William Stephenson, *Sovereign Grace: The Place and Significance of Christian Freedom in John Calvin's Political Thought* (New York: OUP, 1999), 32–5; not to mention Höpfl, *Christian Polity of John Calvin*, 207–17, *et passim*.

[89] Witte, *Reformation of Rights*, 39–80; Mellet, *Les Traités monarchomaques*, 58–61, 128–33, 159–62, *et passim*.

[90] Kingdon, "Calvin's Socio-Political Legacy," 119. Walzer, *Revolution of the Saints*, 57–66.

[91] Nijenhuis, "Limits of Civil Disobedience," 73–94.

he and his fellow reformed Christians are already at war with the Catholics; and second, what I will now demonstrate, that the king is so wedded to idolatry that he must be removed if the true religion is ever to flourish.

Scholars like Caprariis, Crouzet, and Benedict have usefully demonstrated Calvin's willingness to contemplate at least some kinds of active resistance against a government. Caprariis identifies this as a contradiction within Calvin's thought. He notes that Calvin claimed in his first edition of the *Institutio* that he was writing in order to demonstrate to Francis I that those pious believers whom the king had put to death were not the seditious troublemakers described by their enemies. Yet Caprariis argues that this is contradicted by other of Calvin's actions. The contradiction is nicely explained in Benedict's remarks, summarizing Caprariis: "[w]hen Calvin sent suggestions to the faithful within the country indicating to them how they could form properly ordered churches of their own, he clearly implied his willingness to see them take steps that he knew were in violation of the duly established laws, in order to obey the commandments of God."[92] This précis suggests the character of Calvin's political subversion up to, roughly, the 1550s.

But what becomes of it? The answer is that it intensifies, particularly after the watershed changes which occurred in Geneva in the summer of 1555, and that Calvin's training and sending of ministers into France represents a nice window through which to consider this intensification. My exploration of these matters begins with an observation: even with a fairly thorough knowledge of these lectures and even with a general sense of some of the bolder assertions of Calvin about the kings of France staring me in the face, it still came as a surprise to me to see, as I began to study these lectures with this specific subject in mind, just how unremittingly hostile and inflammatory Calvin was towards kings. Calvin can be found as early as 1552 declaring in his Acts commentary that "[i]f a king, or ruler, or

---

[92] Philip Benedict, "The Dynamics of Protestant Militancy: France, 1555–1563," in Philip Benedict et al. (eds), *Reformation, Revolt and Civil War in France and the Netherlands 1555–1585* (Amsterdam: Royal Netherlands Academy of Arts and Sciences, 1999), 35–50, at 39 summarizing Vittorio de Caprariis, *Propaganda e pensiero politico in Francia durante le Guerre di Religione* (Naples: Edizioni scientifiche italiane, 1959), 39. Additionally, see Denis Crouzet, "Calvinism and the Uses of the Political and the Religious (France, ca. 1560–ca. 1572)," in *Reformation, Revolt and Civil War*, 99–113.

magistrate, becomes so lofty that he diminishes the honor and authority of God, he is but a man."[93] But the assertions one finds in these lectures make this sentiment look remarkably tame by comparison. These training lectures do not merely contain strident, aggressive, hateful comments about kings and princes. They are *unrelentingly* strident, aggressive, and hateful against them. They represent a diatribe against monarchs. They are, moreover, remarkably imbalanced. One looks (almost) in vain in these lectures for a comment on the importance of kings, the fact that they are ordained by God, they are called servants of God, and so forth. One such comment exists in these lectures, which will be discussed very soon. But on the whole these lectures contain an onslaught against innumerable aspects of kings, including their morality, treatment of others, their hatred of God and of the gospel, and so forth. It is, if I may say, quite remarkable. It was, in fact, this particular characteristic of these lectures—along with his prayers, which shall be covered soon—that convinced me beyond any reasonable doubt that Calvin intended these lectures for a purpose other than merely teaching his ministerial trainees exegetical skills (as Kingdon proposed) and that the primary purpose which Calvin had in mind in them was to equip teachers who would enter into France and prepare the Huguenot churches to support war, if and when it arose.

The King's Prerogative?

Calvin believed wholeheartedly that it was appropriate for prophets to criticize all, even kings. It was, moreover, his opinion that this was one of the divinely enjoined duties of the prophet.[94] Furthermore, Calvin urged ministers to fear no one, not even a monarch, when speaking on God's behalf. This task of censuring the monarch was not easy. This was in part due to the fact that kings were, Calvin insisted, convinced that they were beyond all reproof. "[I]n the present day," Calvin complained on Amos 5: 10, "those who occupy the seats of judgment wish to be exempt from all reproofs, and would claim for themselves a free liberty in sinning, inasmuch as they think that they

---

[93] CO 48: 109 (on Acts 5: 29). I owe this quotation to Hugues Daussy, "Les Huguenots entre l'obéissance au roi et l'obéissance à Dieu," *Nouvelle Revue du XVIᵉ Siècle*, 22 (2004), 53.

[94] CO 42: 295.

do not belong to the common class of men, and imagine themselves exempt from all reprehension."[95] Yet, though not easy, Calvin ascribed innumerable qualities, from corruption, madness, greed, and arrogance to filth, wickedness, and idolatry to kings and to the king's "counselors, and their chief men," and even their wives and children.[96] He seemed to single out kings, however, as the most sinister and evil of all.

Yet before entering into his overt criticism of them, we should briefly consider how Calvin handled one of the traditional notes struck by Christian thinkers on the civil magistrate, namely, that of obedience to the magistrate as typified by Paul's words in Romans 13: 1ff. and also by 1 Peter 2: 17. Calvin does cite Paul's words on three occasions, the most significant of which appears in his lectures on Jeremiah 27: 6–7. Jeremiah's words relate to God giving many lands— Moab, Tyre, and Sidon, and others—into the hands of Nebuchadnezzar. Calvin's comment is relatively nondescript, but it represents the kindest thing he says in these lectures about kings. "There is no power, says Paul, except from God (Rom. 13: 1) and this judgment is derived from this principle, namely, that all power is from God." God, says Calvin, gives the power to govern to whom he pleases. Those endowed with the sword are God's servants, though they exercise tyranny.[97] This sentiment is, as I say, the strongest endorsement of the king that one finds in these lectures. As such it differs considerably from Calvin's only citation, in these lectures, of Peter's command: "Fear God, honor the king" (1 Peter 2: 17). This comes in his lectures on Daniel 6, in which Daniel is rescued from the lion's den after directly disobeying the king's edict not to pray. Calvin highlights the fact that these two commands (to fear God and to honor the king) must always be kept together. "Let God be feared in the first place, and earthly princes will receive their authority, if only God shines forth," is Calvin's unmistakable emphasis here.[98] Honoring civil authorities is depicted by him almost as something which the authorities must earn. And if these authorities do not recognize this or (worse) if they command things which do not allow one to honor God—as the king did in relation to Daniel—then Calvin's clear

---

[95] CO 43: 79–80 (on Amos 5: 10).   [96] CO 43: 470–1 (on Nahum 2: 11–12).
[97] CO 38: 544. See also CO 40: 663 (on Dan. 4: 17) and CO 40: 712 (on Dan. 5: 18–20).
[98] CO 41: 25.

message is that the believer must follow Daniel and disobey the ruler. More will be said on this theme later, but I wanted simply to take up and analyze these two places where Calvin cites these two *loci classici* on civil government.

Calvin's treatment of these two standard texts reminds us of the point made just a moment ago, namely, that the steady diet which he fed to his trainees in these lectures did *not* contain a fully crafted, well-rounded, balanced rehearsal of views on the magistrate, the obedience due by individuals to the monarch, the question of resistance to civil authority, and so forth. Rather, in these lectures one finds a single-minded anti-monarchical focus, which is aggressive and subversive. Calvin's scant treatment of these two standard texts, therefore, serves as a kind of barometer of his feelings and intentions. As has been noted, "[i]n the sixteenth century, Christian advocates of active resistance, including many Calvinists, had to argue their way around the obvious meaning of the Pauline injunctions in Romans 13, and the extensive tradition built upon them,, in order to make their case."[99] But Calvin's way around it was simply—at least in this venue—to ignore them.

All Monarchs are Selfish, Inhuman, and Mad

> For today, . . . nearly all kings are gross and stupid (*fatui . . . ac bruti*), such that they are like horses and *asini brutorum animalium*.[100]

By contrast, Calvin could never be accused of ignoring the morality of kings. He regularly complained in these training lectures that kings are selfish, inhuman, full of arrogance, greedy, foolish, and mad, and he loved to probe their psychology. Calvin declared at one point, "by this example, we learn that no virtue is so rare in kings as moderation."[101] He observes on Jeremiah 51: 64, "courtly princes are so devoted to themselves and to their own prudence, that they are unwilling to undertake duties which are unpopular."[102] In a lecture on Zephaniah, Calvin pontificates that "kings and others who exercise power are not easily admonished." This, he says, is due to the fact that

---

[99] Kingdon, "Calvin and Calvinists on Resistance to Government," 55.
[100] CO 41: 3 (on Dan. 6: 3–5).   [101] CO 41: 14 (on Dan. 6: 12).
[102] CO 37: 501 (on Jer. 51: 60–4).

they are blinded by the splendor of their fortune and also that "[t]hey think that they are in a certain way exempt from the law, because the station which they occupy is higher."[103] But these sentiments are mild compared with what Calvin is capable of. In comments on Habakkuk 2: 15–16, he observed that when a king wishes "to entice to himself a free city or a lesser prince, he says, 'Look, I seek nothing but to be your friend.'" Yet, Calvin insisted that in doing this, kings were accustomed to perjure themselves. Indeed, he assures his trainees that kings hide their lies for years, mocking God and all humankind in the process. Along similar lines, Calvin avers that "kings pleased themselves with their own greatness, and wish their own pleasure to be adjudged as an oracle."[104] Also: "For we know that wherever there is cunning in the world, it reigns especially in the palaces of princes"[105] Also: "great kings draw human blood and do not care at all when many people perish because of them"[106] All of these remarks, and many more, speak unmistakably to Calvin's own day. He was not merely reflecting on the character of ancient kings, but rather contemporary monarchs, and clearly, given his audience, he had the French king and princes in mind. "In these lectures we may sometimes discern an allegory of French affairs of the times,"[107] as J. T. McNeill has rightly noted.

Calvin's criticisms of the king's conduct are sufficiently scandalous to be considered by the French king as libelous and seditious. His comments on Jeremiah 22: 15 provide us with an excellent example over which to linger for a moment. He begins by simply explaining that, in the passage, Jeremiah "derides the foolish confidence of King Jehoiakim, because he set up empty things against his enemies instead of strong defences." There is nothing surprising *per se* about Calvin's exposition, which seems entirely sensible. It is what directly follows it that is of interest:

> Kings are accustomed to indulging themselves when there is leisure and security; that is, if they do not fear anything. If there is no danger, they freely indulge their own gratifications. And this is common for nearly all of them. For we see that kings especially indulge in excesses when

[103] CO 44: 16 (on Zech. 1: 7–9).   [104] CO 31: 14 (on Dan. 6: 12).
[105] CO 40: 540 (on Dan. 1: 5).   [106] CO 43: 554 (on Hab. 2: 15–16).
[107] John T. McNeill, "Editor's Introduction," in *Calvin; On God and Political Duty* (New York: Macmillan Publishing Co., 1950), p. xx.

there is no war (*ubi nullum . . . bellum*), when no one troubles them, and no one threatens them.[108]

What appears here is indicative of Calvin's custom when speaking about kings, namely, that he immediately moves from the text to comment on "kings" and applies to them negative qualities found in the biblical text, to which he adds others. Continuing his exposition of Jeremiah 22: 15, he enters into a discussion of several alternative interpretations of the passage. Explaining and briefly rebutting each of them (in material which fills approximately one column of the *Calvini Opera*), he then returns to his favored reading of the text. All can see, then, Calvin reiterates, Jehoiakim's foolish ambition which Jeremiah mocks, "for he seemed not to believe himself to be a king unless he were behaving like a madman (*insaniret*)." This summary prompts Calvin to return to his invective against contemporary kings.

As today kings are ashamed to appear humane (*humanum*), and turn all their labors towards exercising tyranny (*tyrannidem*); and they also contrive how they might separate themselves as far as they possible can from the common usage and practice of all (*ab usu communi et vita hominum*).[109]

Thus, Calvin concludes, since kings are like this, it is right and proper that Jeremiah should inveigh against Jehoiakim in the way that he does.

Numerous assertions from Calvin heap abuse on kings, but the example which we have just considered does an especially good job of revealing not only the character of Calvin's teaching on the king but also something about Calvin himself and, by extension, something about what he wanted to achieve through his discussions of kings in these lectures. For this example exposes the deliberateness, even eagerness, which possessed Calvin here. He appears to be pleased to find an opportunity to excoriate kings. He does not, it would seem, want to risk the possibility that these trainees might miss the point that kings are disgustingly indulgent to the point of being embarrassed even to appear as human like the rest of those who inhabit Europe. These sorts of sentiments, one might muse, were intended to do to the current king of France (who by the time Calvin was lecturing on Jeremiah was Charles IX, supported by Catherine de' Medici) what Jeremiah intended to do to Jehoiakim. And yet, whether that be true or not, it seems to me impossible not to draw the conclusion that Calvin wanted to teach his trainees to detest the king of France, to be disgusted by him and his extravagance. This thought will be kept in mind as we continue.

Calvin's "Seditious" Prophets: Monarchs are Tyrannical and Enemies of Christ's Gospel

Calvin instructed his trainees that kings were idolatrous and tyrannical—the just-cited passage from Calvin's lecture on Jeremiah 22: 15 identifies the latter, of course, but these Calvinian accusations need to be examined more thoroughly.

As this analysis commences, it is worth taking a moment to remind ourselves of what was thought about Calvin and his co-religionists by the French Catholics. Barbara Diefendorf's observation may be cited on this point. "We must remember that the 'Lutheran heresy' was not for sixteenth-century Parisians a mere failure of religious orthodoxy; it was a threat to the social order and a danger to the entire community. The Protestants were believed not only to be religious deviants, but also immoral and seditious."[110] As we proceed, this observation will find substantial confirmation. For, in these lectures, Calvin *does* sound seditious; indeed, it is virtually impossible to understand him in any other way so far as the voice of Calvin heard in these orations is concerned. For if the idea of sedition includes within it using language which aims to incite individuals against the authority of a government, then Calvin is seditious. I readily concede that he would not have considered himself to be seditious or guilty of treason. I also concede that Calvin's voice was not the most radical voice addressing the Huguenots. For Viret, Farel, and others were much more vociferous in encouraging open rebellion. All of this I grant. But even granting it, it appears that the opinion of the French Catholics (as registered by Diefendorf) is accurate.

In point of fact, Calvin himself acknowledges, after a certain fashion, the veracity of Diefendorf's reading. When commenting on Amos 7: 10 ("the land is not able to bear all his words"), Calvin observes that two possible interpretations exist on this passage. The first relates to the people who, being offended by the "turbulent doctrine" of the prophet, would complain. They, says Calvin, will

[110] Diefendorf, *Beneath the Cross*, 54.

"hate and detest the Prophet Amos, as a seditious man (*seditiosum*)."
Continuing, Calvin puts these words into the mouths of the French
people. Kings, he says, are "in our day" stirred on by the people in this
manner:

> Why do you delay? For your subjects desire nothing more than that you
> extinguish this evil, and all of them will eagerly assist you. You are in the
> meantime inactive, and your people complain of your delay.[111]

The people think, Calvin explains, the princes are unworthy of
holding their positions, since they allow the ancient rites and ordin-
ances of holy Mother Church to fall into decay. The other possible
meaning of the text which Calvin offers is equally enlightening. Here
he attributes the words of the text to Amaziah the priest of Bethel,
who (in effect) represents the authorities. Amaziah, Calvin explains,
worries that if Amos continues freely to raise tumults, "the whole
kingdom will be on the verge of ruin, for many will follow him."
Calvin elaborates further on Amaziah's fear: "when an open sedition
arises, it cannot be checked without great difficulty. We must therefore hurry, lest Amos should get the upper hand; for there is already
the greatest danger."[112] Both interpretations are intriguing and say an
enormous amount about how Calvin understands his trainees' callings and also about how Calvin perceives the Catholics and authorities with whom his trainees would soon be interacting.

A glance at Calvin's attitude towards kings as expressed in these
lectures confirms this interpretation of him as seditious after the
fashion of Amos. It may be seen that he describes kings to his trainees
as tyrannical, idolatrous, anti-Christian, and Satanic. One of his
milder characterizations of kings' attitudes towards God and the
true religion is seen in comments on Ezekiel 4: 4–8. There he explains
that kings have no other desire than to strengthen their own power.
To this end, Calvin explains that kings pretend, even boast, that they
seek God's glory. "Yet," he contends, "their religion is only a delu-
sion." As long as they keep the people in obedience to them, "whatever kind of worship, and whatever mode of worshipping God, is the
same to them."[113] Likewise, Calvin can slander kings as exercising
their authority solely so that they may remain "in their filth." For this
reason they are "indifferent as to any kind of abomination." The only

---

[111] CO 43: 128.   [112] CO 43: 128.   [113] CO 40: 108 (on Ezek. 4: 4–8).

thing they fear, he explains, is that "any innovation among the common people should take occasion" to arouse them. Therefore, they defend superstitions "with a diabolical pertinacity."[114] Again, Calvin can paint a scenario for his trainees in which someone expresses thanks to God (when speaking to the king) on behalf of one of the king's recent achievements, only to see the king yell violently at the individual, insisting instead that all the praise should go to the king himself.[115] Thus, a general, and extremely intense, antagonism appears in Calvin's analysis.

But in other places Calvin's description is even sharper. There is a rage against truth which Calvin ascribes to kings. We see, first, that Calvin knows, and scoffs at, the idea "that kings, and those in authority, wish to be deemed sacred."[116] Alluding to what I have already discussed, Calvin is fully aware that kings believe themselves to be a special class and sons of God. But to him, this clearly testifies to something sinister. Elaborating, Calvin explains that kings believe themselves beyond reproof, even in relation to teachers sent by God. "Kings and those who occupy the seats of judgment wish to be sacrosanct," and would like to be able to sin freely. In short, Calvin says, kings do not consider themselves to belong to the common class of human beings and "would like to rule without equity, because power is, for them, nothing except unbridled licentiousness (*effraenis licentia*)."[117] This wish, however, does not only exhibit itself in kings possessing an attitude of indifference towards religion. Rather, it exhibits itself in kings raging against God and God's church. "If we enquire," Calvin says on Zechariah 1: 18, "about the condition of the whole world today, we shall find that there is almost no city or people or monarch, or even one of the least princes, whose rage is not exhibited against the church."[118] Kings hate God, Calvin tells his trainees. "If someone were able to enter into the hearts of kings," Calvin insists, "it would be difficult for them to find scarcely one in a hundred who did not despise everything divine." And once again, lest he miss the opportunity, Calvin adds to this sentiment the fact that kings, of course, would never admit to this. They lie about it habitually. They confess themselves, Calvin says, "to enjoy their thrones on account of the grace of God." Yet "they want to be adored in [God's]

[114] CO 44: 349 (on Zech. 13: 4).   [115] CO 43: 516 (on Hab. 1: 16).
[116] CO 43: 79–80 (on Amos 5: 10).   [117] CO 43: 79–80 (on Amos 5: 10).
[118] CO 44: 151 (on Zech. 1: 18).

stead."[119] Thus. Calvin's own animosity is again on show here. Having hurled his sharpest arrows at kings, he is not satisfied but twists the knife one more time—all of this being set out before his ministerial trainees.

Additionally, Calvin seeks to explain to these trainees that there is a kind of method to the kings' madness. He teaches them that kings desire to extinguish the gospel not only because they hate it, but also because they want to keep hold of their own absolute, tyrannical rule and they know they cannot do that unless they extinguish true religion. Not only the Pope, cardinals, and bishops, but also kings are of the belief that "their tyranny cannot stand unless the gospel is abolished."[120] Kings believe, Calvin insists, that they must crush the bringers of the gospel if they are to continue to hold their positions of power. Kings, of course, never speak this way. Kings, as Calvin makes clear, claim to be the defenders of the gospel and the servants of God. Calvin mocks this claim and calls them tyrants and idolaters. He notes that Darius' example (in relation to Daniel in the lion's den) will condemn all those kings who profess themselves to be "catholic kings, or Christians, or defenders of the faith (*protectores fidei*)," mocking (it would appear) the French kings who profess this very thing. These kings do not only bury true piety but also "would willingly extinguish [God's] name from the world." They exercise tyranny over all the pious and establish impious superstitions through their own cruelty. "Darius will be a fit judge for them."[121]

Kings, therefore, Calvin would have his trainees believe, are the civil arm of Romanist idolatry. They seek through their power to abolish the true religion from the earth and are, in this way, like the Israelite kings, whom the prophets attacked so severely. This being so, Calvin is keen to equate every aspect of Roman Catholic worship with the corrupt worship of Israel so roundly condemned by the prophets. He characterizes the Israelite idolatry as the forerunner of Catholic worship, describing both as employing vain ceremonies (*inanibus caeremoniis*) and frivolous puerilities (*frivolis nugis*), being deluded by their own vain imaginations (*suis figmentis*),[122] having recourse to patrons (*patronos*) and mediators (*intermedios*) and worshiping Baal.[123] This, Calvin teaches his trainees, is the religion the king seeks to defend. Functioning behind all of Calvin's language about the

[119] CO 41: 7 (on Dan. 6: 6–7). [120] CO 43: 127 (on Amos 7: 10–13).
[121] CO 41: 30 (on Dan. 6: 25–7). [122] CO 43: 286. [123] CO 42: 235.

king's tyranny and idolatrous longing to abolish the gospel is his deep conviction that true and false worship are so fundamentally incompatible that they are utterly and mutually exclusive.

> Nor is it possible to join together true religion and idolatry. As long, then, as you remain fixed in that false worship to which you have accustomed yourselves, you continue alienated from God.[124]

Therefore, Calvin wishes to inculcate into his trainees that, when the king is striving to support Roman idolatry, he is simultaneously seeking to wipe out all truth.

Having said all this, Calvin turns his rhetoric up a notch higher, declaring explicitly what had, thus far, been left as an implication. He insists that "all earthly power not founded upon Christ must fall."[125] This assertion appears in his dedicatory epistle to his Daniel lectures. Dedicated to "all the pious worshipers of God who desire the kingdom of Christ to be rightly established in France," the missive is dated 19 August 1561. In the letter, Calvin also declares, clearly in reference to the current situation, that "those kings whose sway is most extended shall feel by sorrowful experience how horrible a judgment will fall upon them unless they willingly submit themselves to the power of Christ." His dedication is full of such warnings. One also finds him declaring here that God threatens "speedy destruction" on all kingdoms which obscure Christ's glory by extending themselves too much. The letter, in fact, contains a long invective clearly directed against the king of France which resonates with this same sober tone. A lengthy portion of it follows.

> Moreover, those kings whose domination is the widest, unless they submit themselves to Christ's authority (*imperio*), shall feel by painful experience how horrible a judgment will fall on them. Now, what is less tolerable than to deprive [Christ] of his right, by whose protection their reputation remains secure? For we see how few of kings receive the Son of God; in fact, we see how they move every stone and try every possible means to prevent his entering their lands. Many of their Councilors studiously employ all their industry and influence in order to close every avenue to him. Meanwhile, they set forth the name of Christianity and boast that they are the greatest defenders of the Catholic Faith, although their empty vanity is easily refuted, if people hold the true and

---

[124] CO 43: 73 (on Amos 5: 4–6).
[125] Calvin, *Praelectiones ioannis calvini in librum prophetiarum danielis*, *iii^v.

authentic definition of Christ's kingdom. For his throne or his scepter is nothing but the doctrine of the Evangel, nor does his majesty shine anywhere else or his empire (*imperium*) exist except where all from the greatest to the least hear his voice with the calm docility like sheep, and follow him wherever he calls them. But these kings not only completely reject this doctrine, in which true religion and the lawful worship of God is contained and in which the eternal salvation of humankind and true happiness consists, but with threats and terrors, with the sword and with fire, they also drive it far away from them. They do not omit any work of violence from their efforts to exterminate it.[126]

The sense of prophetic ultimatum here is palpable. Calvin continues in this vein, remarking, in particular, that monarchs think themselves reduced to the level of commoners if they lower "their ensigns of royalty to the Supreme king." In another portion of this dedicatory letter, Calvin returns to pronounce a closing threat to earthly powers. "Let us suppose that all the infernal regions were to offer us battle with all their strength, would God sit by in heaven leisurely and desert and betray his own cause? Moreover, when he had entered into the conflict, would anything—whether it were the crafty cunning of humankind or their furious attacks—deprive him of victory?"[127] The first of the French civil wars would commence in approximately six months from the date of this epistle.[128]

---

[126] Calvin, *Praelectiones ioannis calvini in librum prophetiarum danielis*, *iii^v^–*iv^r^.

[127] Calvin, *Praelectiones ioannis calvini in librum prophetiarum danielis*, *v^r^. There were radical voices in France who were calling for violence in a clear and unambiguous manner. Calvin may come closest to their cadences here in this dedicatory epistle (though this honor might also belong to his sermons from this late period). Again, Nijenhuis, "Limits of Civil Disobedience," 73–94, and Engammare, "Calvin monarchomaque? Du soupçon à l'argument," 207–26.

[128] I might again raise the issue of the scholarly discussion of the question of Calvin's relationship to monarchomaque theory, which is inconclusive at present. Paul-Alexis Mellet, who treats this question in his *Les Traités monarchomaques (1560–1600)*, seems far less inclined to see Calvin as, in any way, similar to the monarchomaque theorists than someone like Engammare. (See Engammare, "Calvin monarchomaque? Du soupçon à l'argument," 207–26; Mellet, *Les Traités monarchomaques*, 58–61; see also 128–33, 159–62, *et passim*). Others have also touched on the idea. Interestingly, Cornel Zwierlein comments: "Si Calvin est monarchomaque, il l'est dans la ligne de son maître Bucer" (Cornel Zwierlein, "La Loi de Dieu et L'Obligation à la Défense: De Florence à Magdeburg 1494–1550," in *Et de sa bouche sortait un glaive: Les Monarchomaques au XVIe siècle* (Geneva: Droz, 2006), 73). It is not clear from Zwierlein's remarks, which continue for a brief paragraph, whether he thinks Calvin could plausibly be linked with the monarchomaques. For more, see the other essays found in *Et de sa bouche sortait un glaive* and also Paul-Alexis Mellet, "'Le Roy des

WARFARE AND PRAYER: ENTREATING
THE LORD OF HOSTS FOR VICTORY
OVER THE GODLESS ENEMY

With his prayers—with which he concluded each of his lectures on
the prophets, covering a period of almost ten years—Calvin sought
the support of God for himself, his ministerial charges, and the pious
remnant in France for the warfare in which they were engaged. These
prayers are not collected in the *Calvini Opera*, which is why I have
referred to them by means of older versions of the lectures. The
editors of the *Calvini Opera* did, however, include some of the
original prefatory material, and specifically *Ioannes Budaeus Christianis Lecturibus S.* in which one finds comments on these prayers. In
particular, there is reference to the fact that the prayers with which
Calvin ended each of his lectures were taken down by the team of
stenographers (Budé, des Gallars, etc), to which I referred earlier, with
the same care and diligence as the lectures.[129] Furthermore, a remark
is made that, while Calvin always began these lectures with the same
opening prayer, he always concluded with a new prayer, given by
God's Spirit and accommodated to the subject of the lecture.[130]

While these prayers of Calvin touch on a wide range of topics (as
one would expect), they are nonetheless full of requests related to war;
indeed requests that refer patently to waging a military campaign
which, while spiritual in nature, is also unmistakably temporal; i.e. it
finds an expression in armed conflict. But a fuller explanation must
accompany this observation.

From his lectures on Hosea, which is to say, from as early as 1556,
he prays about warfare, referring to "war," the notion of "fighting
under the cross," "under your banner," and "under your command."
He prays, for example, at the end of a lecture on Zechariah 9: 12
that "today" they would not look for a redeemer to save them from
their miseries but that they "would carry on warfare under his
cross (*tantum militamus sub cruce eius*)."[131] Similarly, in his prayer
following his lecture on Jonah 1: 13–17, he requests that they

mouches à miel...': Tyrannie présente et royauté parfaite dans les traité monarchomaques," *Archiv für Reformationsgeschichte*, 93 (2002), 71–96.

[129] CO 42; Prolegomena [unnumbered].
[130] CO 42; Prolegomena [unnumbered].
[131] Calvin, *Praelectiones in duodecim Prophetas minores*, 677.

learn to subject their thoughts to God, have regard to God's will, and undertake nothing except what he approves, "so that we may fight under your command (*sub tuis auspiciis*)".[132] He also, incidentally, uses these phrases in the body of the lectures themselves—as when he declares (when treating Hosea 9: 17), "[w]e may then lawfully reprove the papists, and say that God is opposed to them, for we fight under his banner"—but such phrases were more common in his prayers. Noteworthy here is the fact that the above-cited examples come from lectures delivered prior to 1559. We know from a letter from Nicholas Colladon that Calvin was completing the Malachi lectures (and hence, the series on the Minor Prophets) in September 1558.[133]

Calvin also refers in these prayers to strife, conflict, assaults, violence, and the like. He asked in a prayer at the end of his lecture on Daniel 3: 8–18: "When we have learned what worship pleases you, may we constantly persist to the end and never be moved by any threats, or dangers, or violence,..."[134] He prays at the end of his twenty-seventh lecture on Daniel a prayer which includes the sentiment that "we may proceed under the protection of your support against the malice of humankind; and that whenever Satan besieges us from every side and the wicked lay traps for us and we are attacked by the fierceness of wild beasts, may we remain under your protection, and even if we must endure one hundred deaths, may we learn to live and die to you."[135] Likewise, he describes his remnant church as "in danger every day and every moment, not only from the threat of a single raging tyrant, but from the devil who arouses the whole world against us, arming this world's princes and impelling them to destroy us."[136] After his last lecture on the prophet Joel, he asks God to grant to them that they would "persevere in this contest" as they have "in this world, to fight continually, not only with one kind of enemy but with innumerable enemies and not only with flesh and blood but also with the devil, the prince of darkness."[137] He prays at the end of a lecture on Zephaniah 2: 15:

---

[132] Calvin, *Praelectiones in duodecim Prophetas minores*, 344.
[133] CO 21: 88; I owe knowledge of this reference to de Greef, *Writings of John Calvin*, 91.
[134] Calvin, *Praelectiones ioannis calvini in librum prophetiarum danielis*, 36^v–37^r.
[135] Calvin, *Praelectiones ioannis calvini in librum prophetiarum danielis*, 71^v.
[136] Calvin, *Praelectiones ioannis calvini in librum prophetiarum danielis*, 16^r.
[137] Calvin, *Praelectiones in duodecim Prophetas minores*, 222.

Grant, almighty God, as you test us in the warfare of the cross (*sub militia crucis*) and arouse the most powerful enemies whose ferociousness might justly terrify and greatly alarm us if we did not depend on your aid—grant, that we may call to mind how wonderfully you delivered your chosen people in the past (*olim*), and how promptly you brought them help, when they were oppressed and completely overwhelmed, so that we may learn today to flee to your protection, and not to doubt that when you show your favor to us, there is in you sufficient power to preserve us and to overthrow our enemies (*hostes nostros*), no matter how much they may now exult and think that they triumph above the heavens, in order that they may, ultimately, understand by experience that they are earthly and frail, whose life and condition is like the mist which soon vanishes; and may we learn to long for that blessed eternity, which is laid up for us in heaven by Christ our Lord. Amen.[138]

Quoting a full prayer provides us with an opportunity to glimpse in a richer way how Calvin addresses warfare in these prayers—again, all of the just-cited prayers were prayed prior to the Massacre of Vassy.

As the question of meaning is delved into, we should notice two senses of continuity in these prayers. The first relates to the character of war as referred to by Calvin. Examining these prayers, it becomes clear that Calvin does *not* only have spiritual warfare in mind. Though he unmistakably *does* have spiritual warfare in mind, he also conceives of it as possessing a temporal aspect. He and the Huguenots, as I have already said in this monograph, have an Old Testament perspective—an assertion which garners support from the work of Kingdon, Davis, Jouanna, Benedict, and Parker.[139] This perspective dominates his approach to war in these lectures, and it can be seen particularly clearly in these prayers. It is anchored in the covenant bond which, according Calvin, links the *Églises Réformées de France* with the old covenant remnant. So even prior to the commencement of hostilities in March 1562, his prayers reflect the belief that God would support God's people in such hostilities; that God would fight for his people and God's people would fight. The above quotations should make this sufficiently clear, but, unsurprisingly, it becomes clearer when the prayers after the initiation of armed hostilities are examined.

[138] Calvin, *Praelectiones in duodecim Prophetas minores*, 554.
[139] Kingdon, *Geneva and the Coming of the Wars*, 110–13; Davis, "Rites of Violence," 51–91; Jouanna *et al.*, *Histoire et dictionnaire*, 205–12; Benedict, "Prophets in Arms?," 163–96; and Parker, "French Calvinists as the Children of Israel," 227–36.

Once military conflict commences, Calvin betrays an intensity which is striking and is focused squarely upon waging war. Calvin's prayers after the beginning of hostilities cover a range of relevant interests. The following entreaty comes at the end of his lecture on Jeremiah 51: 32.

> Grant, almighty God, as of old (*olim*) you testified your favor towards your Church by not sparing the greatest Monarchies (*tantae Monarchiae*), that we today also might know you to be the same (*eundem*) towards all your faithful people who call upon you. And because the power and cruelty of our enemies are so great, raise up your hand against them, and show that you are the perpetual defender of your Church, so that we may have reason to give glory to your goodness through Christ Jesus our Lord, Amen.[140]

For God to be the defender of the church is plainly for God to fight and win the battle for the Huguenots after the manner of, *inter alia*, Psalm 18 (the issue of the imprecatory prayers will be briefly touched on below). Here the idea of tyrannicide is explicitly addressed, with God's past actions in relation to a tyrannical monarch being recalled as a way to plead to him to behave in the same manner in this present contest. Here Calvin's God is a God of war, who will crush the church's enemies now, just as in the days of Moses, David, or Elijah. Calvin could declare, in direct relationship to the military conflict in which the Huguenots were engaged, that "Satan . . . [is] . . . the captain of our enemies."[141] And he could also, in the very next prayer, pray that their enemies would be confounded just as God used to confound the enemies of his people, Israel.

> Grant almighty God, that since you were formerly (*olim*) so solicitous concerning the salvation of your people that you undertook war for their sake (*bellum eius causa susceperis*) against the most powerful nation, that we today may also know that we will be safe and secure under the protection (*praesidio*) of your hand, and that our enemies will be confounded . . .[142]

The sense of covenantal continuity is profound (a point which is also true of the earlier-cited prayer from Calvin's lectures on Zephaniah 2).

---

[140] Calvin, *Praelectiones in Librum prophetiarum Ieremiae, et Lamentationes* . . . (Geneva: apud I. Crispinum, 1563), 387ʳ.

[141] Calvin, *Praelectiones in Librum prophetiarum Ieremiae, et Lamentationes*, 376ᵛ.

[142] Calvin, *Praelectiones in Librum prophetiarum Ieremiae, et Lamentationes*, 382ᵛ.

For Calvin, the earnest desire of all pious, godly hearts must be trained on the aspiration that the ungodly "papists" be destroyed by the God who was the captain and defender of his church.

> Grant almighty God, that since you formerly (*olim*) exercised your wonderful power in order to help your miserably afflicted people, that today you would manifest the same power towards us; and that you would manifest the same proof of your grace and paternal favor, by raising up your awful hand to destroy all the impious (*ad perdendos omnes impios*) who cruelly oppress your innocent people, in order that having been freed from your hand, we may learn always to give thanks to you...[143]

Calvin's prayers in these lectures are saturated with this notion of covenantal continuity, pleading with God to do in war for the Huguenots what God had done in war for Old Testament Israel.

An additional sense of continuity must be seen as well. This concerns the continuity which characterizes Calvin's prayers before and after armed hostilities have commenced. While Calvin's prayers do, naturally, become more intensely focused on war after the commencement of hostilities, it is crucial to understand that no changes appear in these prayers which find Calvin moving from a non-war mentality to a war mentality. Indeed, one reading through these prayers (or, presumably, one hearing them prayed each week at the conclusion of Calvin's lectures) does not notice a jarring shift in their character with the commencement of war. Rather, there is a seamlessness to the transition; a seamlessness which bespeaks continuity. It is precisely as if Calvin's thinking were: "We have been at war with the papists for years. This war has now taken on a temporal dimension with the commencement of armed hostilities. But it is still the same war. It is a war which will only end once France has become Protestant at all levels of society."

The litmus test of what I am observing is whether the reader can determine which one of his prayers was the first to be prayed following the commencement of the first War of Religion in the spring of 1562. I could not determine this. In point of fact, even before hostilities began, Calvin's prayers sounded the note of war so distinctly that one would think they were already engaged in military conflict. At the end of lecture 60 on Daniel, Calvin prays:

---

[143] Calvin, *Praelectiones in Librum prophetiarum Ieremiae, et Lamentationes*, 380ᵛ.

Grant almighty God, that, having been instructed by your Spirit and also armed by your sacred teaching, we may not only wage war bravely with our open enemies and with those who plainly oppose true religion but also constantly despise all our domestic enemies and apostates, and resist them manfully, and never feel disturbed, even if various troubles should arise against your Church....[144]

Here he speaks not merely of being in danger or exercised by trials but of waging war bravely against a variety of different foes. This was prayed probably a year before Louis of Condé's marshaling of his troops in response to the Massacre of Vassy.[145]

This sense of continuity points to the fact that Calvin's discussions of war, conflicts, fighting, aggression, and the like in both these prayers and in the body of his lectures is not of the character of a response to an interruption. His talk of war is not a reaction to the fact that hostilities had intruded upon their lives and therefore now had to be dealt with. In fact, the presence of this continuity quashes the possibility of such a reading of these lectures. The fact is Calvin was mentioning war, speaking of the Roman Catholics as the "enemy," identifying the monarch as a tyrant and threat, and referring to fighting under the banner of Christ in his prayers five years before the first of the Wars of Religion.

So, then, through his prayers as well, Calvin sought to inculcate into his ministerial trainees lessons related to this war; to prepare them for war and to ensure that, upon their entry into France, they would work to prepare their congregations for war and, specifically armed conflict, if, and when, the opportunity presented itself—remembering of course that Calvin was, all the while, laboring tirelessly to find a lesser magistrate who would commit himself to supporting the French Reformed witness, even if it meant initiating a coup. Though not related to these training lectures, I might also briefly mention Calvin's preoccupation with the singing of Psalms—which were employed by the Huguenots in battle and were referred to

---

[144] Calvin, *Praelectiones ioannis calvini in librum prophetiarum danielis*, 155[r].
[145] From 1563 onwards, his prayers appear to me to be occupied with the language of fear and personal sinfulness. The imprecatory character of his prayers, particularly from 1560 through 1562, is no longer present. It would be hasty to draw conclusions from this observation alone. One example of what I have found appears at the end of his lecture on Ezek. 13: 16. Calvin, *Ioannis Calvini in Viginti prima Ezechielis prophetae capita praelectiones...* (Geneva: ex officina Francisci Perrini, 1565), 222[v].

by Calvin as a "form of public prayers."[146] The first Genevan Psalter appeared in 1562, having been worked on by Clément Marot and (from 1548 onwards) Theodore Beza. It is recorded that the Huguenot armies sang Psalm 68, "Let God arise, let the enemies be scattered," and other imprecatory Psalms before battles and when advancing into combat.[147] Though I do not have the time here to delve more fully into this aspect of Calvin's labors, it would appear that the Psalter fits in with the themes with which Chapters 4 and 5 have been occupied. The question of his views on imprecatory prayer cannot be entered into more deeply here either.[148] Suffice it to say that he plainly deemed the remnant church to be in such dire straits that it was legitimate for him, and for the church, to cry out to God for God's defense, as Moses, Joshua, or David had done in times past (*olim*).

CALVIN'S LECTURES AS WAR PREPARATIONS

In these lectures, Calvin treats the subject of war as a present reality. This he does from as early as 1556. He mentions the Roman Catholics throughout these lectures and consistently labels them as the enemy. They are reprobated by God and idolaters. Their head in the ecclesiastical realm, the Pope, is the Antichrist, and in the civil realm, the king, is a godless tyrant; and the remnant church in France finds themselves at war with them.

Both civil and ecclesiastical realms are subjected to merciless criticism by Calvin, who strives to fill his trainees with the undoubted conviction that the authorities which currently rule France are controlled by the devil. In regard to the civil realm in particular, Calvin

---

[146] *Correspondance des réformateurs dans les pays de langue française*, ed. A. L. Herminjard (Nieuwkoop: Graaf, 1965), iv. 155 as cited in W. Stanford Reid, "The Battle Hymns of the Lord; Calvinist Psalmody of the Sixteenth Century," *Sixteenth Century Journal*, 2/1 (1970), 36–54, esp. 38.

[147] Reid, "Battle Hymns of the Lord," 47.

[148] See Mbunga Mpindi, "Calvin's Hermeneutics of the Imprecations of the Psalter" (Ph.D. thesis, Calvin Theological Seminary, 2004), esp. 100–231; John Thompson, *Reading the Bible with the Dead: What you Can Learn from the History of Exegesis that you Can't Learn from Exegesis Alone* (Grand Rapids, Mich.: Eerdmans, 2007), 49–70 and 237–41.

frequently reiterates in his tutelage of these ministers the idea that kings are inherently evil, and should be opposed as ungodly and Satanic. Calvin plies his trainees with arguments ranging from the lavish lifestyle that kings lead to the fact that they wish to be deemed divine and to extinguish the gospel from the face of the earth. He describes them as inhuman, corrupt, and essentially evil. But most importantly, they are idolaters and sanctioners of idolatry.

In addition to describing the enemy, he prays about them. Calvin prays from 1556 onwards for God's help for the ongoing war in which the remnant church is engaged. This war, as we have seen, seems to have been oriented according to an Old Testament conceptualization of war, such that it included armed conflict. War was approached by Calvin in a positive manner, in the way Samuel or David might have approached it. Calvin never articulates a "just war" argument for his trainees, though he does explain that the king was idolatrous and the Roman church within the country was as well, and, therefore, it was right that they be overthrown as they were wicked and had relinquished their God-given authority. Furthermore, Calvin had, from 1536, propounded the position that a lesser magistrate was not only in the right, but in fact duty-bound, to strive to protect the people from a tyrannical king.[149] Calvin used these lectures, then, in concert with his other efforts, to prepare ministers for France and to prepare the Huguenots to support the initiative of a Prince of the Blood, when one was found. Although the reformer labored strenuously with Antoine of Navarre, it ended up being Louis of Condé who "organized an open revolt against royal authority, seized the city of Orleans as his headquarters, and asked Protestants throughout France to send troops to his support."[150]

In a sense, Calvin's orchestrating of affairs in these lectures represents a remarkable balancing act. First, he wants to instruct his ministers to be convinced that they were already at war and, thus, convinced of the legitimacy of a revolt against the crown, so that the lesser magistrate, when he arises, will have the ground prepared in France; that is, he will have Huguenots ready to join the fight. (Incidentally, Huguenot paramilitary units existed from as early as 1558. Calvin makes no mention of them either positively or negatively in these lectures, but it seems to me impossible that he did not know

---

[149] CO 1: 248 (from 1536 *Institutio*) which appears in *Institutio* 4.20.31 of 1559.
[150] Kingdon, "Calvin's Socio-Political Legacy," 118.

of their existence.) Second, Calvin does *not* want his trainees or their congregations to become so zealous that they take matters into their own hands and initiate armed resistance by themselves. Yet, third, he needed to keep the anti-idolatry zeal of these ministers high, lest his ministerial trainees succumb to fear or, worse, to the arguments of Nicodemite groups who were still active within France. Thus, Calvin (presumably) had to work to strike the right balance. It is worth emphasizing at this point that I am not insisting that Calvin had his heart set upon an armed revolt from early 1556. Rather, I am arguing that he contemplated war at that time (along, presumably, with other options, like Antoine having an opportunity to muscle his way into contention for the throne without the need for revolt) and that, as each year passed, the tensions increased in France, his approaches to Antoine became more and more desperate, and he contemplated armed conflict more seriously. Thus, the balance which he had to strike may, arguably, have changed over time.

One can find examples, particularly after 1561, when he may have failed to strike that balance. Consequently, his ministers and individual evangelicals overstepped their bounds in this way, infuriating Calvin.[151] In point of fact, it is fascinating to note what we find in Kingdon's classic study. There, he records that ministers associated with Geneva, such as Jacques Ruffy, Augustin Marlorat, and Martin Tachard, were linked with some of the violence which arose within France in the late 1550s and early 1560s. Marlorat, for instance, "was accused of preaching war," a charge to which he replied by declaring "that if [I] preached war, it was as [I] learned it in the word of God."[152] On these men, Kingdon writes: "While these shreds of evidence are not conclusive and while there is nothing to tie these inciting activities directly to Geneva, it is clear that in some areas Calvin's envoys were responsible for stimulating war fervor."[153] Despite conceding that it is impossible conclusively to tie this violence to Geneva, Kingdon reiterates the fact that all three of these men "had been carefully trained and were highly regarded by Geneva."[154]

---

[151] Kingdon, *Geneva and the Consolidation of the French Protestant Movement*, 149–98.

[152] Kingdon, *Geneva and the Coming of the Wars*, 111. The report which records his answer is in the third person. I replaced "he" with "I" because it reads better in my paragraph.

[153] Kingdon, *Geneva and the Coming of the Wars*, 111.

[154] Kingdon, *Geneva and the Coming of the Wars*, 111.

I would suggest, however, that my analysis of Calvin's training lectures provides strong evidence linking these Genevan-trained ministers to this violence for, as I have shown, Calvin put the idea of war into their heads. Although it is impossible to say with absolute certainty that Calvin's training lectures are to blame, it would be difficult to imagine that those lectures would *not* inflame some of the ministers to incite acts of aggression. For these training lectures are nothing if not inflammatory.

THE PROPHET AND HIS HOLY WAR

In this chapter, a portion of Calvin's prophetic labors have been examined under a microscope. Specifically, I probed his training of ministers to be sent into France in the late 1550s and into the 1560s until his death. Some, at this point, might mention, by way of objection, Calvin's habit of dismissing the many plots that were hatched to topple the French monarch and also his continual efforts to quell private attempts at rioting, iconoclasm, church seizures, and the like, both being evidence of his conservatism and, thus, contradicting the claims of this chapter. (Indeed, Höpfl goes so far as to say that Calvin instructed churches to refrain from preaching when it was forbidden by the local authorities.[155]) But, on the first of these, while he did dismiss many of these plots as ill-conceived and, in fact, ultimately dismissed the most infamous of them, the Amboise Conspiracy proposed by La Renaudie, yet his opposition was not, and could not have been, a principled one. Rather, he apparently thought the conspiracy was ill-conceived and doomed to failure. On this conspiracy, we know that Calvin remarked that he would have supported the scheme if it had been led by the man "who ought to be chief of the Council of the King according to the laws of France," or in other words, Antoine of Navarre or Louis of Condé, Antoine's

---

[155] Höpfl, *Christian Polity of John Calvin*, 210. He cites letters 3185 and 3188 to support his point, neither of which seems to the present author to carry us towards the conclusion Höpfl asserts in the body of his text, namely, "Calvin counselled submission." Meanwhile he overlooks letters in which Calvin mentions churches having "secret meetings (*secreti conventus*)" (CO 17: 311–12).

brother.[156] We also know that Calvin was involved himself in such plotting. As Dufour has shown, in the summer of 1560 Calvin and Beza were engaged in trying to raise money for troops which they would put at the disposal of Antoine if he were willing to use them for the good of the Huguenot cause.[157] Thus, his could not have been a principled opposition, but rather a pragmatic one. And on the second point, although Calvin sought to quell riots, iconoclasm, and vandalism,[158] this, again, could surely have been for practical reasons. Here I concur entirely with Kingdon, who asserts that Calvin's objecting to such behavior was a sign not of his conservatism but of his pragmaticism. Calvin's disapprobation of such practices, Kingdon argues, is founded on the fact that they "may inflame public opinion without profitable result." Kingdon, furthermore, contends that "here we see again, . . . that Calvin's scruples had a practical base."[159] This reading of the issue fits better with the other material examined above and reveals that these two potentially powerful objections cannot be substantiated.

Calvin appears, in the material covered above, as one intent upon bringing God's kingdom to the world—specifically, France—at great cost. As we know, once he decided to support the plot of Louis of Condé, he did so wholeheartedly and tirelessly. He appeared frequently before the council and conducted numerous business dealings with Bern and other cities. He even went so far as to approve the use of mercenaries and fought to get them paid. He was going to stop at nothing in his quest to not only prepare the French Reformed churches for war with Romanists but ensure they won that war. Money. Mercenaries. Deception. Calvin was going to leave no stone unturned to ensure that France became Protestant. The portion of

---

[156] Henri Naef, *La Conjuration d'Amboise et Genève* (Geneva: Jullien, 1922), 462–3, as cited by Kingdon, *Geneva and the Coming of the Wars of Religion*, 69. See also Kingdon, "Calvin and Calvinists on Resistance to Government," 54–65. I am very aware that Calvin expressed his disapproval of the conspiracy with some vehemence; e.g. to Bullinger in May 1560, CO 18: 83–5. Be that as it may, his attitude was not that ascribed to him by many; see the recent reference to Calvin's adherence to the notion of the "inviolability of rulers" in Daniel H. Nexon, *Struggle for Power in Early Modern Europe*, 245, 247.

[157] Dufour, "L'Affaire de Maligny (Lyon, 4–5 septembre 1560) vue à travers la correspondance de Calvin et de Bèze," 269–80.

[158] He states this in a letter, dated 26 Feb. 1561, to the church of Paris, see CO 18: 376–8, esp. 378.

[159] Kingdon, *Geneva and the Coming of the Wars of Religion*, 111–12.

one of Calvin's letters which Gordon cites is perfect in its communicative force: "The point in question is to find money to support the troops which Messire d'Andelot has levied. This is not the moment to enter into inquiries or disputes in order to find fault with mistakes that have been committed in times past."[160] In fact, Calvin labored strenuously, negotiating loans from other Swiss cities and pontificating against churches in France who were not bearing their share of the burden. He lectured indefatigably, as we have seen, preparing ministers for France who would support the war effort and seek to strengthen the Reformed churches there. He wrote letters to the downtrodden, and to fellow ministers and other friends relating news about the war. He believed unquestionably that this was God's war. God would, so Calvin entreated, crush the enemy as God had done on behalf of Israel so long ago. His was an expansionist, insurrectionist model of reformation. He prayed on one occasion "that we may bravely fight to the end, and never doubt that you will ultimately be the defender (*vindicem*) of your Church, which now seems to be oppressed,"[161] and he seems earnestly to have believed that. He appeared convinced, despite the admission that God's church was oppressed, that this was their moment; that God would, in fact, be the defender of God's church in the war against the "papist" French government. In these ways, Calvin manifested brilliantly the image he had painted in his exposition on Jeremiah 1: 9–10. He was seeking to "reduce the world to order." It will be recalled that, as he continued to expound that passage, he had stated that "when there is no fear of God and no regard for him; when people are led away by the violence of their lusts, no godly teacher can exercise his duty without being prepared for war."[162] This was, I am arguing, precisely what Calvin was prepared for. The idea of bringing God's kingdom into France at a severe cost can be seen in something approaching its more graphic and tragic character now that scholars such as Natalie Zemon Davis[163] have explored the nature and logic of religious violence during the French Wars of Religion. It is not my intention

---

[160] CO 19: 550–1; letter to church in Languedoc, Sept. 1562; see Gordon, *Calvin*, 321–2.

[161] Calvin, *Praelectiones in Librum prophetiarum Ieremiae, et Lamentationes*, 393ᵛ.

[162] CO 37: 478.

[163] Davis, "Rites of Violence," 51–91. See also Natalie Zemon Davis, "Writing 'The Rites of Violence' and Afterward," in *Past and Present,* Suppl. 7: *Ritual and Violence: Natalie Zemon Davis and Early Modern France* (2012), 8–27.

here to explore such issues, but rather to turn attention, as this chapter draws to a close, to the character of Calvin.

That Calvin's endeavors to bring the kingdom of God to France were motivated, in large part, by the conviction he possessed of his own authority as a prophet seems apparent from much of what has been examined above. Calvin, renouncing his own desires and feelings, believed he had been commissioned to impose the kingdom of God upon France. Like Jeremiah, Calvin the prophet had been appointed over nations and kingdoms, and over France, "to uproot and tear down, to destroy and overthrow, to build and to plant."[164]

---

[164] Jer. 1: 9–10.

6

Reducing the World to Order[1]

Calvin believed himself to be a prophet—a finding which, I contend, must be taken more seriously by scholars interested in understanding Calvin and his thinking both about himself and about his times. This study argued that two prophetic traditions existed within Christian thought up to the Early Modern era, one having to do with the reception of supernatural knowledge and the other with scripture interpretation. Calvin held that both were legitimately deemed prophecy, and believed himself a representative of a kind of blending of the two. He held that prophets representing the first tradition had ceased to exist in the post-apostolic era. Thus, Calvin spoke God's word through interpretation of that word; which he also believed was true of Isaiah, Jeremiah, and the other Old Testament prophets; they were interpreters of the Law of Moses. Both Calvin and his old covenant predecessors added nothing to God's word but only explained and applied it to their particular eras—and this they did with absolute authority. Because of the character of the two eras (Old Testament and Early Modern), Calvin's prophetic calling, like that of Isaiah, Jeremiah, or Malachi, entailed fighting idolatry by authoritatively interpreting and applying the scriptures. The eras in which they lived were idolatrous, having departed from God's word, particularly on matters having to do with cultic practice and understanding. Calvin believed himself raised up, therefore, to overturn this idolatry and reestablish the truth of God over God's church. A sense of the scope and authority of this vocation may be grasped when we hear Calvin say that his calling, and that of his ministerial trainees headed into France, was "to reduce the world to order."

[1] CO 37: 480.

Calvin believed that he spoke for God. He was God's mouthpiece in Europe. He believed that he possessed an authority, therefore, that was unrivaled by king, pope, or fellow reformer. This authority verged, I have suggested, on infallibility. It allowed him to diminish the contributions of the greatest minds the church had produced up to his day, from Augustine to Zwingli (calling those contributions wood, hay, and stubble) while holding his own contribution to be sufficiently strong to urge his colleagues upon his death not to change anything in it.

Is this egotism? Is Calvin a megalomaniac? To declare Calvin self-absorbed and arrogant on the basis of the findings of this study is perhaps open for debate, though obviously this would not be the first time such questions were posed. For Calvin, he would likely have said he was as arrogant as Isaiah; as self-absorbed as Ezekiel. He would, and did, declare on a number of occasions that he had given himself over body and soul to God to be governed by God. He was not his own. "If," he might well say to the questioner, "that makes me arrogant, then so be it." In this way, the Calvin depicted in this study, while perhaps seeming distant or unappealing or maybe even insane, was like the authorities whom God had raised up throughout history; like Jeremiah; like Paul. He did not live so as to win friends, but he lived, *he* plainly believed, to dutifully fulfill the calling given him by God.

In Calvin's pursuit of his prophetic calling, he sought to employ drastic measures to secure France for the gospel.[2] These drastic measures included planning for war. In point of fact, the war which commenced in 1562 represents, this monograph argues, the culmination of years of preparation by Calvin. While there are, as has been acknowledged in this study, places within his corpus where he criticizes the war (and various practices of rioting, iconoclasm, etc.), the findings of this study are that these criticisms do not represent solid evidence of his conservatism but ought, rather, to be understood largely as pragmatic assessments. For Calvin, I have argued, pursued and promoted the war, reluctantly but willfully. He did not do this

---

[2] On the strength of feeling Calvin possessed in relation to his homeland, see Engammare, "Une certaine idée de la France chez Jean Calvin l'exilé," 15–27. Calvin also employed drastic measures in reforming Geneva as well, see Naphy, *Calvin and the Consolidation of the Genevan Reformation*; 146–53; Sara Beam, "Rites of Torture in Reformation Geneva," *Past and Present*, suppl. 7: *Ritual and Violence: Natalie Zemon Davis and Early Modern France* (2012), 197–219.

eagerly but because he believed himself called to do it. He pursued this in a calculated manner and with specific ideas of what he wanted to see happen. He did this while simultaneously urging Antoine of Navarre and others to push for reform (presumably, or at least possibly, through various means including peaceful means) within the country. He also did this with the aim that, if it came to war, a lesser magistrate must take charge of such a campaign. And, this study contends, Calvin grew increasingly convinced that it would *have* to come through war; that that was the only option still available. Accordingly, Calvin depicted war, in his training lectures to his ministerial candidates, as a holy calling. This was not a time for the church to engage in conflict resolution, but rather to fight, like the church of old (*olim*).

Interesting here is the fact that Calvin was not an apocalyptic prophet; he pursued this war without the apocalyptic fervor often associated with this kind of pursuit (one thinks, again, of the pursuit of war by the radical arm of the Hussites, following Jan Hus' execution). One could, arguably, more easily imagine Luther pursuing war against, for instance, the Turks, and being driven in that pursuit by an apocalyptic sense that the end of the age was upon him and that victory would draw the curtain on Satan and his minions. But instead, we find Calvin in conflict with the Roman Catholics battling intensely yet with no eschatological fuel to stoke his fires. This seems, in certain ways, to highlight the intensity of Calvin's desire—an intensity and clarity which is particularly apparent if we recall his striving to find the money to pay mercenaries to fight on behalf of and alongside the Huguenot armies. This action communicates so much, not because it sets Calvin in a good or bad light, but because it depicts so plainly how much he wanted to see the Huguenots victorious; how much he wanted to see his vision for reformation implemented in France.

Calvin's intensity contained within it the conviction that war could advance God's kingdom. In this regard, the just-mentioned Hussite Wars and other religiously oriented wars seem to me helpful sources for my understanding of Calvin. This is not because all religiously oriented wars are fundamentally the same, but because all, or at least many of them, share this common conviction about the advancing of God's kingdom—a conviction which is so foreign to the Western world in the twenty-first century. For Calvin, he and his pious fellow evangelicals fought under the banner of Christ, and when the war took the form of armed resistance against the French authorities, he continued to articulate the same message. In all of this, it is the modern West, and not Calvin, which is out of touch with tradition (perhaps happily so).

From this conviction, Calvin prayed. He prayed like Moses or David; imprecating his (and as he saw it, the church's) enemies, and earnestly entreating God to defeat them. He looked specifically at God's ways of delivering his people in the past and desired that God would do the same thing for the Huguenots. By praying in this manner, Calvin betrayed a profound sense of continuity with those in the old covenant community. His prayers entreated God to fight, to defend, to eradicate the enemy. For him, as for Joshua, God was the Lord Sabaoth. God would fight for the Huguenots against the French Catholic armies in precisely the same manner he had for Israel against the Philistines.

What this study has unearthed, then, is a Calvin who, in certain key ways, was like an Old Testament figure. Some of these ways have been noted in previous paragraphs, but we still might reflect upon the assertion for a moment longer. Calvin was, of course, still the humanist, still the Genevan pastor, still the cutting-edge theologian, but in certain ways he lived in the mental world of Elijah, David, and Ezekiel. Moreover and more particularly, he believed that he possessed their authority. Of course, Paul would be the name to have recourse to if one were to locate Calvin within a New Testament world of meaning (though, as this monograph makes clear, the Pauline office of prophet was essentially poisoned as a possible identity for Calvin because of the Anabaptists' claims to that office). And no doubt Calvin identified with Paul powerfully and often. But because the Calvin uncovered in this study is an idol fighter and possessed such a clear conception of his own authority over earthly rulers, the names of Elijah, Jeremiah, and Ezekiel are more fitting.

Possessing the authority of a Jeremiah or an Elijah, Calvin did not conceive of himself simply as one among many laboring to find the truth of God in sixteenth-century Europe. Rather, he saw himself as *the* voice of God in Europe; this was particularly true by the late 1540s, by which time Luther, Oecolampadius, Capito, and Zwingli had all died. Calvin was one of very few left who spoke the word of God purely. If Servetus or Castellio (or for that matter, Bullinger) agreed with him, that was good, but if they disagreed with him, then they disagreed with God *ipso facto*. In my reading of Calvin, this seems absolutely undeniable. He believed he was right *simpliciter*. All the rest of the world could disagree with him, but if they did, they were wrong. The idea that *he* was wrong was something which I do not think he even contemplated, at least in relation to the public persona which he fashioned.

This account of Calvin's prophetic awareness and authority is intended to serve as a contribution to the ongoing study of this man as a man; as a figure who occupied the sixteenth century, rather than merely a theologian abstracted from his era. It may thrill or disappoint, but it has endeavored to unearth something of Calvin's character and self-belief, something of the role which he occupied in the Early Modern world, and, indeed (he believed), in subsequent ages. This study has found Calvin to be a reformer who was willing to see, and even contribute to, his country being plunged into war for the sake of the gospel. The clear sense which Calvin had of the situation in France was that his homeland was in the grip of something diabolical which required a radical solution which God had called him to apply. He pursued that solution, working tirelessly to find a Prince of the Blood ready to work for reform in the country, and he contemplated a variety of means, including revolt against the monarch, to achieve it. He employed these means not because he himself longed to employ them but rather because, denying himself, he took up God's calling to employ them. Similarly, Calvin worked tirelessly to rush minister-prophets into France who would both spread the message that resistance was required and also be ready to take over spiritual control of the country during and after the commencement of armed military resistance. For Calvin to do less than that would, it seems, have been for him to disavow the calling God had given him. He had already had the specter of Jonah thrust at him by Bucer years earlier. One can imagine, as he contemplated the situation in France in the late 1550s and early 1560s, that such a ghost may well have revisited him again, rekindling in him the prophetic calling he had received so many years before.

Bibliography

Primary Sources

Biblia latina cum glossa ordinaria Walafridi Strabonis aliorumque et interlineari Anselmi Laudunensis. Strasbourg: Adolf Rusch, for Anton Koberger, c.1480.

Albertus Magnus. *S.D.E. Alberti Magni . . . Opera Omnia.* 19 vols. Münster i. W: Aschendorff, 1952.

Ambrosiaster. *Divi Ambrosii episcope Mediolanensis omnia . . .* Basel: A. Petri, 1516.

Aquinas, Thomas. *Sancti Thomae Aquinatis doctoris angelici Opera Omnia . . .* Parma: P. Fiaccadori, 1852–73.

——*S. Thomae Aquinatis . . . super Evangelium S. Matthaei Lectura,* ed. P. Raphaelis Cai OP. Taurini: Marietti, 1951.

——*St Thomas Aquinas Summa Theologiae,* vol. 45 *(2a2ae. 171–178) Prophecy and Other Charisms,* tr. Roland Potter OP. Cambridge: Cambridge University Press, 2006.

Bibliander, Theodor. *Oratio Theodori Bibliandri ad enarrationem Esaiae prophetarum principis dicta . . .* Zurich: Froschouerus, 1532.

——*Propheta Nahvm Ivxta Veritatem Hebraicam, Latine redditus per Theodorum Bibliandrum; adiecta exegesi, qua uersionis ratio redditur, & authoris diuini sententia explicatur.* Zurich: Froschouerus, 1534.

Brenz, Johannes. *In Epistolam, quam apostolus Paulus ad Romanos scripsit, commentariorum libri tres.* Tübingen: Georgius Gruppenbachius, 1588.

Bucer, Martin. *Epistola D. Pauli ad Ephesios, . . .* Strasbourg: s.n., 1527.

——*Enarrationes perpetuæ in Sacra Quatuor Evangelia, recognitæ nuper [et] locis compluribus auctæ . . .* Argentorati: Georgius Ulricherus Andlanus, 1530.

Bugenhagen, Johannes. *Annotationes Ioan. Bugenhagii Pomerani in X. epistolas Pauli, scilicet, ad Ephesios, . . . Hebraeos.* Strassburg: Apud Iohannem Hervagium, 1524.

Bullinger, Heinrich. *De prophetae officio, et quomodo digne administrari posit, oratio.* Zurich: Froschouerus, 1532.

——*In priorem d. Pauli ad Corinthios epistolam, Heinrychi Bullingeri commentarius.* Zurich: Froschouerus, 1534.

——*De scripturae sanctae authoritate . . . perfectione, deque Episcoporum, . . . Libri duo.* Zurich: Froschouerus, 1538.

——*De origine erroris libri duo.* Zurich: Froschouerus, 1539.

——*In Apocalypsim conciones centum.* Basel: Johannes Oporin 1557.

——*Heinrychi Bullingeri Jeremias fidelissimus et laboriosissimus Dei Propheta . . . concionibus CLXX.* Zurich: C. Froschouerus, 1575.

——*Reformationsgeschichte,* i, ed. J. J. Hottinger and and H. H. Vögeli, repr. Zurich: Nova-Buchhandlung, 1984.

Calvin, John. *Ioannis Calvini Commentarii in Isaiam prophetam . . .* Geneva: ex officina Ioannis Crispini, 1551.

——*Ioannis Calvini in Viginti prima Ezechielis prophetae capita praelectiones . . .* Geneva: ex officina Francisci Perrini, 1565.

——*Praelectiones ioannis calvini in librum prophetiarum danielis, . . .* s.l.: apud Bartholomaeum Vincentium, 1571.

——*Praelectiones in Librum prophetiarum Jeremiae, et Lamentationes . . .* Geneva: Héritiers d'Eustache Vignon, 1589.

——*Ioannis Calvini Opera Quae Supersunt Omnia,* 59 vols. Ed. Wilhelm Baum, Eduard Cunitz, and Eduard Reuss, Corpus Reformatorum, 29–87. Brunswick: C. A. Schwetschke, 1863–1900.

——*Opera Selecta.* ed. Peter Barth. 5 vols. Munich: Chr. Kaiser Verlag, 1926–36.

——*Supplementa Calviniana. Sermons inédits.* Ed. Erwin Mühlhaupt *et al.* Neukirchen-Vluyn: Neukirchener Verlag, 1936–.

——*Iohannis Calvini Commentarius in epistolam Pauli ad Romanos,* ed. T. H. L. Parker. Leiden: Brill, 1981.

——*John Calvin,* ed. G. R. Potter and M. Greengrass. New York: St Martin's Press, 1983.

——*Ioannis Calvini Epistolae,* i. *1530–sep. 1538,* ed. Cornelis Augustijn and Frans Peter van Stam. Geneva: Droz, 2005.

Capito, Wolfgang. *In Habakuk prophetam.* Strasbourg: Vvolphium Cephalaeum, 1526.

——*In Epistolam Apostoli Pauli ad Romanos, Commentarii.* Basel: Hervagius, 1555.

——*The Correspondence of Wolfgang Capito,* ed. Erika Rummel, with Milton Kooistra and tr. 2 vols. Toronto: University of Toronto Press, 2009.

Denis the Carthusian. *D. Dionysii Carthusiani insigne opus commentariorum in Psalmos omnes Davidicos,* Cologne: apud Haeredes J. Quentelii & G. Calenium, 1558.

Erasmus, Desiderius. *Novum instrumentum.* Basel: Johann Froben, 1516; repr. Stuttgart-Bad Cannstatt: Frommann-Holzboog, 1986.

Estius, Guilielmus. *Estius in Omnes Canonicas Apostolorum Epistolas.* Paris: Mogunriae, 1841.

François Lambert of Avignon. *Praefatio in In Primum Duodecim Prophetarum, nempe, Oseam . . .* Strasbourg: Johan Hervagium, 1525.

——*Commentarii de Prophetia, Eruditione et Linguis . . .* Strasbourg: Johan Hervagium, 1526.

Gregory the Great. *Homélies sur Ézéchiel*. Latin text, introduction, tr., and notes by Charles Morel SJ. Paris: Les Éditions du Cerf, 1986.

Gwalther, Rudolph. *In D. Pauli apostoli epistolam ad Romanos homiliae.* Zurich: Froschauerus, 1566.

——*In prophetas duodecimo, quos vocant minores, Rodolphi Gualtheri . . . homiliae.* Zurich: Froschoverus, 1577.

——*Isaias: in Isaiam prophetam Rodolphi Gvaltheri Tigurini homiliae CCCXXVII.* Zurich: Froschouerus, 1583.

——*In Epistolam D. Pauli Apostoli ad Corinthios Priorem.* Zurich: Froschouerus, 1590.

Hoffman, Melchior. *Das XII. Capitel des propheten Danielis ausgelegt, . . . christen nutzlich zu wissen.* Stockholm: Königliche Druckerei, 1526.

Hugh of St Cher. *Théorie de la prophétie et philosophie de la connaissance aux environs de 1230: La Contribution d'Hugues de Saint-Cher (Ms. Douai 434, Question 481)*, ed. Jean-Pierre Torrell OP. Leuven: Spicilegium Sacrum Lovanense, 1977.

Jerome. *Commentaire sur Saint Matthieu.* Latin text, introduction, tr., and notes by Émile Bonnard. Paris: Sources chrétiennes, 1977.

Jud, Leo. *Catechismus brevissima Christianae religionis formula, . . . in communem omnium piorum utilitatem excusa.* Zurich: Froschouerus, 1539.

Junillus Africanus. *Exegesis and Empire in the Early Byzantine Mediterranean; Junillus Africanus and the Instituta Regularia Divinae Legis,* ed. Michael Maas, with Edward G. Mathews, Jr., Latin text est. Heinrich Kihn, tr. Michael Maas. Tübingen: Mohr Siebeck, 2003.

Luther, Martin. *D. Martin Luthers Werke: Kritische Gesamtausgabe*, Weimar: Hermann Bohlaus, 1883–1987.

——*Luther's Works,* ed. Jaroslav Pelikan and Helmut T. Lehman, St Louis: Concordia, 1955–76.

Melanchthon, Philip. *Commentarii in epistolam Pauli ad Romanos hoc anno M.D.XL. recogniti & locupletati.* Strasbourg: Apud Cratonem Mylium, 1540.

——*Corpus Reformatorum: Philippi Melanthonis opera quae supersunt omnia.* 28 vols., ed. Karl Bretschneider and Heinrich Bindseil. Halle: A. Schwetschke & Sons, 1834–60.

Morely, Jean. *Traicté de la discipline & police chrestienne.* Lyon: Jean de Tournes, 1562.

Musculus, Wolfgang. *In Epistolam Apostoli Pauli ad Romanos, Commentarii.* Basel: Joannem Hervagius, 1555.

——*In Sacrosanctum Davidis Psalterium Commentarii: In Quibus Et Reliqua . . .* Basel: Joannem Hervagius, 1556.

——*In Esaiam Prophetam Commentarii . . .* Basel: Joannem Hervagius, 1557.

——*In ambas apostoli Pauli ad Corinthios epistolas, commentarii.* Basel: Joannem Hervagius, 1559.

——*Loci Communes.* Basel: Joannem hervagium, 1564.

——*In Mosis Genesim plenissimi Commentarii.* Basel: Joannem hervagium, 1565.

——*In Epistolas Apostoli Pauli ad Galatas, et Ephesios Commentarii.* Basel: Hervagius, 1569.

Nicholas of Lyra. *Lyra Biblia Latina: Biblia Latina cum postillis Nicolai de Lyra et expositionibus Guillelmi Britonis in omnes prologos S. Hieronymi et additionibus Pauli Burgensis replicisque Matthiae Doering.* Nuremberg: Anton Koberger, 1483.

Oecolampadius, Iohannes. *In Epistolam B. Pauli Apost. Ad Rhomanos Adnontationes a Ioanne Oecolampadio Basileae praelectae, & denuo recognitae.* Basel: Andr. Cratandrum, 1526.

——*D. D. Ioannis Oecolampadii et Huldrichii Zwinglii Epistolarum libri quatuor.* Basel: [R. Winter], 1536.

Olevianus, Gaspar. *In epistolam D. Pauli Apostoli ad Romanos notae, ex Gasparis Oleviani concionibus excerptae, & a Theodoro Beza editae . . .* Geneva: Apud Eustathium Vignon, 1579.

Patrologiae cursus completus, series Graeca. 161 vols., ed. Jacques Paul Migne. Paris: Garnier, 1857–99: vol. 30: Basil the Great, *Enarratio in Isaiam Profetam;* vol. 80: Cyril of Alexandria, *In Ezekiel;* vol. 22: Eusebius, *Demonstratio Evangel. v Prol;* vol. 56: John Chrysostom, *Homiliae in Isaiae;* vol. 80: Theodoretus of Cyrus, *In Psalm. Praef.*

Patrologiae cursus completus, series latina. 221 vols., ed. Jacques Paul Migne. Paris: Garnier, 1844–1904: vol. 34: Augustine, *Super Gen. ad litt. Libri duodecim;* vol 153: Bruno the Carthusian. *Expositio In Epistolas Sancti Pauli;* vol. 70: Cassiodorus. *In Psalterium Praefatio;* vol. 117: Haymo of Halberstadt. *In Divi Pauli Epistolas Expositio.* and *Enarratio In Duodecim Prophetas Minores;* vol. 181: Herveus Burgidolensis. *Commentaria In Epistolas Divi Pauli;* vol. 82: Isidore of Seville. *Etymologiarum Libri Viginti;* vol 25: Jerome. *Commentariorum In Amos Prophetam Libri Tres;* vol. 28: Jerome. *Prolog.I & II Para;* vol. 150: Lanfranc of Bec. *In Epistolam I ad Corinthios;* vol. 191: Peter Lombard. *Prologo super Psalmos;* vol. 30: Pseudo-Jerome. *Commentarius In Epistolas Sancti Pauli [Incertus];* vol 112: Rhabanus Maurus. *Enarrationum In Epistolas Beati Pauli;* vol. 114: Walafrid Strabo (Anselm of Loan). *Glossa Ordinaria;* vol. 180: William of St Thierry. *Expositio In Epistolam Ad Romanos.*

Pellican, Conrad. *In omnes apostolicas epistolas, Pauli, Petri, Iacobi, Ioannis et Iudae D. Chuonradi Pellicani . . .* Zurich: Officina Froschoviana, 1539.

——*In Prophetas Maiores et Minores, ut vulgo vocantur, hoc est, in Isaiam, Ieremiam, . . . Commentarii Conradi Pellicani . . .* Zurich: Christoph. Froschouerus, 1582.

188   *Bibliography*

Savonarola, Girolamo. *Compendio di Rivelazioni; Trattato sul Governo della città di Firenze.* Casale Monferrato: Piemme, 1996.

Vermigli, Peter Martyr. *In Epistolam S. Pauli Apostoli ad Rom. D. Petri Martyris, Vermilii Florentini, . . . commentarii doctissimi, cum tractatione perutili rerum & locorum, qui ad eam epistolam pertinent.* Basel: Petrum Pernam, 1560.

——*Defensio Doctrinae veteris & Apostolicae de sacrosancto Eucharistiae Sacramento . . .* Zurich: Froschouerus, 1562.

——*Est regum libri Duo posteriores cum commentariis Petri Martyris Vermilii.* Zurich: Froschouerus, 1566.

——*In duos libros Samuelis prophetæ qui uulgo priores libros Regum appellantur D. Petri Martyris Vermilii . . . Commentarii doctissimi, cum rerum & locorum plurimorum tractatione perutili.* Zurich: Froschouerus, 1567.

——*In Primum librum Mosis, qui vulgo Genesis dicitur, commentarii doctissimi D. Petri Martyris, Vermilii Florentini, . . . nunc denuo in lucem editi.* Zurich: Froschoerus, 1579.

——*In Selectissimam D. Pauli Apostoli Primum ad Corinthios Epistolam Commentarii.* Zurich: Froschoerus, 1579.

Zwingli, Ulrich. *De Vera et Falsa Religione . . . Commentarius.* Zurich: Froscherus, 1525.

——*In Cata Baptistarvm Strophas Elenchus Huldrichi Zuinglij.* Zurich: Froschouerus, 1527.

——*Annotatiunculae per Leonem Iudae, ex ore Zvinglij in utranq; Pauli ad Corinthios Epistolam publice exponentis conceptae.* Zurich: Froschouerus, 1528.

——*D. D. Ioannis Oecolampadii et Huldrichii Zwinglii Epistolarum libri quatuor.* Basel: [R. Winter], 1536.

——*Sämtliche Werke,* ed. Emil Egli, Georg Finsler, and Walther Köhler. Berlin: Schwetschke, 1905–59.

Secondary Sources

Alphandéry, Paul. "Prophètes et ministère prophétique dans le Moyen Age latin." *Revue d'Histoire et de Philosophie Religieuses,* 12 (1932), 334–59.

Ash, J. L. "The Decline of Ecstatic Prophecy in the Early Church." *Theological Studies,* 37 (1976), 227–52.

Balserak, Jon. "'There Will Always Be Prophets;' Deuteronomy 18:14–22 and Calvin's Prophetic Awareness." In Herman Selderhuis (ed.), *Saint or Sinner? Papers from the International Conference on the Anniversary of John Calvin's 500th birthday in Putten, the Netherlands.* Tübingen: Mohr Siebeck, 2010, 85–112.

——*Establishing the Remnant Church in France: Calvin's Lectures on the Minor Prophets, 1556–1559.* Leiden: Brill, 2011.

—— "'We Need Teachers Today, Not Prophets;' Peter Martyr Vermigli's Exposition of Prophecy." *Archiv für Reformationsgeschichte*, 103 (2012), 148–72.

—— "Examining the Myth of Calvin as a Lover of Order." In Peter Opitz (ed.), *The Myth of the Reformation*. Göttingen: Vandenhoeck & Ruprecht, 2013, 160–75.

Barnes, Robin. *Prophecy and Gnosis: Apocalypticism in the Wake of the Lutheran Reformation.* Stanford, Calif.: Stanford University Press, 1988.

Beam, Sara. "Rites of Torture in Reformation Geneva." *Past and Present*, Suppl. 7: "Ritual and Violence: Natalie Zemon Davis and Early Modern France" (2012), 197–219.

Beckwith, Sarah. *Christ's Body: Identity, Culture, and Society in Late Medieval Writings.* London: Routledge, 1993.

Benedict, Philip. *Rouen during the Wars of Religion*. Cambridge: Cambridge University Press, 1981.

—— "The Dynamics of Protestant Militancy: France, 1555–1563." In Philip Benedict, G. Marnef, H. Van Nierop, and M. Venard (eds), *Reformation, Revolt and Civil War in France and the Netherlands 1555–1585*. Amsterdam: Royal Netherlands Academy of Arts and Sciences, 1999, 35–50.

—— "Prophets in Arms? Ministers in War, Ministers on War: France 1562–74." *Past and Present*, Suppl. 7: *Ritual and Violence: Natalie Zemon Davis and Early Modern France* (2012), 163–96.

—— and Nicolas Fornerod. "Les 2,150 'églises' réformées de France de 1561–1562." *Revue historique*, 311/3 (2009), 559–60.

Benoit, Daniel, *et al. Calvin à Strasbourg, 1538–1541*. Strasbourg: Oberlin, 1938.

Bilinkoff, Jodi. "A Spanish Prophetess and her Patrons: The Case of Maria de Santo Domingo." *Sixteenth Century Journal*, 23/1 (1992), 21–34.

Blacketer, Raymond. "The Moribund Moralist: Ethical Lessons in Calvin's Commentary on Joshua." In Wim Janse and Barbara Pitkin (eds), *The Formation of Clerical and Confessional Identities in Early Modern Europe*. Leiden: Brill, 2006, 149–68.

Bloch, Marc. *Les Rois thaumaturges: Etude sur le caractère surnaturel attribué à la puissance royale particulièrement en France et en Angleterre*. Oxford: Oxford University Press, 1924.

Boer, Erik de. "The Presence and Participation of Laypeople in the *Congrégations* of the Company of Pastors in Geneva." *Sixteenth Century Journal*, 35/3 (2004), 651–70.

—— *The Genevan School of the Prophets: The Congrégations of the Company of Pastors and their Influence in Sixteenth Century Europe*. Geneva: Droz, 2012.

Bohatec, Josef. *Calvins Lehre von Staat und Kirche mit besonderer Berücksichtigung des Organismusgedankens*. Breslau: M. & H. Marcus, 1937.

Boisson, Didier, and Hugues Daussy. *Les Protestants dans la France moderne.* Paris: Éditions Belin, 2006.

Bolliger, Daniel. "Bullinger on Church Authority: The Transformation of the Prophetic Role in Christian Ministry." In Bruce Gordon and Emidio Campi (eds), *Architect of Reformation: An Introduction to Heinrich Bullinger, 1504–1575.* Grand Rapids, Mich.: Baker, 2004, 159–77.

Borgeaud, Charles. *Histoire de l'Université de Genève par Charles Borgeaud . . . Ouvrage publié sous les auspices du Sénat universitaire et de la Société académique,* i. *L'Académie de Calvin, 1559–1798.* Geneva: George, 1900.

Bouwsma, William. *John Calvin: A Sixteenth Century Portrait.* Oxford: Oxford University Press, 1988.

Brady, Jr., Thomas A. *Ruling Class, Regime and Reformation at Strasbourg, 1520–1555.* Leiden: Brill, 1978.

Bryson, David. *Queen Jeanne and the Promised Land: Dynasty, Homeland, Religion and Violence in Sixteenth-Century France.* Leiden: Brill, 1999.

Burnett, Amy Nelson. *Teaching the Reformation: Ministers and their Message in Basel, 1529–1629.* New York: Oxford University Press, 2006.

Büsser, Fritz. *Calvins Urteil über sich Selbst.* Zurich: Zwingli-Verlag, 1950.

——"Der Prophet-Gedanken zu Zwinglis Theologie." *Zwingliana,* 13 (1969), 7–18.

——*Huldrych Zwingli: Reformation als prophetischer Auftrag,* Zürich: TVZ, 1973.

——*Heinrich Bullinger (1504–1575): Leben, Werk und Wirkung,* 2 vols. Zurich: TVZ, 2004–5.

——and Alfred Schindler, eds. *Die Prophezei: Humanismus und Reformation in Zürich: Ausgewählte Aufsätze und Vorträge.* Bern: Lang, 1994.

Caciola, Nancy. *Discerning Spirits: Divine and Demonic Possession in the Middle Ages.* New York: Cornell University Press, 2003.

Campi, Emidio, and Christian Moser. "Loved and Feared: Calvin and the Swiss Confederation." In Martin Ernst Hirzel and Martin Sallmann (eds), *Calvin's Impact on Church and Society, 1509–2009.* Grand Rapids, Mich.: Eerdmans, 2009, 14–34.

——"Calvin, the Swiss Reformed Churches, and the European Reformation," in *Calvin and his Influence, 1509–2009.* Oxford: Oxford University Press, 2011, 119–43.

Caprariis, Vittorio de. *Propaganda e pensiero politico in Francia durante le Guerre di Religione.* Naples: Edizioni scientifiche italiane, 1959.

Cassan, Michel. *Le Temps des guerres de religion: Le Cas du Limousin, vers 1530—vers 1630.* Paris: Publisud, 1996.

Chenevière, Marc-Edouard. *La Pensée politique de Calvin.* Paris: Éditions Je Sers, 1937.

Cholakian, Patricia Francis. *Marguerite de Navarre: Mother of the Renaissance.* New York: Columbia University Press, 2006.

Chomarat, Michel. "De quelques dates clairement exprimées par Michel Nostradamus, dans ses 'Prophéties'." In *Prophètes et prophétie au XVIe siècle*. Paris: Presses de l'École Normale Supérieure, 1998, 83–93.

Chrisman, Miriam. *Strasbourg and the Reform: A Study in the Process of Change*. New Haven: Yale University Press, 1967, 177–200.

——*Lay Culture, Learned Culture: Books and Social Change in Strasbourg, 1480–1599*. New Haven: Yale University Press, 1982.

Chung-Kim, Esther. *Inventing Authority: The Use of the Church Fathers in Reformation Debates over the Eucharist*. Waco, Tex.: Baylor University Press, 2011.

Cottret, Bernard. *Calvin: Biographie*. Paris: Éditions Jean-Claude Lattès, 1995.

Courtenay, William J. *Covenant and Causality in Medieval Thought: Studies in Philosophy, Theology and Economic Practice*. London: Variorum Reprints, 1984.

Crouzet, Denis. *Les Guerriers de Dieu: La Violence au temps des troubles de religion (vers 1525–vers 1610)*. 2 vols. Seyssel: Champ Vallon, 1990.

——*La Genèse de la réforme française: 1520–1560*. Paris: Sedes, 1996.

——"Calvinism and the Uses of the Political and the Religious (France, ca. 1560–ca. 1572)." In Philip Benedict, G. Marnef, H. Van Nierop, and M. Venard (eds), *Reformation, Revolt and Civil War in France and the Netherlands 1555–1585*. Amsterdam: Royal Netherlands Academy of Arts and Sciences, 1999, 99–113.

——*Jean Calvin: Vies parallèles*. Paris: Fayard, 2000.

Daussy, Hugues. "Les Huguenots entre l'obéissance au roi et l'obéissance à Dieu." *Nouvelle Revue du XVIe Siècle*, 22 (2004), 49–69.

Davis, Natalie Zemon. "The Rites of Violence: Religious Riots in Sixteenth-Century France." *Past and Present*, 59 (1973), 51–93.

——*Society and Culture in Early Modern France*. Stanford, Calif.: Stanford University Press, 1975.

——"Writing 'The Rites of Violence' and Afterward." *Past and Present*, Suppl. 7: *Ritual and Violence: Natalie Zemon Davis and Early Modern France* (2012), 8–27.

Denis, Philippe. "La Prophétie dans les Églises de la Réforme au xvie siècle." *Revue d'Histoire ecclésiastique*, 72 (1977), 289–316.

——"Calvin et les églises d'étrangers au XVIe siècle: Comment un ministre intervient dans une église autre que la sienne." In *Calvinus Ecclesiae Genevensis Custos : Die Referate des Congrès International des Recherches Calviniennes . . . Vom 6. bis 9. September 1982 in Genf*. Frankfurt am Main: Peter Lang Verlag, 1984, 69–92.

Deppermann, Klaus. *Melchior Hoffman: Soziale Unruhen und apokalyptische Visionen im Zeitalter der Reformation*. Göttingen: Vandenhoeck & Ruprecht, 1979.

——*Melchior Hoffman: Social Unrest and Apocalyptic Visions in the Age of Reformation*. Tr. Malcolm Wren. Edinburgh: T&T Clark, 1987.

Diefendorf, Barbara. "Prologue to a Massacre: Popular Unrest in Paris, 1557–1572." *American Historical Review*, 90/5 (1985), 1067–91.

—— "Simon Vigor: A Radical Preacher in Sixteenth-Century Paris." *Sixteenth Century Journal*, 18/3 (1987), 399–410.

—— *Beneath the Cross: Catholics and Huguenots in Sixteenth-Century Paris*. New York: Oxford University Press, 1991.

Donnelly, John Patrick, compiler. *A Bibliography of the Works of Peter Martyr Vermigli*, Kirksville, Mo.: Truman State University Press, 1990.

Doumergue, Émile. *Jean Calvin, les hommes et les choses de son temps*. 7 vols. Lausanne: G. Bridel & Cie., 1899–1927.

Droz, Eugénie. *Chemins de l'hérésie: Textes et documents*. 4 vols. Geneva: Slatkine Reprints, 1970–6.

Dufour, Alain. "L'Affaire de Maligny (Lyon, 4–5 septembre 1560) vue à travers la correspondance de Calvin et de Bèze." *Cahiers d'Histoire*, 8 (1963), 269–80.

—— *Théodore de Bèze, Histoire littéraire de la France publée par l'Académie des Inscriptions et Belles-Lettres*, vol. 42. Paris: Diffusion de Boccard, 2002, 315–470.

Eire, Carlos. *War Against the Idols: The Reformation of Worship from Erasmus to Calvin*. Cambridge: Cambridge University Press, 1986.

Elias, Norbert. *Über den Prozess der Zivilisation: Soziogenetische und psychogenetische Untersuchungen*. 2 vols. Basel: Haus zum Falken, 1939.

Elwood, Christopher. *The Body Broken: The Calvinist Doctrine of the Eucharist and the Symbolization of Power in Sixteenth-Century France*. New York: Oxford University Press, 1999.

Engammare, Max. "Calvin: A Prophet without a Prophecy." In John Leith and Robert Johnson (eds), *Calvin Studies IX: Papers Presented at the Ninth Colloquium on Calvin Studies, Davidson College, January 30–31, 1998*. Davidson, NC: Davidson College, 1998, 88–107.

—— "Calvin monarchomaque? Du soupçon à l'argument." *Archiv für Reformationsgeschichte*, 89 (1998), 207–26.

—— "Review of Jean Calvin: Vies parallèles." *Bibliothèque d'Humanisme et Renaissance*, 62/3 (2000), 732–9.

—— "Calvin lecteur de la Bible en chaire." In David F. Wright, Anthony N. S. Lane, and Jon Balserak (eds), *Calvinus Evangelii Propugnator: Calvin, Champion of the Gospel. Papers from the International Congress on Calvin Research Seoul, 1998*. Grand Rapids, Mich.: CRC Production Services, 2006, 147–60.

—— "Humanism, Hebraism and Scriptural Hermeneutics." In Torrance Kirby, Emidio Campi, and Frank A. James III (eds), *A Companion to Peter Martyr Vermigli*. Leiden: Brill, 2009, 161–74.

—— "Une certaine idée de la France chez Jean Calvin l'exilé." *Société de l'Histoire du Protestantisme Français*, 155 (2009), 15–27.

Erikson, Erik H. *Young Man Luther: A Study in Psychoanalysis and History.* New York: Norton, 1958.

Ferzoco, George. "The Processo Castellano and the Canonization of Catherine of Siena." In Carolyn Muessig, George Ferzoco, and Beverly Mayne Kienzle (eds), *A Companion to Catherine of Siena.* Leiden: Brill, 2009, 185–201.

Fogelqvist, Ingvar. *Apostacy and Reform in the Revelations of St. Birgitta.* Stockholm: Almqvist & Wiksell International, 1993.

Friesen, Abraham. *Erasmus, the Anabaptists, and the Great Commission.* Grand Rapids, Mich.: Eerdmans, 1998.

Gal, Stéphane. *Grenoble au temps de la Ligue: Étude politique, sociale et religieuse d'une cité en crise, vers 1562–vers 1598.* Grenoble: Presses Universitaires de Grenoble, 2000.

Ganoczy, Alexandre. *Calvin, théologien de l'Église et du ministère.* Paris: Éditions du Cerf, 1964.

——*Le Jeune Calvin: Genèse et évolution de sa vocation réformatrice.* Wiesbaden: Franz Steiner Verlag, 1966.

——"Calvin avait-il conscience de réformer l'Eglise?" *Revue de Théologie et de Philosophie Lausanne,* 118/2 (1986), 161–77.

——*The Young Calvin,* tr. David Foxgrover and Wade Provo. Philadelphia: Westminster Press, 1987.

Garrison-Estèbe, Janine. *Protestants du Midi, 1559–1598.* Toulouse: Privat, 1980.

Giesendorf, P. F., ed. *Le Livre des habitants de Genève,* i. *1555–1572.* Geneva: Droz, 1957.

Gilmont, Jean-François. *Jean Calvin et le livre imprimé.* Geneva: Librairie Droz, 1997.

——*John Calvin and the Printed Book.* Tr. Karin Maag. Kirksville, Mo.: Truman State University Press, 2005.

——and Rodolphe Peter, eds. *Bibliotheca Calviniana: Les Œuvres de Jean Calvin publiées au XVIe siècle.* 3 vols. Geneva: Droz, 1991–2000.

Ginzburg, Carlo. *Il Nicodemismo, Simulazione e dissimulazione religiosa nell' Europa del '500.* Turin: Einaudi Editore, 1970.

Goertz, Hans-Jürgen. *Thomas Müntzer: Mystiker, Apokalyptiker, Revolutionär.* Munich: C. H. Beck, 1989.

——*Thomas Müntzer: Apocalyptic Mystic and Revolutionary,* trans. Jocelyn Jacquiery. Edinburgh: T&T Clark, 1993.

Göing, Anja-Silvia. "Die Ausbildung reformierter Prediger in Zürich 1531–1575: Vorstellung eines pädagogischen Projekts." In H. J. Selderhuis and Markus Wriedt (eds), *Bildung und Konfession: Theologenausbildung im Zeitalter der Konfessionalisierung.* Tübingen: Mohr Siebeck, 2006, 293–310.

Gordon, Bruce. "Calvin and the Swiss Reformed Churches." In Andrew Pettegree, Alastair Duke, and Gillian Lewis (eds), *Calvinism in Europe 1540–1620.* Cambridge: Cambridge University Press, 1994, 64–81.

Gordon, Bruce. "Toleration in the Early Swiss Reformation: The Art and Politics of Niklaus Manuel of Berne." In Ole Peter Grell, Bob Scribner, and Robert William Scribner (eds), *Tolerance and Intolerance in the European Reformation*. Cambridge: Cambridge University Press, 1996, 128–44.

——*The Swiss Reformation*. Manchester: University of Manchester Press, 2002.

——*Calvin*. New Haven: Yale University Press, 2009.

——"'Christo testimonium reddunt omnes scripturae': Theodor Bibliander's Oration on Isaiah (1532) and Commentary on Nahum (1534)." In Bruce Gordon and Matthew McLean.(eds), *Shaping the Bible in the Reformation: Books, Scholars and their Readers in the Sixteenth Century*. Leiden: Brill, 2012, 107–41.

Greef, Wulfert de. *The Writings of John Calvin; Expanded Edition*. Philadelphia: Westminster/John Knox, 2008.

Greenblatt, Stephen. *Renaissance Self-Fashioning from More to Shakespeare*. Chicago: University of Chicago Press, 1980.

Greengrass, Mark. *The French Reformation*. Oxford: Blackwell, 1987.

Hällström, Gunnar af. *Charismatic Succession: A Study on Origen's Concept of Prophecy*. Helsinki: Finnish Exegetical Society, 1985.

Hancock, Ralph. *Calvin and the Foundations of Modern Politics*. Ithaca, NY, and London: Cornell University Press, 1989, 70–81.

Harms, Frederik A. V. *In God's Custody: The Church, a History of Divine Protection. A Study of John Calvin's Ecclesiology Based on his Commentary on the Minor Prophets*. Göttingen:.Vandenhoeck & Ruprecht, 2009.

Haude, Sigrun. "Gender Roles and Perspectives among Anabaptist and Spiritualist Groups." In James M. Stayer and John D. Roth (eds), *A Companion to Anabaptism and Spiritualism, 1521–1700*. Leiden: Brill, 2007, 425–66.

Heller, Henry. "Putting History Back into the Religious Wars: A Reply to Mack P. Holt." *French Historical Studies*, 19/3 (1996), 853–61.

Herminjard, A. L. *Correspondance des réformateurs dans les pays de langue française*. Nieuwkoop: Graaf, 1965.

Higman, Francis. "The Question of Nicodemism." In Wilhelm Niesel (ed.), *Calvinus Ecclesiae Genevensis Custos: Die Referate des Congrès International des Recherches Calviniennes . . . Vom 6. bis 9. September 1982 in Genf*. Frankfurt am Main: Peter Lang Verlag, 1984, 165–70.

Hofheinz, Marco. "De munere prophetico: Variationen reformierter Auslegung des prophetischen Amtes. Zur theologiegeschichtlichen Entwicklung eines dogmatischen Topos vor der Aufklärung (von Zwingli bis Lampe)." In Calvins M. Hofheinz, W. Lienemann and M. Sallmann (eds), *Calvins Erbe: Beiträge zur Wirkungsgeschichte Johannes*. Göttingen: Vandenhoeck & Ruprecht, 2011, 115–68.

Holder, R. Ward. "Calvin and Tradition: Tracing Expansion, Locating Development, Suggesting Authority." *Toronto Journal of Theology*, 25/2 (2009), 215–26.

——"Calvin's Theology: Tradition and Renewal." In Herman Selderhuis (ed.), *The Calvin Handbook*. Grand Rapids, Mich.: Eerdmans, 2009, 384–95.

Holt, Mack. "Putting Religion Back into the Wars of Religion." *French Historical Studies*, 18/2 (1993), 524–51.

——"Religion, Historical Method, and Historical Forces: A Rejoinder." *French Historical Studies*, 19/3 (1996), 863–73.

——*The French Wars of Religion, 1562–1629*. 2nd edn. Cambridge: Cambridge University Press, 2005.

Hoogstra, J. T., ed. *John Calvin Contemporary Prophet: A Symposium*. Grand Rapids, Mich.: Baker, 1959.

Höpfl, Harro. *The Christian Polity of John Calvin*. Cambridge: Cambridge University Press, 1982.

Izbicki, Thomas M., and Christopher M. Bellitto, eds. *Reform and Renewal in the Middle Ages and the Renaissance: Studies in Honor of Louis Pascoe, S.J.* Leiden: Brill, 2000.

Jahn, Johann Gottlieb. *Geschichte des Schmalkaldischen Krieges: Eine reformationsgeschichtliche Denkschrift zur Erinnerung an das, für die ganze damalige protestantische Kirche verhängnisvolle Jahrzehend von 1537 bis 1547*. Leipzig: Reclam, 1837.

Jouanna, Arlette. *Le Devoir de révolte: La Noblesse française et la gestation de l'État moderne (1559–1661)*. [Paris]: Fayard, *c*.1989.

——*et al*. *Histoire et dictionnaire des Guerres de Religion*. Paris: Robert Laffont, 1998.

Kagan, Richard. *Lucrecia's Dreams; Politics and Prophecy in Sixteenth-Century Spain*. Berkeley, Calif.: University of California Press, 1995.

Kaiser, Wolfgang. *Marseille au temps des troubles, 1559–1596*. Paris: École des Hautes Études en Sciences Sociales, 1991.

Keller, Abraham. "Calvin and the Question of War." *Modern Language Quarterly*, 11/3 (1950), 272–80.

Kerby-Fulton, Kathryn. *Reformist Apocalypticism and 'Piers Plowman.'* Cambridge: Cambridge University Press, 1990.

——"Prophet and Reformer: 'Smoke in the Vineyard'." In Barbara Newman (ed.), *Voice of the Living Light: Hildegard of Bingen and her World*. Berkeley, Calif.: University of California Berkeley Press, 1998.

Kienzle, Beverly Mayne. "Defending the Lord's Vineyard: Hildegard of Bingen's Preaching against the Cathars." In Carolyn Muessig (ed.), *Medieval Monastic Preaching*. Leiden: Brill, 1998.

Kingdon, Robert. *Geneva and the Coming Wars of Religion in France, 1555–1563*. Geneva: Droz, 1956.

——*Geneva and the Consolidation of the French Protestant Movement, 1564–1572*. Geneva: Droz, 1967.

——"Calvin's Socio-Political Legacy: Collective Government, Resistance to Tyranny, Discipline." In David Foxgrover (ed.), *The Legacy of John Calvin*. Grand Rapids, Mich.: CRC Publication Services, 2000, 112–23.

——"Calvin and Calvinists on Resistance to Government." In David F. Wright, Anthony N. S. Lane, and Jon Balserak (eds), *Calvinus Evangelii Propugnator: Calvin, Champion of the Gospel. Papers from the International Congress on Calvin Research Seoul, 1998*. Grand Rapids, Mich.: CRC Production Services, 2006, 54–65.

Kirby, Torrance, Emidio Campi, and Frank A. James III, eds. *Companion to Peter Martyr Vermigli*. Brill: Leiden, 2009.

Knecht, Robert J. *The French Wars of Religion 1559–1598*, 2nd edn. New York: Longman, 1996.

Kolfhaus, Wilhelm. "Der Verkehr Calvins mit Bullinger." In Josef Bohatec (ed.), *Calvinstudien: Festschrift zum 400. Geburtstage Johann Calvins*. Leipzig: Haupt, 1909, 27–125.

Kusukawa, Sachiko. *The Transformation of Natural Philosophy: The Case of Philip Melanchthon*. Cambridge: Cambridge University Press, 1995.

Ladner, Gerhart. *The Idea of Reform: Its Impact on Christian Thought and Action in the Age of the Fathers*. New York: Holt, Rinehart & Winston, 1967.

Lane, Anthony N. S. *John Calvin; Student of the Church Fathers*. Edinburgh: T&T Clark, 1999.

Lerner, Robert E. "Medieval Prophecy and Religious Dissent." *Past and Present*, 72 (1976), 3–24.

——*The Powers of Prophecy: The Cedar of Lebanon Vision from the Mongol Onslaught to the Dawn of the Enlightenment*. Berkeley, Calif.: University of California Press, 1983.

Lillback, Peter A. *The Binding of God: Calvin's Role in the Development of Covenant Theology*. Grand Rapids, Mich.: Baker, 2001.

Link, Christian. *Johannes Calvin: Humanist, Reformator, Lehrer der Kirche*. Zurich: TVZ, 2009.

Locher, Gottfried. *Die Zwinglische Reformation im Rahmen der europäischen Kirchengeschichte*. Göttingen: Vandenhoeck & Ruprecht, 1979.

——*Zwingli's Thought: New Perspectives*. Leiden: Brill, 1981.

Maag, Karin. *Seminary or University? The Genevan Academy and Reformed Higher Education, 1560–1620*. Aldershot: Ashgate, 1995.

——"Calvin and Students." In Herman Selderhuis (ed.), *Calvin Handbook*. Grand Rapids, Mich.: Eerdmans, 2008, 165–71.

—— "Recruiting and Training Pastors: The Genevan Model and Alternative Approaches." In *Revisiting Geneva: Robert Kingdon and the Coming of the French Wars of Religion.* St Andrews: Centre for French History and Culture of the University of St Andrews, 2012, 10–22.

Maas, Anthony John. *Christ in Type and Prophecy.* New York: Benziger Brothers, 1893.

McGinn, Bernard. "Awaiting an End: Research in Medieval Apocalypticism 1974–1981." *Medievalia et Humanistica,* ns 11 (1982), 263–89.

—— "Early Apocalypticism: The Ongoing Debate." In C. A. Patrides and J. Wittreich (eds), *The Apocalypse in English Renaissance Thought and Literature.* Ithaca, NY: Cornell University Press, 1984, 2–39.

—— *The Calabrian Abbot: Joachim of Fiore in the History of Western Thought.* New York: Macmillan Publishing Co., 1985.

—— *Antichrist: Two Thousand Years of the Human Fascination with Evil.* New York: Columbia University Press, 2000.

McGrath, Alister. "John Calvin and Late Mediaeval Thought: A Study in Late Mediaeval Influences upon Calvin's Theological Development." *Archiv für Reformationsgeschichte,* 77 (1986), 58–78.

McKee, Elsie A. *Elders and the Plural Ministry; The Role of Exegetical History in Illuminating John Calvin's Theology.* Geneva: Droz, 1988.

Mellet, Paul-Alexis. "'Le roy des mouches à miel...': Tyrannie présente et royauté parfaite dans les traité monarchomaques." *Archiv für Reformationsgeschichte,* 93 (2002), 71–96.

—— ed. *Et de sa bouche sortait un glaive: Les Monarchomaques au XVIe siècle.* Geneva: Droz, 2006.

—— *Les Traités monarchomaques: Confusion des temps, résistance armée et monarchie parfaite (1560–1600).* Geneva: Droz, 2007.

Mentzer, Raymond A. *Heresy Proceedings in Languedoc, 1500–1560.* Philadelphia: American Philosophical Society, 1984.

—— "Calvin and France." In Herman Selderhuis (ed.), *Calvin Handbook.* Grand Rapids, Mich.: Eerdmans, 2008, 78–87.

Millet, Olivier. *Calvin et la dynamique de la parole: Étude de rhétorique réformée.* Geneva: Editions Slatkine, 1992.

—— "Eloquence des prophètes bibliques et prédication inspirée: La 'Prophétie' réformée au XVIe siècle." In *Prophètes et prophétie au XVIe siècle.* Paris: Presses de l'École Normale Supérieure, 1998, 65–82.

—— "Calvin's Self-Awareness as Author." In Irena Backus and Philip Benedict (eds), *Calvin and his Influence, 1509–2009.* Oxford: Oxford University Press, 2011, 84–101.

Minnis, A. J. *Medieval Theory of Authorship: Scholastic Literary Attitudes in the Later Middle Ages.* London: Scolar Press, 1984.

—— A. B. Scott, and David Wallace, eds. *Medieval Literary Theory and Criticism c.1100–c.1375.* Oxford: Oxford University Press, 1988.

Monheit, Michael. "Review of Jean Calvin. Vies parallèles." *Sixteenth Century Journal*, 33/3 (2002), 854–6.

Monter, William. *Judging the French Reformation: Heresy Trials by Sixteenth-Century Parlements*. Cambridge, Mass.: Harvard University Press, 1999.

Mouton, Jean-Luc. *Calvin*. Paris: Gallimard, 2009.

Morisi-Guerra, Anna. "The *Apocalypsis Nova*: A Plan for Reform." In Marjorie Reeves (ed.), *Prophetic Rome in the High Renaissance Period*. Oxford: Clarendon Press, 1992, 27–50.

Moser, Christian. *Theodor Bibliander (1505–1564) Annotierte Bibliographie der gedruckten Werke*. Zurich: TVZ, 2009.

Mpindi, Mbunga. "Calvin's Hermeneutics of the Imprecations of the Psalter." Unpublished Ph.D. thesis, Calvin Theological Seminary, 2004.

Muller, Richard. "The Hermeneutic of Promise and Fulfilment in Calvin's Exegesis of the Old Testament Prophecies of the Kingdom." In David Steinmetz (ed.), *The Bible in the Sixteenth Century*. Durham, NC: Duke University Press, 1990, 68–82.

——*The Unaccommodated Calvin: Studies in the Foundation of a Theological Tradition*. New York: Oxford University Press, 2000.

Naef, Henri. *La Conjuration d'Amboise et Genève*. Geneva: Jullien, 1922.

Naphy, William. *Calvin and the Consolidation of the Genevan Reformation*. Manchester: University of Manchester Press, 1994.

Nasrallah, Laura. *An Ecstasy of Folly: Prophecy and Authority in Early Christianity*. Cambridge, Mass.: Harvard University Press, 2003.

Netanyahu, Benzion. *Don Isaac Abravanel: Statesman and Philosopher*. New York: Cornell University Press, 1998.

Neuser, Wilhelm. *Johann Calvin: Leben und Werk in seiner Frühzeit 1509–1541*. Göttingen: Vandenhoeck & Ruprecht, 2009, 144–51.

Nexon, Daniel H. *The Struggle for Power in Early Modern Europe: Religious Conflict, Dynastic Empires, and International Change*. Princeton: Princeton University Press, 2009, 235–64.

Nijenhuis, Willem. "The Limits of Civil Disobedience in Calvin's Last-Known Sermons: Development of his Ideas on the Right of Civil Resistance." In *Ecclesia Reformata*, ii. *Studies on the Reformation*. Leiden: Brill, 1994, 73–94.

Oberman, Heiko. "Martin Luther: Vorläufer der Reformation." In Eberhard Jüngel, Johannes Wallmann, and Wilfrid Werbeck (eds), *Verifikationem: Festschrift für Gerhard Ebeling zum 70 Geburstag*. Tübingen: J. C. B. Mohr, 1982, 91–119.

——"Europa Afflicta: The Reformation of the Refugees." *Archiv für Reformationsgeschichte*, 83 (1992), 91–111.

——"One Epoch: Three Reformations." In *The Reformation: Roots and Ramifications*. Tr. Andrew Colin Gow. Edinburgh: T&T Clark, 1994, 201–20.

——"Hus and Luther: Prophets of a Radical Reformation." In C. Pater and R. Peterson (eds), *The Contentious Triangle: Church, State, and University.* Kirksville, Mo.: Truman State University Press, 1999, 135–67.

——*John Calvin and the Reformation of the Refugees.* Geneva: Droz, 2009.

Olson, Jeannine. *Calvin and Social Welfare: Deacons and the Bourse française.* London and Toronto: Associated University Presses; Selinsgrove, Pa.: Susquehanna University Press, 1989.

van Oort, Johannes. "John Calvin and the Church Fathers." In Irena Backus (ed.), *The Reception of the Church Fathers in the West.* Leiden: Brill, 1997, 661–700.

Opitz, Peter. *Calvin: Theologische Hermeneutik.* Neukirchen-Vluyn: Neukirchener Verlag, 1994.

——ed. *Calvin im Kontext der Schweizer Reformation: Historishe und theologische Beiträge zur Calvinforschung.* Zurich: TVZ, 2003.

——"Von prophetischer Existenz zur Prophetie als Pädagogik: Zu Bullingers Lehre vom munus propheticum." In Emidio Campi and Peter Opitz (eds), *Heinrich Bullinger: Life—Thought—Influence. Zurich, Aug. 25–29, 2004 International Congress Heinrich Bullinger (1504–1575).* 2 vols. Zurich: TVZ, 2007, ii. 493–513.

——*Leben und Werk Johannes Calvins.* Göttingen: Vandenhoeck & Ruprecht, 2009.

Pannier, Jacques. *Calvin à Strasbourg.* Strasbourg: Impr. alsacienne, 1925.

Parker, Charles H. "French Calvinists as the Children of Israel: An Old Testament Self-Consciousness in Jean Crespin's Histoire des Martyrs before the Wars of Religion." *Sixteenth Century Journal,* 24/2 (1993), 227–36.

Parker, T. H. L. *John Calvin: A Biography.* London: J. M. Dent & Sons, 1975.

——*Calvin's Old Testament Commentaries.* Edinburgh: T&T Clark, 1986.

Pellerin, Daniel. "Calvin: Militant or Man of Peace?" *Review of Politics,* 65 (2003), 35–59.

Peter, Rodolphe, ed. *Sermons sur les livres de Jérémie et des Lamentations. SC* 6: XIV–XVI.

Peterson, Rodney. "Bullinger's Prophets of the 'Restitutio'." In Mark S. Burrows and Paul Rorem (eds), *Biblical Hermeneutics in Historical Perspective.* Grand Rapids, Mich.: Eerdmans, 1991, 245–60.

——*Preaching in the Last Days: The Theme of the 'Two Witnesses' in the Sixteenth and Seventeenth Centuries.* New York: Oxford University Press, 1993.

Pfister, Oskar. *Das Christentum und die Angst: Eine religionspsychologische, historische und religionshygienische Untersuchung.* Zurich: Artemis, 1944.

——*Christianity and Fear: A Study in History and in the Psychology and Hygiene of Religion.* London: Allen & Unwin, 1948.

Pfister, Rudolph. *Kirchengeschichte der Schweiz,* ii. *Von der Reformation bis zum zweiten Villmerger Krieg.* Zurich: Zwingli Verlag, 1979.

Pitkin, Barbara. "Prophecy and History in Calvin's Lectures on Daniel (1561)." In Katharina Bracht and David S. du Toit (eds), *Die Geschichte der Daniel-Auslegung in Judentum, Christentum und Islam. Studien zur Kommentierung des Danielbuches in Literatur und Kunst.* Berlin: de Gruyter, 2007, 323–47.

Preuss, Hans. *Martin Luther: Der Prophet.* Gütersloh: C. Bertelsmann, 1933.

Reeves, Marjorie. *The Influence of Prophecy in the Later Middle Ages: A Study in Joachimism.* Oxford: Oxford University Press, 1969.

——"History and Prophecy in Medieval Thought." *Medievalia et Humanistica,* ns 5 (1974), 51–75.

——"The Medieval Heritage." In Marjorie Reeves (ed.), *Prophetic Rome in the High Renaissance Period.* Oxford: Clarendon Press, 1992, 3–26.

Reid, Jonathan. *King's Sister–Queen of Dissent: Marguerite of Navarre (1492–1549) and her Evangelical Network.* Leiden: Brill, 2009.

Reid, W. Stanford. "The Battle Hymns of the Lord: Calvinist Psalmody of the Sixteenth Century." *Sixteenth Century Journal,* 2/1 (1970), 36–54.

Reuter, Karl. *Das Grundverständnis der Theologie Calvins.* Neukirchen-Vluyn: Neukirchener Verlag, 1963.

Roberts, Penny. *A City in Conflict; Troyes during the French Wars of Religion.* Manchester: University of Manchester Press, 1996.

——"The Most Crucial Battle of the Wars of Religion? The Conflict over Sites of Reformed Worship in Sixteenth-Century France." *Archiv für Reformationsgeschichte,* 89 (1998), 247–67.

Roelker, Nancy Lyman. *Queen of Navarre: Jeanne d'Albret, 1528–1572.* Cambridge, Mass.: Harvard University Press, 1968.

——*One King, One Faith: The Parlement of Paris and the Religious Reformations of the Sixteenth Century.* Berkeley, Calif.: University of California Press, 1996.

Roget, Amédée. *Histoire du peuple de Genève depuis la Réforme jusqu'à l'Escalade.* 7 vols. Geneva: Jullien, 1870–83.

Roussel, Bernard. "Des auteurs." In Guy Bedouelle and Bernard Roussel (eds), *Le Temps des Réformes et la Bible: Bible de tous les temps.* 5 vols. Paris: Beauchesne, 1989, v. 199–305.

Saebø, Magne, ed. *Hebrew Bible: Old Testament.* 2 vols. Göttingen: Vandenhoeck & Ruprecht, 2008.

Schalk, Ellery. *From Valor to Pedigree: Ideas of Nobility in France in the Sixteenth and Seventeenth Centuries.* Princeton: University of Princeton Press, 1986.

Schramm, Percy. *Der König von Frankreich: Das Wesen der Monarchie vom 9. zum 16. Jahrhundert, ein Kapitel aus der Geschichte des abendländischen Staates.* Weimar: H. Böhlaus Nachfolger, 1939.

Schreiner, Susan. *Are You Alone Wise? The Search for Certainty in the Early Modern Era.* Oxford: Oxford University Press, 2011.

Schubert, Hans von. "Calvin." In Erich Marcks and Karl Alexander von Müller (eds), *Meister der Politik: Eine weltgeschichtliche Reihe von Bildnissen*, 2 vols. Berlin: Deutsche Verlags-Anstalt, 1923, 68–9.

Schummer, Léopold. *Le Ministère pastoral dans l'Institution Chrétienne de Calvin à la lumière du troisième sacrement.* Wiesbaden: Franz Steiner Verlag, 1965.

Soergel, Philip M. *Miracles and the Protestant Imagination: The Evangelical Wonder Book in Reformation Germany.* New York: Oxford University Press, 2012.

Spierling, Karen. *Infant Baptism in Reformation Geneva: The Shaping of a Community, 1536–1564.* Philadelphia: Westminster/John Knox, 2009.

Spijker, Willem van't. *The Ecclesiastical Offices in the Thought of Martin Bucer.* Tr. John Vriend and Lyle Bierma. Leiden: Brill, 1996.

Springer, Michael. *Restoring Christ's Church: John Lasco and the Forma ac ratio.* Aldershot: Ashgate, 2007.

Sproxton, Judy. *Violence and Religion: Attitudes towards militancy in the French Civil Wars.* London: Routledge, 1995.

Stauffer, Richard. "Les Discours à la première personne dans les sermones de Calvin." In *Regards contemporains sur Jean Calvin: Actes du Colloque Calvin.* Paris: Presses Universitaires de France, 1965, 206–38.

Stephenson, William. *Sovereign Grace: The Place and Significance of Christian Freedom in John Calvin's Political Thought.* New York: Oxford University Press, 1999.

Strayer, Joseph R. "France: The Holy Land, the Chosen People, and the Most Christian King." In Theodore Rabb and Jerrold Seigel (eds), *Action and Conviction in Early Modern Europe: Essays in Memory of E. H. Harbison.* Princeton: Princeton University Press, 1969, 3–16.

Sunshine, Glenn. *Reforming French Protestantism: The Development of Huguenot Ecclesiastical Institutions, 1557–1572.* Kirksville, Mo.: Truman State University Press, 2003.

Sypher, G. Wylie. "'Faisant ce qu'il leur vient a plaisir': The Image of Protestantism in French Catholic Polemic on the Eve of the Religious Wars." *Sixteenth Century Journal*, 11/2 (1980), 59–84.

Tavard, George. "Calvin and the Nicodemites." In Randall C. Zachman (ed.), *John Calvin and Roman Catholicism: Critique and Engagement, Then and Now.* Grand Rapids, Mich.: Baker Book House, 2008, 59–78.

Thompson, John. *John Calvin and the Daughters of Sarah: Women in Regular and Exceptional Roles in the Exegesis of Calvin, his Predecessors, and his Contemporaries.* Geneva: Droz, 1992.

—— "Patriarchy and Prophetesses: Tradition and Innovation in Vermigli's Doctrine of Woman." In Frank A. James III (ed.), *Peter Martyr Vermigli and the European Reformations.* Leiden: Brill, 2004, 139–58.

Thompson, John. *Reading the Bible with the Dead: What you Can Learn from the History of Exegesis that you Can't Learn from Exegesis Alone.* Grand Rapids, Mich.: Eerdmans, 2007.

Torrance, T. F. *The Hermeneutics of John Calvin.* Edinburgh: Scottish Academic Press, 1988.

Troeltsch, Ernst. *The Social Teachings of the Christian Churches*, ii. Tr. Olive Wyon. London: Allen & Unwin, 1949.

Valois, Noel. "Le Roi très chrétien." In *La France Chrétienne dans l'Histoire.* Paris: SHF, 1896, 314–27.

Vénard, Marc. *Réforme protestante, réforme catholique dans la province d'Avignon, XVIᵉ siècle.* Paris: Cerf, 1993.

Voaden, Rosalynn. *God's Word, Women's Voices: The Discernment of Spirits in the Writing of Late-Medieval Women Visionaries.* Rochester, NY: Boydell & Brewer, 1999.

Vogler, Günter. "Thomas Müntzer: Irrweg oder Alternative? Plädoyer für eine andere Sicht." *Archiv für Reformationsgeschichte*, 103 (2012), 11–39.

Wallace, Ronald S. *Calvin, Geneva and the Reformation: A Study of Calvin as Social Reformer, Churchman, Pastor and Theologian.* Edinburgh: Scottish Academic Press, 1988.

Walzer, Michael. *The Revolution of the Saints: A Study in the Origins of Radical Politics.* Cambridge, Mass.: Harvard University Press, 1965.

Wendel, François. *Calvin: Sources et évolution de sa pensée religieuse.* Paris: Presses Universitaires de France., 1950.

——*Calvin: The Origins and Developments of his Religious Thought.* Tr. Philip Mairet. Durham, NC: Labyrinth Press, 1987.

Wernle, Paul. *Calvin und Basel bis zum Tod des Myconius 1535–1552.* Basel: Reinhardt, 1909.

Whitford, David. "Robbing Paul to Pay Peter: The Reception of Paul in Sixteenth Century Political Theology." In R. Ward Holder (ed.), *A Companion to Paul in the Reformation.* Leiden: Brill, 2009, 573–606.

Wilcox, Peter. "L'Envoi des pasteurs aux Eglises de France: Trois listes établies par Colladon (1561–1562)." *Bulletin de la Société de l'histoire du protestantisme français*, 139 (1993), 347–74.

——"The Lectures of John Calvin and the Nature of his Audience." *Archiv für Reformationsgeschichte*, 87 (1996), 136–48.

Williams, George. *The Radical Reformation.* Philadelphia: Westminster Press, 1975.

Witte, John R. *The Reformation of Rights.* Cambridge: University of Cambridge Press, 2007.

Wolin, Sheldon. "Calvin and the Reformation: The Political Education of Protestantism." *American Political Science Review*, 51/2 (1957), 428–53.

Wright, David F. "Why was Calvin so Severe a Critic of Nicodemism?" In David F. Wright, Anthony N.S. Lane, and Jon Balserak (eds), *Calvinus*

Bibliography 203

Evangelii Propugnator: Calvin, Champion of the Gospel. Papers from the International Congress on Calvin Research Seoul, 1998. Grand Rapids, Mich.: CRC Production Services, 2006, 66–90.

Zachman, Randall. *John Calvin as Teacher, Pastor, and Theologian.* Grand Rapids, Mich.: Baker Academic, 2006.

Zagorin, Perez. *Ways of Lying; Dissimulation, Persecution, and Conformity in Early Modern Europe.* Cambridge, Mass.: Cambridge University Press, 1990.

Ziolkowski, Jan. "The Nature of Prophecy in Geoffrey of Monmouth's Vita Merlini." In James Kugel (ed.), *Poetry and Prophecy: The Beginnings of a Literary Tradition.* London: Cornell University Press, 1990, 151–62.

Zuidema, Jason. *Peter Martyr Vermigli (1499–1562) and the Outward Instruments of Divine Grace.* Göttingen: Vandenhoeck & Ruprecht, 2008.

Zwierlein, Cornel. "La Loi de Dieu et l'obligation à la défense: De Florence à Magdeburg 1494–1550." In Paul-Alexis Mellet (ed.), *Et de sa Bouche Sortait un Glaive; Les Monarchomaques au XVIᵉ Siècle.* Geneva: Droz, 2006, 31–75.

Index